AWARENESS OF MORTALITY

Edited by
Jeffrey Kauffman

Death, Value and Meaning Series
Series Editor: John D. Morgan

Baywood Publishing Company, Inc.
AMITYVILLE, NEW YORK

Library of Congress Catalog Number: 95-7706
ISBN: 0-89502-174-4 (Cloth)
ISBN: 0-89503-173-6 (Paper)

Library of Congress Cataloging-in-Publication Data

Awareness of mortality / edited by Jeffrey Kauffman.
    p.   cm. - - (Death, value, and meaning series)
    Includes bibliographical references and index.
    ISBN 0-89503-174-4 (cloth). - - ISBN 0-89503-173-6 (pbk.)
    1. Death.   I. Kauffman, Jeffrey.   II. Series.
  BD444.A93 1995
  128'.5- -dc20   95-7706
                                                  CIP

Dedicated to the memory of my parents
Florence Packer Kauffman and Raymond Kauffman,
both of whom died during the time
this book was in preparation.

Acknowledgments

I thank Jack Morgan for giving me the opportunity to edit this book. From our initial discussions and throughout the course of putting it together, I have always been able to depend on him. I am deeply grateful to Terry Rando for her warm and very generous encouragement, support, and guidance. I thank Robert Kastenbaum and Ken Doka for their support and advice. I met these and many other wonderful colleagues through my association with the Association of Death Education and Counseling (ADEC).

I acknowledge my teachers in philosophy at the Graduate Faculty of the New School for Social Research in the 1960s, especially Seth Benardeti. I also thank my teachers in psychoanalysis, Abraham Bronson Feldman and Gunther Abraham.

I thank Lucy McIlvaine for typing. I recognize the importance in my life of Alan, Shelly and Will. My relationship with my son, Daniel, is a source of deep satisfaction and happiness.

Hilda has been my friend, inspiration, spiritual companion, and teacher of my heart.

Table of Contents

Introduction: Changing Planes

On my way to the 1991 Association for Death Education and Counseling Conference in Duluth, Minnesota, I had to change planes in Minneapolis. I saw Jack Morgan waiting for a flight out to Duluth, and went over to talk to him. We talked about how philosophical issues are marginalized in the thanatological literature. I expressed my opinion that philosophical questioning was basic to thanatology, and too much neglected.

Philosophical thanatology is an important part of the foundation and of the evolving dialogue of thanatology. It is the reflective discipline of processing the life experiences that death confronts us with, the reflective discipline of engaging the deepest and the hardest questions of human nature, the ultimate questions that are present in the day to day experiences of the thanatologist. Without a viable and developing philosophical thanatology, the broader field of thanatology cannot take its bearings on deeper issues or grapple with problems of meaning, purpose, dignity, consciousness, transcendence, selfhood, etc. Without philosophical thanatology, thanatology as a discipline may fail to achieve maturity as a field of study and practice. As thanatology evolves, it needs to continue to affirm the compassion at the heart of its practices, to become more disciplined in its awareness of mortality, and to nurture the link between these.

That conversation eventually led to this book. But who would read a book like this? Thanatologists are, generally, *doers*. We do research, we teach, we provide care for the dying and bereaved. This book, however, is not about doing anything. It is about questioning and reflecting.

Insofar as awareness of mortality is the most fundamental part of thanatology, this book may be for all thanatologists. Yet, not all thanatologists will choose to question and reflect.

In an important sense, philosophical thanatology may have more to do with the private concerns than the professional concerns of the thanatologist, (though private concerns feed professional ones).

Finally, in thanatology, awareness of mortality is the alpha and omega of all that we do. Awareness of mortality is where we start, where we are headed, and its significance saturates the meaning of all that is in between. For us thanatologists, awareness of mortality is the touchstone of our work, of all our doings, and of our being. All of us who work in the field of death and dying are, beyond our projects and practices, working on our awareness of mortality. It is implicit in all we do. *Awareness of Mortality* is a contribution toward making this most implicit background of our doings, an explicit theme for passionate, intellectual inquiry.

PART I

Posing Questions

This book is not about answers. It is about questions. Moreover, it is about the act of questioning. Awareness of mortality grows as we are able to reach beyond answers, and revitalize our questions. As we keep questioning alive and safe from the satisfaction, closure and illusion of answers, we nurture awareness of mortality. A crucial part of the discipline of philosophical thanatology is to identify our answers, so that they may be turned back into questions. One task of philosophical thanatology is to depose the sovereignty of the unquestioned, to break through the muteness of the not yet questioned and the comfort of the already answered—and achieve a disquieting state of being in question. Philosophical thanatology is an awareness of mortality disciplined by strength of soul that keeps open the difficult and painful questions of mortality.

In the opening chapter Kastenbaum raises questions about what we can expect from philosophy, and what we, as thanatologists, expect from ourselves. His playfulness in this chapter provides a light approach to the sobering questions at hand. The play is, however, not without irony and the easy reading of the text gently veils a more difficult and disturbing meaning.

Kastenbaum introduces the concept of "mortality attacks." Rather than the more philosophical and perhaps enigmatic concept "awareness of mortality," he presents mortality as an attack. This is a more robust term and is closer to the immediate painful reality of death. He describes three ways to treat a mortality attack: 1) the use of philosophy as a pharmaceutical; 2) the use of philosophy as a consolation; and 3) the consoling relationship. Philosophy as pharmaceutical makes one feel better in the face of mortality attacks; philosophy as consolation is "mediated and supported by rational discourse." Kastenbaum considers Boethius' *Philosophy of Consolation*, written in the immediacy of Boethius' death sentence, as a model text for philosophical thanatology. He says that for Boethius consolation 1) is earned through rigorous and enlightened discourse; 2) is bitter to the taste; 3) requires genuine risk of despair; and 4) is accessible only by overcoming a spiritual amnesia. The final treatment for mortality attacks is the consoling relationship in which consolation is found in the empathy and care of another human being.

The other chapter in this section, Roy's *Dying and Death Late in the Twentieth Century* is an examination of ethical consciousness. Roy articulates the primacy of human dignity in ethical decision-making and in awareness of mortality in general. He places before us the ethical dilemma and significance of bringing unspoken assumptions into awareness and into speech. This argument for the priority of questions over answers is multidimensional and consists of: 1) his openness to call into question his own established points of view; 2) his recognition of totalitarian tendencies within thanatological liberalism; 3) his assertion that thanatological ethics is not interested in right answers, but in teaching us to articulate compelling questions, and that a key ethical task is to identify and bring into question our own "right answers"; and 4) his most disturbing insight that "we are cut off from the deepest questions our intelligence would ask . . . " Attempting to hold together in tension the contradictory experiences of transcendent hope and laughter, and of agonized protest, Roy, in this chapter, works at the boundaries of the human spirit.

In both of these chapters, as throughout this book, the intellectual pursuits of philosophical thanatology are profoundly bound up with compassion, or, as Kallenberg (Chapter 5) writes "action supported by love." Awareness of mortality is both a compassionate and a mysterious act.

CHAPTER 1

What Should We Expect From Philosophy?

Robert Kastenbaum

People who respond when the call goes out for a death counselor or educator might claim to be the spiritual progeny of the man who is most closely associated with the development of the Western philosophical tradition. Socrates attained so great a reputation that his predecessors have been crowded into a motley drawer labeled "preSocratic thinkers." It must be admitted that Socrates was by no means the first philosopher, and, further, that his words come down to us through the intermediation of a student whose own contributions to the message are impossible to gauge. Who knows how much Plato altered, improved, or simply made up? Nevertheless, Socrates is enshrined in Western tradition as the father of both philosophy and death studies. "For is not philosophy the study of death?" he asked, and nobody rose to challenge him—for the moment.

Today's death educators and counselors might find it useful to examine what has been inherited from both the founding father and the many subsequent contributors to the never-ending philosophical dialogue. One point is evident at the outset: we cannot simply take this inheritance to the bank. All is not free and clear. Each gleaming insight from philosophy's treasure trove was mined within a particular context by people who had to cope with the conflicts, stresses, and challenges of the day as well as the fundamental mysteries of existence. The particularities of these circumstances and the varied socio- intellectual labyrinth through which they have passed, generation after generation, encumber the heritage.

This difficulty is already evident with Socrates/Plato. Are we at liberty to take just what we like from their worldview, and arbitrarily dispense with those facets that make us feel uncomfortable? For example, can we align ourselves wholly with the condemned man who showed such consideration to his executioner as

3

well as his friends, and yet dissociate ourselves from the disconcertingly modern vision of an oppressive State in the hands of biotechnicians? Left to Socrates/Plato we would not even have the right to sing the blues:

> This is the point to which, above all, the attention of our rules should be directed—that music and gymnastic be preserved in their original form, and no innovation made. . . . And when any one says that mankind must regard the newest song which the singers have, they will be afraid that he may be praising not new songs, but a new kind of song; and this ought not to be praised [1, p. 345].

And so we would have had no Palestrina masses for the dead, no Mozart or Brahms' Requiems, no country cry-in-my-beer tunes, no radiant gospel expressions of faith, no gut-aching blues, and no astonishing rap song eulogy to the slain member of a teen gang [2]—to sample just a few "new kinds of song" since the would-be city fathers imagined their Republic. Would we care to purchase our philosophy of life and death at the cost of a grim, oppressive, and technocratic State?

Other philosophies that might compete for our allegiance also are booby-trapped with assumptions, assertions, and commands that might trouble today's death educator and counselor. For example, Heidegger was not only "widely considered the central figure in contemporary existentialist thought" [3, p. 459], but also perhaps the most influential contributor to the philosophy of death in the postWorld War II years. Can we and should we ignore his enthusiastic embrace of Nazism—and his insistence that true philosophical discourse is possible only in the German and Greek languages? For another example, consider the promising combination of a certifiably great philosopher and a message that many would like to hear. Descartes concluded that the soul escapes the dying body for much the same reasons that rats desert a sinking ship. The soul is definitely not a biodegradable substance. Instead:

> The soul is of such a nature that it has no relation to extension, nor to the dimensions or other properties of the matter composing the body, but only to the whole assemblage of its organs. . . . It does not become smaller on the removal of a part of the body. When, however, the assemblage of the bodily organs disintegrates, it itself, in its entirety, withdraws from the body [4, Article V].

It might be tempting to call on Descartes' testimonial as a philosophical pillar to support one's own inclination to believe in survival of death. However, one must then also be prepared to persuade contemporary biological scientists that this extraordinary nonmaterial substance, the soul, has its headquarters in the pineal gland, one of the most humble structures in the central nervous system. Chances are that not many death counselors and educators would take up Descartes' seventeenth-century neurophysiology as proof that the destructible body has an immortal soul that can beat a hasty departure when the going gets rough. Without a device such as the pineal gland to rely upon, however, Descartes' interactive dualism becomes a separatism in which body and soul know each other not. These examples could be multiplied as one moves from philosopher to philosopher. Some of the most appealing ideas either require assumptions or deliver consequences that are difficult to endorse today.

Caution is advisable in drawing upon even the most familiar components of our philosophical heritage. The core issues and concepts often have been tarnished and trivialized by indifferent handling. What first appeared as a rough-edged and provocative thought may have become smoothed into a bromide; an admission of ignorance may have been transformed into a testament of faith. The possibility of misinterpretation increases when we venture toward views that are remote from our own tradition. The Navajo philosophy of death and mourning, for example, resists easy comprehension by outsiders who have no way of thinking and feeling themselves into the distinctive worldview within which life as well as death take their meaning. Furthermore, we might also feel disoriented when confronting the turbulence of new ideas that have not yet been tamed, named, and neutered by the gatekeepers of academia. (Their motto: "Wait until it stops moving, then put it in a box—or a book!")

It would be a waste of time and perhaps a self-deception to shuffle through the worn index cards to offer a textbookish survey of philosophical ideas about death. Instead, it could be more useful to encounter freshly both what is alive in death philosophy and what is in our own minds and hearts.

PURPOSE AND METHOD

This chapter has the limited purpose of exploring some of the challenges that confront us in making a useful connection between the death-related issues of today and the perdurable philosophical enterprise. Each of us will answer the "should" question for ourselves. In fact, we will answer this question *out* of ourselves. Socrates would be the first to light up in glee as we expose our own assumptions and needs by the type of demands we make upon philosophy. We begin with a brief dialogue overheard (or overimagined) after hours at a meeting of the Association for Death Education and Counseling.

Dialogue Fragment:
Take Two Clichés and Call Me in the Morning

Rigor: And so, friend, would you not agree that although all philosophers are mortals, not all mortals are philosophers?

Mortis: Agreed.

R: What sign, then, distinguishes the philosopher from others?

M: Two signs. A larger hat size to accommodate the hyperdeveloped brain, and a well-corrugated brow—for every deep wrinkle of thought must surely produce its outward mark.

R: *Helas!* I now understand why you still wear a child's cap atop a brow as smooth as an egg. I restate the question: What do we mean, friend, when we characterize a person as being "philosophical?"

M: Tedious, passive, and in all likelihood a born loser.

R: May the gods forgive you, I cannot!

M: Did I forget: *boring*?

R: Before the lightning strikes—apologize!

M: Certainly: I deeply *regret* the fact that the term "philosophical" has come to signify passivity in the face of adversity, withdrawal from the robust skirmishes of life, and escapist fantasies masquerading as wisdom.

· R: *(Butting M in the stomach and throwing wild punches)* Die, scoundrel, die!

M: *(Unperturbed)*. But how? Nonchalantly? Enigmatically? How about: beatitudinously?

R: No! Writhing in pain, gasping for breath, and begging for mercy!

M: Hardly philosophical, that. How about the standard wan philosophical smile?

R: Suffer, damn you!

M: Well, all right: but only stoically!

(The beating continues, but more from duty than pleasure)

PHILOSOPHY AS PHARMACEUTICAL FOR MORTALITY ATTACKS

No wonder that Mortis is being so thoroughly pummeled. Deserves it, doesn't he, for exposing the game? Generally speaking, "being philosophical about death" does carry the connotations that he was nervy enough to identify. There is a strong tendency to reach for that vial labeled "philosophy" when one is anxious, depressed, or experiencing other symptoms that are common during a mortality attack. Many prefer philosophy in its readily available over-the-counter forms: mass media-promulgated and commercialized concoctions, often consisting of treatises whose first two words are "How to . . ." These promises to relieve our pain—including both the pain of thought and the thought of pain—by confiding the secrets of certitude and serenity. Few big sellers in the Phony Philosophy section offer to multiply our doubts and knock the props from under our shaky assumptions. Some readers brave the domain of serious philosophy or theology, but only to turn back hastily after a dose of murky Heidegger syrup or an allergic reaction to Hegel, if not blessed with a fortuitous postNietzchean high. Few will embark upon systematic philosophical studies, perhaps suspecting this to be another one of those fates worse than death. What many seek are the reputed consolations and certitudes of philosophy delivered on demand and at discount by smiling MacDisney faces.

Philosophy-as-pharmaceutical probably should be evaluated as one would any other drug. Does it relieve those distressing symptoms of mortal vulnerability? Are we able to get on with our normal routines? More ambitiously: does it actually cure what ails us, as distinguished from dulling symptom awareness? And then there are the cost-benefit factors: 1) is the expense within our means: 2) are there dangerous side-effects?

Perhaps as death educators and counselors we need to consider these questions with particular care because we find ourselves in the position to influence others in their times of doubt or crisis. Are we in the business of calming fears and doubts either by dispensing philosophical bromides, or by providing quasi-philosophical creditation for wishes and fantasies? Is it our mission to pour soothing ointments, even if this means dulling the senses? An instructor who sees him/herself as Dr. Feelgood might well see philosophy as just one more resource among others to achieve this objective.

Question: Should this be our identity and goal of choice?

Question: Does using philosophy for this purpose actually produce the desired result in reducing the symptoms of mortality attacks?

Question: Does it also produce the desired result in "curing" dread, conflict, or other negative correlates of death awareness?

Question: Does utilizing philosophy as pharmaceutical cost something in the way of opportunities missed for self development and exercise of critical thinking?

Question: Is there more or less to philosophy than its role as a semantic tranquilizer?

In pursuing questions such as these, one might begin by monitoring the information, concepts, and attitudes that one has become accustomed to conveying as educator or counselor. For example, am I using primary sources or relying mostly on other people's selections and interpretations? Do I present philosophical ideas within the context of their total system and historical context, or as little more than detachable slogans? When philosophy enters my classroom or counseling office, does it usually serve the purpose of raising or answering questions? Are opposing views offered and discussed, or do I simply lay out my favored concepts for captive client or audience?

At one extreme, a death educator/counselor might be working primarily on the personal agenda of sedating his/her own death—related anxieties through selective and simplistic applications of a philosophical position that one finds comfortable. At the other extreme, one might take on the mission of confronting others with the strongest possible opposing positions to stimulate critical thinking and the development of more sophisticated conceptions, even at the possible cost of heightened anxiety.

The effects of exposure to philosophical discourse in death education and counseling can be evaluated both with respect to the teacher/counselor's objectives and to whatever values are cherished by an external observer or observers. For example, Dr. Feelgood may succeed in the sense that his/her students have compiled a choice collection of inspirational and compensatory statements about death—but Dr. Headstrong may see this instead as abject failure because the students have not been challenged to work out personal positions based on rigorous comparison of opposing views.

PHILOSOPHY AS CONSOLATION

It has already been suggested that philosophy is most often looked to as a source of consolation when mortality is at issue. Furthermore, it has been strongly implied that the consoling effect frequently is sought by dispensing philosophy as though a feel-good drug. It is time now to propose a distinction between sedation and consolation. Some presentations made in the name of philosophy do boil down to groundless assertions. The banality is masked by emotional flavorings and/or claims upon authority. Repeating something often enough is also a well known technique for instilling belief in a "philosophy" that is little more than a conditioned association. When words are used to produce a drug-like effect (in Western society, sedation more often than intoxication, although the exceptions are intriguing), then we are in the presence of philosophy-as-pharmaceutical.

It is possible, however, to influence feelings through cognition as well as the other way around. If one attends to a sustained philosophical argument and finds it persuasive, then there may well be emotional and attitudinal consequences. Therefore, one might turn to philosophy for a sense of consolation that is mediated and supported by rational discourse. In other words, consolation could be regarded as a reward that has been earned through rigorous and enlightening discourse. Consolation achieved through the disciplined exercise of one's highest mental facilities would seem to be not only different from, but, also superior to the passive consumption of philosophical opiates.

Perhaps no title in this area is more promising and no single work more famous than the last book written by Anicius Manlius Severinus Boethius: *On the Consolation of Philosophy* [5]. The reputation he brought to this work and the circumstances under which it was written have contributed to its renown. Boethius was among the culture elite in Rome, five centuries into the Christian era. He led an active live as a high level statesman, while somehow finding the time to write on logic, mathematics, education, theology, and other subjects as well as translating and commenting on the works of Aristotle and Porphyry. Had he not written *Consolation,* Boethius would still have a place in history as a scholar who influenced medieval thinkers even more than those of his own time. Here, then, was a disciplined and accomplished thinker who was very much part of the real world.

By his early forties, Boethius seemed to have everything: family, wealth, reputation, a position of high governmental influence, and a first-rate mind that was being applied productively to a variety of scholarly and applied projects. Despite—or because—of this enviable standing, Boethius was charged with treason and sacrilege, among other offenses, imprisoned, and sentenced to death. The historical perspective suggests that he was guilty only of following his judgment and conscience while in the dangerous terrain between warring political constituencies. Nearly a thousand years after Socrates' accepted the cup of hem- lock, Boethius became another prominent thinker who had been branded by his society as a criminal ripe for execution.

It was under these circumstances that Boethius wrote *The Consolation of Philosophy*. The major elements were all in place for a "natural experiment" on the power of philosophy to generate consolation from misfortune: a learned and disciplined thinker under the sentence of death for having pursued what he regarded as the right and proper path. As already mentioned, the book did strike a responsive chord that has continued to resonate through history. Therefore, one might think that *The Consolation of Philosophy* would be well established as a core reading both for the seeker of ready inspiration and the serious student of thanatology. *Choral response: "Not!"* Instead of occupying a central place in the renewed search for guidance and meaning, this classic seems to have been neglected by the death awareness movement both in its academic/ professional and popular manifestations.

Even a very brief characterization of Boethius' contribution may tell us some- thing useful, then, about the whole consolation enterprise as well as this famous but obscure work.

Consolation is an extended meditation in which misfortune provides the oppor- tunity to consider the nature of ethics, wisdom, and one's relationship to God. It differs from most other philosophical discourses on these subjects by having so firm an anchor in the real life predicament of a particular person, the author. A person could easily give into rage and despair when unjustly deprived of personal liberty as well as all the palpable fruits of one's achievement—and, furthermore, placed in the helpless situation of awaiting the impending execution that might come at any time.

There is a potential sense of bonding or empathy, then, between a doubting, confused, or anguished reader and Boethius. The author who is attempting to provide consolation is not a distant figure engaged in dispensing sage advice from a protected position—it's that poor devil locked away in a cell, listening for the footsteps of his executioners. If credibility is a consideration, then Boethius surely qualifies as do few other philosophers.

Consolation could have taken the form of passionate assertions. In trying to rally his own spirits, Boethius might have repeated and embellished on articles of faith and the assurances given in scripture or by esteemed authorities. Had he followed this course, *Consolation*, would have been just one more collection of inspirational sayings—and perhaps more popular today if less significant in the history of thought. Another possibility open to Boethius was to turn on the full power of his analytic intelligence. This must have been a tempting possibility because sustained logical analysis was one of his specialties and also could have provided an absorbing keep-busy activity to defend against constant apprehension regarding his situation. Had this been Boethius' approach, *Consolation* probably would have taken the form of an admirable but dry tome with very limited appeal.

What he actually gave the world with *Consolation* was something a good deal more creative than either of the above alternatives. The logical workings are there all right, and so are the inspirational outcomes—but both are integrated into what perhaps can best be described as a multi-media theatrical production. Of course, this production all takes place within the confines of one's own private stage, but there may be more gain than loss in this restriction. *Consolation* proceeds by first person prose narrative, by poetry, by song, by prayer, and by dialogue. Boethius was too much the disciplined logician to settle for mere assertions, and too much the skilled communicator to settle for quasi-mathematical arguments. And so, within his prison cell, Boethius conjured up a sort of entertainment whose profoundly serious intent could be conveyed with a keen sense of pacing, and climax-building, along with subtle glints of humor.

For substance, Boethius could draw upon the best of classical philosophy and the still-emerging Christian theology. His skill in utilizing these sources for his urgent purposes provided subsequent generations of theologians and other scholars with a convenient and persuasive document.

At this point we have before us a work that does offer the *Consolation* promised in its title, and does so through "earning" its conclusions by a resolute process of rational analysis that is made less demanding to the reader by its lyrical-dramatic form. Boethius even makes himself a character in the drama, interacting with *Philosophia*, a beautiful and virtuous lady who is the personification of elevated thought. It does not require a Jungian to recognize that Boethius has here provided still another bridge for the questing reader by 1) recognizing the divided forces and impulses within each of us, 2) personifying these as female and male principles, and 3) implying that discovering the supreme good and therefore the right course of action requires a wholeness of self which, in turn, must be achieved through open dialogue between the "ying and yang."

A person who has unexpectedly lost a loved one, or who faces his/her own imminent death might well identify with Boethius when he interrogates God:

> Creator of the star-filled universe, seated upon your eternal throne You move the heavens in their swift orbits. You hold the stars in their assigned paths, so that sometimes the shining moon is full in the light of her brother sun and hides the lesser stars. . . . Nothing escapes Your ancient law; nothing can avoid the work of its proper station. You govern all things, each according to its destined purpose. Human acts alone, O Rule of All, You refuse to restrain

within just bounds. *Why should uncertain Fortune control our lives?*
[5, pp. 14-15, italics added].

As this passage demonstrates, Boethius keeps the main points to the fore and is neither stodgy nor pedantic in expression. Why, then, when so many seek consolation, have so few turned to Boethius in recent years?

Philosophia may have the answer for us. At one point she has already earned Boethius' gratitude for having explained (in song) the relationship between love, wisdom, and misfortune. But she warns him that "You will find what I have yet to say bitter to the taste . . . " [5, p. 42]. This bitter medicine for the soul includes her unmasking and rejection of the values that most people live by. Most of us suffer from a kind of spiritual amnesia that must be overcome before we can set our feet on the right path: "In spite of its hazy memory, the human soul seeks to return to true good; but, like the drunken man who cannot find his way home, the soul no longer knows what its good is" [5, p. 45].

Apparently, most of us do not want consolation at the price demanded of us by Boethius, and, therefore, even less so at the price exacted by philosophers who are not as reader-friendly in their presentations. Boethius expects the reader to bring something of his/her own to the enterprise. For example, readers should be able to follow arguments and counterarguments and sustain a line of reasoning over time. Furthermore, readers should be ready to take some risks that are contingent upon these arguments. If I really hope for earned consolation, then I must take the risk (along with Boethius) that the adversarial argument will prove more convincing. In other words, consolation is not guaranteed, and despair is a real possibility.

But Does Philosophy Really Console Us?

The Consolation of Philosophy has been taken here as a prime example of the intersection between rigorous intellectual discourse and the quest for solace in the face of misfortune, loss, and death. Despite its admirable qualities, Boethius' masterpiece may not be attractive to contemporary seekers because it requires effort and does not guarantee feelgoods. The intellectual effort demanded of *Consolation* is relatively light compared with many other philosophical tracts, but it does ask for involvement and persistence: an uncommitted pass-through would be a meaningless if not trivializing exercise. Even with an attentive reading, however, one might well decide that there is little personal consolation to be found here. Perhaps there is now too much distance between this fifth-century Roman statesman and our own times. Or perhaps we find ourselves less convinced by Philosophia's answers than by Boethius' questions. Essentially, then, philosophically-informed consolations may fail to cure our mortality attacks because they ask more of our minds than we are prepared to give, or because we take away more doubts and worries that we brought with us.

The possibility that philosophical inquiry might confirm our worst fears, generate fears worse still, or confuse us through the interminable scrimmage of argumentation is a risk that should be acknowledged. If consolation is not a sure thing even with a diligent, obliging, and problem-focused guide such as Boethius, then it becomes an even more effortful and uncertain pursuit when we turn to philosophers at large. William James prefaced his 1904 lecture on the moral equivalence of war with the *caveat*: "I am only a philosopher, and there is only one thing that a philosopher can be relied on to do, and that is to contradict other philosophers" [6, p. 240]. Indeed, much philosophical discourse is devoted to knocking over the towers of blocks laboriously constructed by previous players, a game that might not appeal to readers who really want to know how philosophy can help them cope with their mortality attacks.

This leads us to another acknowledgment that could throw an even colder bucket of water on the whole quest for philosophical consolation, insight, and meaning with respect to death-related issues. Contrary to what some of us might like to believe, most philosophers have offered very little that is enlightening on the subject of death. There are legions of philosophers who have either ignored the subject or dealt with it in a passing and peripheral manner. Despite Socrates/Plato's assertion that philosophy is fundamentally the study of death, many thinkers have taken divergent courses without ever seeming to find the occasion to meditate on mortality no matter how many treatises they produce on epistemology, metaphysics, aesthetics, or ethics.

This curious disinterest (or avoidance) can be found among both ancients and moderns. For example, Aristotle's few words about death consists of a detached-sounding naturalistic explanation of how things die (it's sort of a pre-cryonic theory of temperature regulation). On the twentieth-century scene, few philosophers made death a salient topic until the existential approach emerged from the horrors of World War II. One of the few contemporary philosophers to devote himself systematically to mortality as the central issue was Jacques Choron, who served in the later years of his life as a valuable mentor to workers in the field of suicide research and prevention after writing a pair of philosophical-historical books that are well worth seeking out [7, 8]. It was emblematic of the times that even as the death awareness movement was struggling into existence, Choron was being isolated and even mocked by the philosophical establishment because he was so foolish as to waste his time dealing with death rather than any of the more trendy issues of academic philosophy.

In examining the psychologists' construction of death, I found that the major reference works in psychology gave little or no attention to thoughts, feelings, relationships and actions as they pertain to death [9]. The situation in philosophy is not as different as one might suppose. For example, one can move across several centuries and a thousand or so pages without encountering a reference to death in some stretches of Copleston's nine volume history of philosophy [10]. This set is an impressive achievement for a single author who, as a priest, would not lack familiarity with the central role of death in Church doctrine and ritual. That death is given so little salience through nearly five thousand pages of text cannot be charged as a quirk of Father Copleston's, but rather stands in testimony to philosophy's falling away from the problem of death. In fact, when death is brought forward as a topic, it is usually done so in the guise of immortality, i.e., discussing death only to deny death.

Readers new to philosophy, then, will not necessarily find penetrating discussions of death in any abundance. In this sense, we have been both favored and misled by complications that select a few enticing or provocative nuggets. For example, in *The Oxford Book of Death*, we are offered Montaigne's elegant observation: "It is uncertain where death looks for us; let us expect her everywhere: the premeditation of death, is a forethinking of liberty" [11, p. 29]. This is a rather promising statement (and kindred to Boethius' dialogue with Philosophia), so we might expect that it is but a hint of the treasure that Montaigne holds in store. In actuality, however, Montaigne did not say write that much about death—and so it goes. Readers of the death literature often come across such snippets and might well assume that philosophy is chock full of rigorous, profound, original, and systematic contributions to the understanding of death. (*Choral repeat: Not!*) To be sure, there are rewarding essays to be found, but first-rate philosophical discourses on death do not lie about on every side like golden nuggets.

And there is at least one more little problem with extracting consolation from philosophy. Not everybody responds decisively to cognitive/semantic input. Words on a page may have little power to influence a person in significant matters. This unresponsiveness can derive from a limited ability to follow rigorous argumentation, but it can also be more a matter of basic temperament. So this is where we make one further distinction about sources of consolation.

THE CONSOLING RELATIONSHIP

Earlier we explored the inclination to use philosophy as though a drug that might dull or happily befuddle our sensibilities and therefore relieve us of having to face mortal issues. An alternative approach was then illustrated through Boethius' masterwork. Much more deserving of the term "philosophical," this approach would offer consolation by engaging the rational side of our own nature in a systematic round of argument and counterargument. In concluding this brief exploration, I had to propose several qualifications, including the fact of individual differences. Just as some of us will not be enticed by philosophy as pharmaceutical, so some of us will not be truly consoled by thought alone, no mater how logical or rigorous.

This leaves us with a source of consolation not yet mentioned here, but which seems to be most suited to the temperament and needs of death educators and counselors. *Consolation may come in its most persuasive and acceptable form when it comes through a relationship.* A smile. A touch. An embrace. A few words that are significant not so much for their content as for their context and for their affirmation of a continuing relationship. These are the relational counterparts to the drug and syllogism. A person struggling with doubt, loss, and stress may find a measure of consolation and confidence through the supportive presence of other people.

It is far beyond the scope of this chapter to press an inquiry into the how and why of what we might call *relational consolation*. A few basic points can be suggested, however, for further study:

- Relational consolation probably draws its primary strength from early developmental experiences in which the young and vulnerable feel comforted by the presence as well as the actions of others; it is therefore a rooted experience with its own credibility base. One scarcely has to ask why an infant feels more secure when mother is there.
- Death-related issues often center on the loss of relationships. Again, there is a natural credibility involved when consolation is provided by companionship and togetherness—living proof that one is not alone when fearing loss of relationship.
- For reasons such as these, relational consolation does not require the escapism and deceit that is often associated with philosophy as drug, nor the flash of rational swords in combat, whose outcome can be far from certain, as in the traditional cognitive-philosophical approach.
- Generally, traditional consolation does not answer the cognitive philosophical questions, at least, not on a cognitive level. On the other hand, relational consolation need not contribute to falsification. The relationship itself seems to speak: "Here we are . . . and we are in it together . . . so let's go on together." There are implicit cognitive philosophies within relationship consolation that could be articulated, although not on this occasion. Just as cognitive/rational consolation touches on feelings and relationships when it is effective, so relational consolation is a way of expressing concepts and beliefs through human interaction.
- Death educators and counselors often have superior relational skills that they rely upon constantly in their work. The same may be said for many service-providers such as hospice staff and volunteers. Much of what is accomplished for dying and grieving people could be construed as relational consolation which, in turn, houses powerful if not fully articulate philosophies.

OK, NOW: WHAT CAN WE REALLY EXPECT
FROM PHILOSOPHY?

May I suggest—simply suggest—the two following propositions as realistic expectations of Philosophia for people who devote themselves to death education, counseling, and related activities.

1. *Many of the potential rewards are to be found in philosophical writings that are not focused on death.* Reference is made particularly to epistemology, the study of knowledge or, more specifically, of knowing. The assumptions, concepts and process of communication in death-related situations are highly vulnerable to epistemological error. We may not know what we think we know nor communicate what we believe we have communicated—and thereby contribute inadvertently to folly, suffering, and missed opportunities. Furthermore, because such concepts as "death," "dead," "dying," "terminal illness," "stages," and the like are far from simple, we can prepare ourselves to deal more with them in a less naive manner. The epistemological literature is vast and varied. One might begin with A. J. Ayer's *The Problem of Knowledge* [12] and then move to Bertrand Russell's *An Inquiry into Meaning and Truth* [13], and on from there in whatever direction one feels most impelled.

2. *We can use philosophical studies to stimulate our own self-development and thereby become more useful to students, clients, and others.* This was also at the core both of Socrates' quest and his method. Through lively and unsparing questioning of our own ideas and motives we begin to discover who we really are—and without true self-knowledge, we are in no position to appreciate philosophical insights. In trying to answer the question, *What is Philosophy?*, Ortega y Gasset reminds us of an incident in Egyptian mythology. Osiris has died and Isis "his beloved, eager to bring him back to life, makes him swallow the eye of the falcon, Horus. From then on the eye appears in all the hieratical drawings of Egyptian civilization, representing the first attribute of life—the act of seeing oneself" [14, p. 217]. This incident is very close in spirit to the Delphic oracle's celebrated advice to Socrates: "Know thyself." We might, then, seek out Philosophia as part of our quest for self-awareness and self-knowledge. This enterprise will not necessarily reveal to us either the secrets of life and death or a source of infallible consolation. It might be of great value, however, in preparing us to recognize truth, beauty, and goodness where ever and whenever we chance upon it. As more developed and self-aware selves we will be better able to appreciate life with both all its uncertainties and that one big certainty, respecting both our potentials and our limits.

Again, Ortega y Gasset:

> To live is not to enter by choice into a place which has been chosen earlier according to one's taste, as one might choose a theatre after dinner; it is to find oneself suddenly fallen, submerged, projected without knowing how, into a world which cannot be changed, into the world of now. Our life begins with

the astonishing and continuous surprise of existence. . . . Fundamentally, life is always unforeseen [14, p. 220].

REFERENCES

1. Plato, The Republic, in *The Dialogues of Plato*, Benjamin Jowett (trans.), Encyclopaedia Brittanica, Chicago, pp. 295-441, 1971.
2. J. Holveck, *Grief Reactions within the Adolescent Gang System*, Department of Communication, Arizona State University: Term Paper, 1992.
3. M. Grene, Martin Heidegger, in *The Encyclopedia of Philosophy*, P. Edwards (ed.), Volumes 3 and 4, Macmillan, New York, pp. 459-465, 1972.
4. R. Descartes, *On the Passions of the Soul*, 1646.
5. A. M. S. Boethius, *The Consolation of Philosophy*, R. Green (trans.), Bobbs- Merrill, Indianapolis, (Original work, 524), 1962.
6. W. James, Remarks at the Peace Banquet and the Moral Equivalence of War, in *William James*, M. Knight (ed.), Penguin, London, (Original work, 1904), pp. 240-248, 1954.
7. J. Choron, *Death and Western Thought*, Collier-Macmillan, New York, 1963.
8. J. Choron, *Death and Modern Man*, Collier Books, New York, 1971.
9. R. Kastenbaum, *The Psychology of Death* (Revised Edition), Springer, New York, 1992.
10. F. Copleston, *A History of Philosophy*, (Nine volumes reprinted in three.) Doubleday/Image, New York (Original work, 1946-1953), 1985.
11. D. J. Enright, (ed.), *The Oxford Book of Death*, Oxford University Press, Oxford, 1987.
12. A. J. Ayer, *The Problem of Knowledge*, Penguin Books, Baltimore, 1957.
13. B. Russell, *An Inquiry into Meaning and Truth*, Penguin Books, Baltimore, 1965.
14. J. Ortega y Gasset, *What is Philosophy?*, W. W. Norton, New York, 1964.

CHAPTER 2

Dying and Death—Late in the Twentieth Century

David J. Roy

"Our unspoken assumptions have the force of revelation."
Seamus Heaney [1, p. 19]

Montaigne said: "It is dying, not death, that I fear." That rings true today. We speak a great deal about dying—in hospitals, in academia, and even in the courts of law—and the stress in our talk is on dying with dignity. The phrase means so many important things, such as: controlling pain, managing symptoms, calming anxieties, comforting the dying and their families, knowing when and how to retire from insensitive technological prolongation of life, assuring quality of life when cure is no longer possible, and helping families live through their grief.

The acts we increasingly contemplate and discuss, in the name of giving dying patients maximal control over their dying, are challenging assumptions of Western civilizations about how far our dominion over human life, our own life included, really should extend. Yet while we openly and even passionately discuss the ways of dying, we seem to have signed a solemn pact with silence on the matter of death. To replace thought on death we seem to have substituted discourse and research about what we can somehow manage, and that is dying. We don't know how to manage death, so what could we possibly think or say about that?

I would like to speak of some unspoken assumptions that influence and control our words and deeds, and even our silence, as we face dying and death late in this century. I write predominantly in the first person because I am not a neutral objective observer describing correlations between realities in which I am uninvolved. I cannot assume that others will be able to reproduce or discover in their own experience the insights, the uncertainties, the anxieties, and, perhaps, the glimmers of hope that I have found in mine.

DYING . . . A STRUGGLE FOR DIGNITY?

In his story about the death of Ivan Ilyitch, Tolstoi asked "And the *mujiks* (the peasants), how do the *mujiks* die?" If Phillippe Ariès is correct [2], the peasants died the way Solzhenitzen described the dying of older folk in *The Cancer Ward*: no puffing up of themselves, no fighting against death, no pretending they weren't going to die, no stalling about squaring things away. They prepared themselves quietly and they departed easily "as if they were just moving into a new house" [3].

If that is how the *mujiks* died, it is not how many people today think they will die. People today fear loss of control when the time comes to die. They fear "a twilight life tethered to feeding tubes or respirators" [4, p. 553].

Blaise Pascal said that a human being, even when subjected to the laws of nature that dictate descent into death, remains superior to the entire universe. This is so, because a human being can know that he or she dies, while the universe knows nothing about what it does. The balancing truth is that human dignity does not reside in the power for thought and knowledge alone. Dignity comes to mature expression in the power to act knowledgeably and sensibly and to command respect for one's considered and cherished intentions.

Patients surviving on mandatory life-support technology are not always able to act in accordance with their considered and cherished intentions. They would often need help to act, and they cannot always command attention, understanding, and respect from doctors, nurses, or hospital administrators for a choice and decision that seemingly contradict a *raison d'être* of medicine, the saving of life. These patients may well wonder about the worth of being superior to the universe when they feel inferior and enslaved to a life-support medicine because of their inability to command if, when, and for how long, it will be used.

So, in the last decades of this century "dying with dignity" has become a rallying cry of opposition to degrading and useless prolongation of biological life, when a patient's organism, though still minimally functional, can no longer support or permit the exercise of intelligent and personal control over life's events. The trend of thought in both ethics and law has strengthened over the last twenty years against senseless tethering of people to life-prolongation technology.

Yet, we are not always able to act according to the same categories in which we think. We think in terms of autonomy, consent, and respect for a patient's individuality and life plans. Often, though, we act according to an absolute save-life-at-all-costs ethic, even at costs of suffering that sick people are unable to bear. The Cartesian *Cogito* is also still very much alive and very active. Health care professionals may well accept the principle that prolongation of life to the bitter end, and under suffering the patient finds intolerable, is not the right thing to do and yet balk at discontinuing life-prolonging treatment from a patient who is conscious, lucid, and is likely, with life support, to live for a good while.

Canada offers a recent poignant example. Nancy B., a twenty-four-year-old woman in a Quebec City hospital was afflicted with Guillain-Barré syndrome, a progressive neuromuscular disorder. Her respiratory muscles had deteriorated irreversibly and she had been in the hospital on a respirator support for two and a half years. Nancy could do nothing by or for herself, had no privacy, and repeatedly asked for the respirator to be disconnected so that her condition and nature could take its course. The respirator could keep her lungs going, but it would never get her going again.

The professionals charged with Nancy's care were uncertain of the legal consequences of disconnecting the respirator because Nancy would surely die quite rapidly without respirator support. So the case went to court. The judge decided that Nancy's request should be respected, that her request was not equivalent to suicide and that disconnecting the respirator was neither homicide nor euthanasia. Nancy's request was a refusal to be enslaved to a machine and it was also an affirmation that to be bearably alive requires more than being just a functioning brain.

The ethical and legal distinctions we make between allowing patients to die, suicide, and euthanasia are justifiable and logically defensible. But these distinctions often seem very thin to many people and they often fail to free doctors from the perception that in disconnecting respirators they have executed their patients. Philosophers are working overtime late in the century to shape and purify the concepts we need to frame and justify the decisions we have to make for realities we never had to face earlier.

DYING . . . PAIN OR PEACE?

Doctors should not be forced by any law of the state or by any dictate of mortality to stand by, helpless and hands tied, and to go just so far, and no farther, and not far enough in using whatever means are proportionate and effective in relieving dying patients from pain. Constant, wracking, and mind-twisting pain separates persons from themselves and from their loved ones. It shatters human integrity. Adequate control of pain, a prerequisite for an integrated human life, and for dying as an integrated human being, is the goal that should govern both the choice and combination of analgesics as well as the route, dosage, and frequency of administration.

It is foolish to deny patients relief from pain because of fears and uncertainties that analgesics, in doses needed for effective relief, may shorten life. A dying patient receiving frequent injections for pain control will eventually die after one of these injections. No one can really say the patient died *because* of the last injection [5, p. 84].

Methods exist today to control pain while maintaining consciousness. Yet, there is some controversy about whether these methods always work in the last days of life of people dying from advanced cancer. Some claim, others deny, that in these last days there is a crescendo of pain requiring sedation into unconsciousness as the only effective relief [6-8].

Those who argue for the ethical and legal justification of euthanasia must wonder about the clarity of the arbitrariness of the distinction between inducing unconsciousness and rapidly terminating life if and when dying persons experience a crescendo of unmanageable pain in the last days of life.

IS THERE ONLY ONE RIGHT WAY TO DIE?

My own words are coming back to haunt me and my unspoken assumptions are hounding me.

A number of years ago, I wrote that we would all do well to go slowly in fixing the modes of dignity in dying. The one attitude we must criticize, I emphasized, is thanatological totalitarianism, the idea that there is only one right way to die. I implied that there are many ways to die with dignity and that resigned acceptance of imminent death is no more an expression of human dignity than is Dylan Thomas' admonition to rail against the dying of the light and to go raging into that gentle night.

I was thinking then of *attitudes*, not *acts*, and I was quite comfortable with my thanatological liberalism. I was opposed to the idea that dignity in dying required people to exhibit the poise and the sentiments of acceptance of death. But I was assuming all along that rectitude, if not dignity, demanded of people that they accept—this means, that they await—their time, their moment of death.

This assumption, some would say, is a very theocratic assumption, is now, late in this century, being brought out into the open and into question. Should my thanatological liberalism tolerate the same diversity of acts as it would of attitudes?

Liberation from enslavement to life-prolonging technology, mentioned previously, is for some people not quite enough. I knew of a young man in the terminal stages of AIDS. He had a head full of projects and wanted to live. Yet, knowing he would inevitably die soon from AIDS, he asked for sufficient drugs and instructions in how to use them so that he could time his death to occur before he was led away and lost his mental competence. That is what he did as his dark days of increasing loss of function began to accumulate. He organized a farewell dinner for his friends, said his good-byes, took his drugs and died during the night.

Is this decision to advance one's death any less right or honorable or courageous than awaiting one's moment of death with quiet acceptance and resignation?

I have always admired Bridgman's philosophical reflections on physics, but one of his existential *pensées* still sends a chill up my spine. In his *Reflections of a Physicist*, Percy Williams Bridgman wrote: "Beyond the public level, waiting for a deeper analysis, is the private level. It is on the private level that I realize my essential isolation, here is my awful freedom that I can hardly face" [19, p. 75]. And how did he face his spreading inoperable cancer? Guy T. Emery, reviewer of a recently published Bridgman biography, describes Bridgman's way of facing death as stoic, rational, and straightforward. He didn't *await* death. He wrapped up work on his collected papers, wrote a note, and—awful freedom in essential isolation—he shot himself [10, p. 109].

That's how Bridgman died. He was aware of his essential isolation, and, though I had never met him, I, as a physics student, was aware of his presence in the original and penetrating ideas with which I had to grapple. I could never bring myself to judge his way of facing his impending demise and death from cancer. It would seem terribly wrong of me to presume the understanding and the capacity, let alone the right, to judge his act. But I cannot suppress my questions. Are human beings really so essentially isolated as he thought? Does his "awful freedom," and mine, or anyone else's include mastery over the time of one's death? Is the decision to await death and to pass through the disintegration and the losses of dying any less rational or straightforward than the decision to assume control and determine the time of one's death?

BEFORE DEATH . . . FREEING TIME . . . FOR WHAT?

Pain as we all know, is only one of suffering's dimensions. We suffer and hurt as persons, not just as brains in bodies. Eric Cassell has reminded us that persons suffer most profoundly when they face impending disintegration or destruction. The suffering proceeds "until the threat of disintegration has passed or until the integrity of the person can be restored in some other manner" [11, p. 6].

Death means destruction and disintegration. There is not much that anyone can do to make his threat pass in advanced terminal conditions. Can the integrity of persons be maintained or restored in the face of such threats?

How can any human being help another faced with the threat of impending disintegration to raise the enormous strength required to say, with the poet G. M. Hopkins, "I'll not despair, . . . not untwist, slack they may be, these last strands of man in me?" [12, p. 99].

The time of dying is a time for questions that shake the foundation of one's existence and threaten to expose the emptiness of one's dearest dreams. These questions may be only sensed, anxiously, or they may be faced lucidly in all their starkness—questions to which no one has ever given completely quieting answers.

How can one help another human being to face such questions if not by awakening him or her to an act of the spirit, an act of hope, that keeps one from falling apart when every empirical datum indicates one's impending biological disintegration and social disappearance?

The poet, whose name I do not know, captured the high demand of ministering to the spiritual needs of the dying when he wrote: "Such a price/The gods exact for song—/That we become what we sing . . . " Only someone who has "become the song"—and there are many such songs—can activate in another the tremendous forces of the spirit required to counter the emptying echo of the cry: This is pain! To think, to speak, to love and yet—to have to die!

It is profoundly depersonalizing to sense that one is nothing more than a sequence of moments signaling little more than one's impending disappearance. Unrelenting pain and symptom distress can bind a dying person's consciousness to the fragmenting moment-after-moment passage of his own time. If a person's time is bound to pain and distress, it cannot be used for anything else, it can't be integrated into a unique act of the spirit that would bind the person together and to someone else. So the great efforts of palliative medicine and palliative care to "control" pain and "manage" symptoms really serve the deeper existential purpose of freeing a dying person's time. This is so terribly crucial, when there is so little time left.

Freeing a dying person's time? For what? The lines of Czeslaw Milosz's poem, "Earth Again," intimate a bold and almost incredible answer. One frees a dying person's time "so that for a short moment there is no death and time does not unreel like a skein of yarn thrown into an abyss" [13, p. 8].

The poet sings, rather than states, that certain moments of time can be so charged with life that they burst forth from entropy's downward sweep, escape death's gravitation, and hover above the course of biology and history as permanent signals of human transcendence. These moments, shaped together by the human spirit's highest concentrations of power, hold together and last forever, untouched by the biological pull toward decomposition of the person's body and its return to the earth. These are unique configurations of time, forever redeemed, whatever may happen afterwards; moments of time fused into a personal identity that will never pass away, even if there is no one around who remembers.

That's just a poem, some will say and you can do anything with words. It is possible, perhaps, for us as persons to do with real acts of presence and personal gift what the poet has done with words?

IN THE FACE OF DEATH . . . WHAT CAN WE DO?

One night, not so long ago, in the middle of a dinner among four friends, a doctor, pained and reflective over the deaths of so many of the AIDS patients in his care, asked me: "Do you think there *is* life after death? Doesn't the law of entropy govern everything? Aren't we, small and insignificant, caught for a short time, our lifetime, between two impenetrable darknesses: where we have come from and where we are going?"

I knew I couldn't, in the seconds of a respectably short pause, come up with any striking metaphysical answers as to what people might *think* or *say* about death. So I picked the questions about what people might possibly *do* in the face of death and its darkness.

Well, what *might* people possibly do? Hold hands, I said. We all have to enter that darkness, so we might do it together, holding hands, as did the two officers, about to be executed, at the end of the film *Breaker Morant*. And laugh, I said, we might laugh. My friends looked at me oddly and I had to explain that I did not mean the cynical, empty laugh that banalizes real evil. I meant the full blooming cosmic laugh, that spontaneous response to a release from dread coming with the sudden realization: "Oh, is *that* all it is!" But that explanation didn't carry the evening either. So I was pressed to admit: to laugh because I know I'm bigger and more lasting, that death can only happen if I know how to do that most mighty of human acts, to hope.

So, what might people *do* in the face of death and its darkness? I know of only three alternatives: distraction, despair, or hope. Or is there something else?

A little boy in France startled George Steiner on the occasion of Jean-Paul Sartre's funeral. There were throngs and throngs of people in the funeral cortege and Steiner asked a little boy, "What's going on?" The boy answered, *"Une manif contre la mort de Sartre"*; indeed, a manif(estation), a demonstration against death, against the death of Sartre [14, p. 3].

So there is something else one can do in the face of death: one can demonstrate against it. So, at least, thinks the primitive mind. People in earlier generations and in other cultures, more primitive than we—we may think—thought and spoke of death with hatred, as they would of an enemy to be conquered, as of an enemy to be taunted: "O death, where *is* thy sting, *where* thy victory?"

Who today could possibly be so uninhibited, so nakedly primitive as to admit a hatred of death? We live in a culture of high science and technology, so we laudably marshal and perfect the surgery, drugs, and technology that empower us to *postpone* death, as we often do so masterfully. *Postpone* death, yes, but *face* death when it can no longer be postponed? Well, it's not true to say we do not think about death. We do, at least in academic circles. We can hold our own with educated people of the past and, as they have done, we too know how to philosophize and say a great number of clever things about death as a biological necessity, about death as a part of the natural order of things, about death in the context of the field theory of modern physics, about the mind-body duality, and . . . and . . . and.

We live in a culture, it is assumed, of high education. Though we can tolerate a degree of metaphysical discourse about matters unthinkable, we acutely resent embarrassingly anthropomorphic and primitive displays of hatred, hubris, or despair against death. Better the rational stance of calm silence in the face of a fate that is biologically necessary, inevitable, and universal. Better not to ask the primitive questions that make people queasy because no one knows how to answer them, except, perhaps, with the mumbled symbols of some ancient religion.

So, we increasingly and successfully socialize ourselves into silence about any questions that would direct us beyond the boundaries of what "human agency can alleviate" [15, p. 62]. We shrink away from the thrust of our own intelligence when it would drag us, if given free rein, into a darkness where no data, no concepts, no hypotheses, and no proof could silence or calm the dread and the rage with which an awakened human spirit should tremble in confronting the apparently all-too-real and inevitable fate of personal extinction.

> Below the surface-stream, shallow and light,
> Of what we *say* we feel—below the stream
> As light, of what we *think* we feel—there flows
> With noiseless current strong, obscure and deep,
> The central stream of what we feel indeed.... [16, p. 413].

The great repression and distraction of late twentieth-century culture forces us increasingly into silence about "what we feel indeed" on the frontier of death's darkness. We are cut off from the deepest questions our own intelligence would ask, because these are questions to which neither we ourselves, nor any other human agency, can adequately respond. So, we are not simply silent about these questions, we rather learn not to ask them anymore. How could we, when the language we would need, even just to phrase the questions, let alone to speak meaningfully to them, is now largely dead?

In classicist cultures language was held together, taut, tight, and vibrant by a single set of beliefs and ideals that were both the standard and the space of thought and discourse for all human beings in all times and places. But we live in a fractured and fragmented post-classicist world. If to hope is to believe, we no longer share the same beliefs, and who would dare speak of his or her own beliefs, except in the comforting circle of cultic friends?

Our science, in a post-classicist world, is not a ready-made achievement stored for all time in a great book, but an ongoing process that no library, let alone any single mind, is expected to encompass [17, p. 241]. Our ethics, likewise, are not a simple inheritance of principle, completed and ready for universal application. And this is our condition too when we meet one another at the frontiers of death. We no longer have *one* great book from which we can read words of strength and promise to awaken acts of hope in people who tremble when cumulative losses and impending death crack the protective shell of everyday routine thoughts, images, and dreams.

FACING DEATH . . . ON THE BOUNDARIES
OF HUMANISM

One of my friends at that same dinner not so long ago wondered if he would ever find the strength of faith to face his own death, and the death of his loved ones calmly, and without a crushing sense of despair. I rather brutally asked him: "What do you want to be? Stronger than Jesus?" What did I mean? Well, that central figure, if one can believe the narratives of his life, died with two seemingly diametrically opposed cries: "Father, into Thy hands I commend my spirit," and "My God, my God, why have You abandoned me?" If these are the overtones and undertones of the human spirit on the boundaries of humanism, can we do anything better on those boundaries that hold these two seemingly contradictory experiences together in tension? Is that the way of not untwisting, slack they maybe, these last strands of man in me?

REFERENCES

1. S. Heaney, *The Haw Lantern*, Faber and Faber, London, Boston, 1987.
2. P. Ariès, *Western Attitudes Toward Death: From the Middle Ages to the Present*, The Johns Hopkins University Press, Baltimore and London, pp. 1-25, 1974.
3. A. Solzhenitzen, *Cancer Ward*, New York, pp. 96-97, 1969.
4. Final Exit: Euthanasia Guide sells out, *Nature, 352*, 1991.
5. H. Trowell, *The Unfinished Debate on Euthanasia*, SCM Press, London, 1973.
6. V. Ventafridda, et al., Symptom Prevalence and Control During Cancer Patients' Last Days of Life, *Journal of Palliative Care, 6*:3, pp. 7-11, 1990.
7. B. Mount, A Final Crescendo of Pain?, *Journal of Palliative Care, 6*:3, pp. 5-6, 1990.
8. R. Fainsinger, et al., Symptom Control During the Last Week of Life on a Palliative Care Unit, *Journal of Palliative Care, 7*:1, pp. 5-11, 1991.
9. P. W. Bridgman, *Reflections of a Physicist*, Philosophical Library, New York, 1950.
10. G. T. Emery, No Holds Barred, *Nature, 351*, 1991.
11. E. Cassell, The Nature of Suffering and the Goals of Medicine, *The New England Journal of Medicine, 306*, 1982.
12. G. M. Hopkins, Carrion Comfort, in *The Poems of Gerard Manley Hopkins*, W. H. Gardnor and N. H. MacKenzie (eds.), Oxford University Press, Oxford, New York, Toronto, 1980.
13. C. Milosz, *Unattainable Earth*, translated by the author and Robert Hags, The Ecco Press, New York, 1986.
14. G. Sleiner, Sartre in Purgatory, *The Times Library Supplement*, May 3, 1991.
15. P. Ramsey, The Indignity of "Death with Dignity," *The Hastings Center Studies, 2*, 1974.
16. M. Arnold, St. Paul and Protestantism, in *After Babel: Aspects of Language and Translation*, G. Sleiner (ed.), Oxford University Press, New York, 1975.
17. B. Lonergan, Dimensions of Meaning, in *Collected Works of Bernard Lonergan, Vol. 4*, F. E. Crowe and R. M. Doran (eds.), University of Toronto Press, Toronto, 1988.

PART II

Perspectives in Philosophical Thanatology

The trauma of death, which is at the heart of awareness of mortality, may shake the very foundations of our assumptive world. The questions about the meaning of life and death that the bereaved may be compelled to think about are the same questions that philosophical thanatology must confront with disciplined intellectual passion. As both Pletcher and Morgan point out in different ways, the experienced meaninglessness of death and life forces us to ask in a basic, if not a radical way, about the meaning of human existence. The awareness of mortality of the various authors in this section raises questions about the meaning of human consciousness (Kauffman), the meaning of individuality and freedom (Warren), the meaning of suffering (Kallenberg), the meaning of death as transcendence (Morgan), the meaning of meaning (Pletcher), and the meaning of selfhood and mystery (Tomer).

Philosophical thanatology has the responsibility to question presuppositions; to address topics that lie beyond the scope of empirical data; to be a context for processing the experience of mortality, the search for meaning, and the exploration of transcendence; to prod the self to question itself; to disturb quiescent consciousness; to strengthen the tolerance for the painfulness of mortality; to foster intellectual discipline in thanatology; and, to provide a place within thanatology for rational discourse and dialogue. In "Part II: Perspectives in Philosophical Thanatology," examples of philosophical reflections that address some of these issues are presented.

Morgan introduces the reader to the classical philosophical problem of the immortality of the soul. He presents an argument for the immortality of the soul as a response to the pain experienced in, e.g., the thought "What gives meaning to the life condemned to death." On the journey of the human soul, Morgan says, death is the awakening to self-consciousness, independence and activity: Death is the awakening to God.

27

Warren urges us to recognize how the sociopolitical collectivization of the meaning of death prevents the development of individuality. Groups (national, ethnic, religious, etc.) restrain our freedom to reflect upon our own individual meaning of death. Building upon Kierkegaard, Heidegger, Steiner and Marcuse, he helps us recognize the connectedness of freedom and individual identity to the project of philosophical thanatology.

Kallenberg reflects on the eternal question of suffering, and the need for every historical period and for each individual to raise this question anew. He considers the effects of secularization and technology on the dilemma of finding meaning in suffering in the modern world. A basic attitude of trust, he suggests, is needed to constitute a sense of meaning. He explores both the existential quest for meaning and the general philosophical question whether suffering and death have any meaning at all.

Pletcher writes about the philosophical problem of meaning. He explores the relationship between awareness of death and meaning in life. He argues that "awareness of death is awareness of the possibility that our life can have meaning, not because of life's intrinsic value, but because of its limitations and impermanence."

Kauffman develops a thanatocentric theory of consciousness in which the very existence of human consciousness is understood to arise out of and to be coextensive with mortality. He described the development of consciousness from embeddedness in a rudimentary mortality awareness to a more differentiated awareness of mortality. This is a process in which death, disassociated from consciousness as objectification and as otherness, returns to consciousness as a self-awareness of mortality. In Kauffman's account, awareness of mortality is paradoxical, and is an awareness of the mystery of death at the center of human consciousness.

In the concluding chapter of this section, Tomer explores the relationship between personal identity and death concerns. He invites the reader to enter into some puzzles or thought experiments that may bring about changes in the perception of oneself and effect one's concerns about death. These puzzles lead Tomer to the liberation of the self and to a redemptive "heartfelt mystery based on reflection." Tomer sees transcendence as part of a developmental process. He concludes this chapter with the illuminating proposal that in the final stage of development, there is renunciation of the principle of individuality as a way to deal with the mystery of death.

CHAPTER 3

Immortality

John Morgan

Ivan Ilych's life was "most simple and most ordinary and therefore most terrible" [1, p. 16]. He served as a public administrator, had a marriage of convenience, and fathered children. Having injured himself in a seemingly minor manner, he was now dying a painful death [1, p. 24]. His physicians treated him indifferently, now knowing or at least, not telling him a correct diagnosis and prognosis [1, p. 34]. His wife hated him, saw him as inept and believed that his illness was his own fault and remained aloof [1, p. 37]. His fellow workers treated him in a merely correct manner [1, p. 38]. Meditating on the fate that awaited him, we find him: " . . . agonizingly, unbearably miserable. 'It is impossible that all men have doomed to suffer this awful horror' " [1, p. 42].

We see a similar fatalism and despair in the song that Peggy Lee recorded a few years ago entitled *Is That All There Is?* [2]. The song chronicled several events in a young girl's life, each ending in the disappointment exemplified by the question, "Is that all there is?" Just before the end of the song, Miss Lee anticipates our question "Why doesn't she end it all?" with the response that she is not ready for "that final disappointment."

These fundamentally pessimistic views of human existence are not rare. They are common in the work of the French philosopher Albert Camus, in his plays, novels and essays. The question "Why not commit suicide?" for Camus means: "what reason do I have to continue living when life simply doesn't make sense?" [3, p. 4]. One looks for some sort of meaning in one's life and expects the world to give an answer. According to Camus, there isn't any meaning in the world [3, p. 16]. The world is simply there [3, p. 16]. What is absurd is looking for meaning. The senselessness of life stems, for Camus, from the fact that we demand explanations for the way the world is and while many theories are proposed, none is satisfactory [3, p. 21].

"Any thoughtful man might well imagine that he could have devised a cosmic operation less replete with frustration, suffering, and indignity" [4, p. 17]. The purpose of this chapter is to explore the question implicit in the remarks of Albert Camus, Ivan Ilych, and Peggy Lee. Is the fate of humans to live trivial lives, to suffer disappointment after disappointment until that final disappointment, death? Is it possible that life has a meaning, and that death is something other than an *"awful horror?"* **What gives meaning to a life condemned to death?** From time immemorial, theologians, philosophers, and non-professional thinkers alike have thought that some meaning to life is found in immortality—the continued existence of the person after death.

THE MEANING OF THE TERM

"Immortality" has several meanings. According to Lifton, aside from the philosophical, literal sense of "not subject to death," there are also the biological, the theological, the artistic or creative, and the natural [5, p. 22]. I will use the term in its literal sense, the idea that some aspect of the human person is not subject to death. Thus, the way I am using the term, immortality is natural, as opposed to the Christian sense of resurrection in which a specific act of God occurs to reverse death.

HUMAN KNOWING CAPACITY

When Socrates, Plato's teacher, was condemned to death, rather than plead for mercy as his accusers had hoped [6, p. 417], Socrates announced: "Wherefore, O Judges, be of good cheer about death, and know of a certainty that no evil can happen to a good man, either in life or after death" [6, p. 423]. Socrates' response differs from Illych's, Camus', and from that implicit in Peggy Lee because they differ in their views of the human knowing capacity. The ancient philosophers who held that the person is immortal, did so because of epistemological foundations which I believe continue to be sound.

The basic problem of epistemology (theory of knowledge) and thus of all philosophy is what has been called the question of universals. By a universal is meant a knowing awareness that is applicable to two or more instances of the referent of that awareness. For example, the idea "paper" can be used to mean the substance on which these words are written, the thing that is delivered to one's doorstep in the morning, or the thing in which a gift is wrapped. Each of these things are in some sense paper. Yet each specific instance to which the idea "paper" refers is different. To be more exact I will limit myself to paper meaning "a physical object made from wood or other pulp for the purpose of receiving and storing visible character." The way the terms are used, *papers* are individual examples of paper, the generic. *Paper* refers to individuals, paper is the universal, the idea, the generalization. The history of thought has used many expressions for this awareness.

Individuals are "one out of many." What this means is that there are many pieces of paper in the universe, and the one that I see in front of me is "one out of many." There are many pieces of chalk in the world, and the one in my hand in class is "one out of many." The accurate meaning of the word individual is "one out of many."[1] A universal refers to an awareness that "is equally applicable to more than one individual or more than one instance of the same individual." The idea paper applies equally to each of the many individual pieces of *paper* on my desk. The idea mother applies equally to the many persons who are *mothers* as well as the many experiences that one has of his/her individual *mother*.

Seemingly the only things that come into daily experience are individual things—this piece of paper in front of me, the piece of paper which is a memo from the department chairman, the piece of paper on which the first page of the newspaper is printed. I have experienced only individual pieces of *paper*, but I know intellectually that they all are subsumable under the same or the same idea, *paper*.

A different example might be easier. As strange as it may seem, we have never heard *music*. What we have heard is individual events of the "the rhythmic progression of sound." Yet, the question "Do you like music?" is a meaningful question. The hearer is aware of his/her liking music as a whole, not simply the individual experiences which s/he has had. Even such a specific piece of music as Beethoven's Ninth Symphony is a universal. We have heard only individual renditions of that symphony. Thus when asked if we like it, we do not respond that we like the individual sensations we heard, but we like our "universalized" experience of Beethoven's Ninth, or of music.

Plato [6] and Aristotle [7] noticed this aspect about the human mind twenty-five centuries ago when they said that we are capable of perceiving the difference between "white" and "this white thing" [7, p. 701]. There is a difference between knowing the thing and knowing the idea. **The "problem" of universals is this: we experience only individual things, but we think only in universal concepts.**

One of the basic principles of philosophy is that there must be a sufficient reason for every event [8, p. 35]. This transcending of the limitations of experience sense data must be caused by, or rooted in something. It doesn't seem as though the physical world can be the reason for generalizations, the world doesn't have paper-in-general, or *mother-in-general*, *music-in-general* or anything else in-general. The world has "*this paper*," "*this mother*," or "*this music*." If this

---

[1] Thus when one says that "I am not being treated as an individual," they are in error. To be treated as a sex object, a cog in the wheel of industry, or as gun fodder for the military industrial complex is precisely to be treated as an individual—one out of many. What they are *not* being treated as is a *person*, a unique substance of a rational nature. (Boethius).

experience occurs and it is not rooted in the thing known, the physical world, then it must be rooted in the knower.

THE SOUL

In order to explain the idea of soul, at least in Western philosophical thought, one has to look at how the Greeks of the Golden Age explained change. A century after Thales (Bakewell, [9]), asked the questions from which we date the origin of philosophy [9, p. 1], Thinkers had reached an impasse. Heraclitus [9, p. 28], define the original matter of the universe as *fire*, belived that the universe, as is a fire in a fireplace, is in constant change and that stability is an illusion. Parmenides, on the other hand, seemingly the first to arrive at the abstract term *being*, held that all things are a part of one vast all, and that changes is an illusion [10, p. 11]. Plato hinted at a solution to the problem in the Parmenides [10, p. 98] but his student, Aristotle, gave a fuller explanation. Change for Aristotle is explained by the hypothesis, the hylemorphic theory, that there are two fundamental *principles of being*, matter and form [11, p. 229]. Matter is amorphous, without determination, infinite possibility; form is determination, specification. Thus the piece of paper in front of me is **matter specified by form to be a particular thing**. Change is the infinite potentiality of matter losing one set of characteristics, forms, or receiving others. Thus neither Heraclitus or Parmenides are fully right or fully wrong. The world is stable because matter is stable, the world is in flux, because matter continually loses and receives forms.

We see in our experience two fundamentally different types of things. There are those things which are fundamentally passive, that is, they react to light, react to chemicals and heat, but seemingly do not initiate their own activity. If I want this piece of paper to move from one place on the desk to another I, or some other external force, have to move it. All the coaxing in the world will not get the paper to move itself. On the other hand, there are things in the world which are self-moving. A plant takes nutrients from the soil and converts them into itself, an animal moves to a sunny window, the person decides to go to university. We call this ability to move oneself *life*, and it is found generically in plants, animals, and persons.

In order to differentiate the specifying agent in a living individual, Plato and Aristotle call this specifying agent *soul*, rather than form. Thus soul in Greek thought refers to the "source of activities of a living thing," or the "form of a living thing." Aristotle's technical definition of the soul is "the first act of a body capable of vital activity" [12, p. 555]. Thus plants are besouled, as are animals and persons.

There is a long history to the idea of a soul and to the human recognition that life differs from non-life. "There appears to be a universal tendency to conceive of each person as possessing a vital substance, and élan vital, that animates his behavior and quickens his body" [13, p. 222]. The word soul is an Anglo-Saxon term referring to the controlling agency, governing the vital principle in humans [14, p. 222]. The equivalent Greek term is *psyche* or *pneuma* and the latin term is *anima* [15, p. 542]. The original meaning of the idea "soul" is breath in both Greek philosophy and the Hebrew Bible. In Greek life the *psyche* was a subtle, animating principle which left the body at death; in the rites of Dionysus the *psyche* was for the first time regarded as a principle superior to the body, and imprisoned by it, and the Pythagoreans held the *psyche* to be the "harmony" of the body [15, p. 566].

> From primitive peoples as the Australian aborigines to the most sophisticated of the world religions, beliefs in the existence of an individual "soul" have persisted, conceivably with a capacity both to antedate and to survive the individual organism or body. The persistence of that belief and the factors giving rise to it provide the framework for the problematic of death in the Western world [14, p. 256].

THE CHARACTERISTICS OF SOUL

The person is a unified being. For the sake of convenience, we speak of hands, feet, liver, and other parts, but in reality we are an intrinsic unity such that the fundamental activity of the part would be different apart from the whole than when it is in the whole. Thus for most of our activity, we can say that the whole person acts. However, since a thing can act only to the extent that it is, if we see activities which transcend the powers of the body, then we can hold the position that the soul is acting independently of the body.

It seems that the soul operates independently of the body in thinking. It is true that all the raw material of thought comes through organic senses, however, that does not imply that it remains organic. Body by its very nature is in space and time. What we mean by individuality is occurrence within a specific space and at a specific time. Thus if Aristotle, Plato, and Aquinas are correct that thinking is not individuated, then the thinking capacity of the person is doing something that a body cannot do, generalize. I think that then following examples might be helpful.

1. The statement "Dr. Morgan taught Anselm's argument for the existence of God in San Diego in 1963, in Montreal in 1974 and in London (Ontario) in 1977" is a true statement. What is the mind doing in making that assertion? Does it not seem that the mind is transcending the limits of space and time? The mind can think of itself in Los Angeles thirty years ago, the body cannot present itself as such.

2. Because the mind gets its information from the body while the body has images of reality, we tend to confuse the two. However, the following example may show that the mind is doing something different than does the body. I know

the difference between a plane, closed, three-sided figure (a triangle), and a plane, closed, four-sided figure (a rectangle). Because the mind and body operate together when I think of these examples, I think the meanings of triangle and square while my memory (a sense organ) pictures them. However, this is not always the case. I know the difference between a plane, closed figure of 7,312 sides and a plane, closed figure of 7,313 sides—but I cannot picture them. The mind is dependent on the body for information. That does not imply that the mind is dependent on the body for being. I am dependent on a movie screen for information, but that does not stop me from getting up and walking out.

3. The mind can reflect upon itself. Let us use the following as a definition of mind: "that capacity to know in a non-individualized way." Any definition would do, but that definition is consistent with what has been said so far. Who made up that definition of mind? The mind defined itself by reflecting on its activities. I can make one physical thing touch another physical thing; I can make one part of a physical thing (a piece of paper) touch another part of the same thing; but I cannot make the same part bend back on itself. While you can use the tip of the index finger of the right hand to touch anything, including the tip of the index finger on the left hand, what the tip of the index finger on the right hand cannot do is touch the tip of the index finger of the right hand. Physical things cannot reflect on themselves, the mind can. This capacity to transcend the limits of material things is called *spirituality*.

IMMORTALITY

If the soul does something that the body cannot do, think, then there is no reason to think that the death of the body necessarily entails the death of the soul. We can destroy something by breaking it into component parts or destroying that upon which it depends for existence. But the soul has no parts, and as we have seen it is dependent upon body for *operation*, but not for *existence*. As a simple (partless) substance, the soul is intrinsically immortal [15, pp. 439-440].

What does the soul do after death? "Aye, there's the rub" [17, p. 47]. Speaking without an appeal to faith, we have no knowledge of life after death. Since the soul is dependent on the body for learning, nothing new could be learned after death. Is the soul dependent on the body for remembering what has already been known? In this life we do not remember except through the stimulation of the senses. However, Aquinas holds that in this life the manner of being of the soul is to be united to the body and to operate that way. He does not believe that implies the same thing after death [18, p. 77]. Maybe disembodied souls operate differently. Aquinas also holds that since the soul's way of being is to be united with a body, God would not have created an intrinsically defective being—a soul without a body [19, p. 332]. He uses this as an argument for the resurrection of the body [19, p. 332].

The Near Death experiences have many common elements

> an out-of-body experience during which one's body is viewed and conversa-
> tions are overheard; a feeling of peace; travelling through a tunnel; meeting or
> seeing a dead relative, beings of light, or historical religious figures; a life
> review, in which the events in one's life are re-evaluated in the light of greater
> understanding; experiences in preternatural realms of light; being told to
> return to life to complete unfinished business; and a deep feeling of sadness
> upon leaving this blissful dimension [20, p. 73].

In addition, emphasis is placed on seeing medical procedure while one was out of
the body and clinically dead. In some cases these experiences were such that they
could not have been seen on television medical shows [21, p. 35]. If such really
happen, there is additional evidence for the ability of the human knowing capacity
to transcend the limits of the body.

THE HUMAN JOURNEY

Who is the I that undergoes death? We are so used to filling out resumes that we
sometimes may believe that the "I" that each of us consists of is a long series of
independent characteristics. Yet someone could know all that objective data about
us, and not really know us. We could surprise even those who live with us most
intimately. In moments of self-pity, we state that "nobody understands me." But
perhaps the reality is that nobody understands anyone, and we face that reality
only in such moments. Jose Ortega y Gasset described the person as a "radical
solitude" [22, p. 140], that is, at the very root (radix) of us, there is an ultimate
incommunicability and loneliness.

This realization that we are not our resume, that no list of characteristics no
matter how long can enclose us is called the "subjectivity" [23, p. 15]. Life does
not consist of objective characteristics but is a process of creating the person we
are to become from the biological raw material as well as the events of biography.

> The unborn child obviously is given an existence he did not request, a heritage
> and environment he could not choose. He did not select his parents or his race,
> or the time and place of his birth. He is borne along on the preexisting currents
> of family and society. Soon, however, the conscious self awakens and he rises
> high enough above the currents to accept or fight their obscure forces. Born
> into a community whose structure was imposed on him, he gradually become
> aware of his personal autonomy. His actions become increasingly inde-
> pendent; the environment that once held him widens; self-consciousness
> deepens; he realizes more and more his capacity for deepening the type of
> relationship he wants to maintain with his given situation [24, p. 130].

Life is continual self-development and self independence. As the human being progresses from conception to maturity the balance between passive response to stimuli and active initiation of activity tips more heavily toward the activity side. Full activity, however, cannot occur while we are still bound by the body since the body provides such powerful stimuli. Full activity, therefore, would seem to be possible only on a departure from the body [24, p. 132]. In old age the person is preparing to leave an environment no longer capable of supporting his growth [24, p. 131]. Death finally emerges as: "man's first completely personal act, and is, therefore, by reason of its very being, the place above all others for the awakening of consciousness, for freedom, for the encounter with God, for the final decision about eternal destiny" [24, p. 129]. This is a spiritual journey, the independence of the person from the limits of the here and now. "By *spiritual* I allude to the journey of the soul—not to religion itself but to the drive in humankind that gives rise to religion in the first place" [25, p. 8]. The spiritual is the human striving toward meaning, the search for a sense of belonging [25, p. 8], the sense of belonging in the universe and a vibrant awareness of the oneness of everything. "To love God is to be in love with the universe. This all might be viewed as Idea One of the spiritual path" [25, p. 13].

> The foetus is subjected to the most painful crisis of its prenatal life precisely when it is about to be born: it is squeezed, constricted, almost strangles, and finally expelled, with no knowledge for it of free air, space, light and love awaiting it beyond the passage. Immediately before death, this other great passage, man suffers biological dissolution. As Shakespeare expressed it: "He shuffles off this mortal coil." With no experience of what he is about to become, he fights for air and feels as if he were being expelled from his body. It is clear, therefore, that the positive meaning of this event cannot be revealed by the preparatory phase, the expulsion: the pains of birth are not yet birth itself, and old age and dying are not yet the stage at which the spiritual person is delivered from the material body [26, p. 188].

Departure from the material body in which passivity prevails would appears as a necessary condition of full activity [26, p. 189]. The meaning of this earthly adventure is to train the spiritual person for that free act whereby he is to establish his own being. Man is incarnated spirit whom is in the act of *becoming* before he attains the fulness of his *being* [26, p. 196].

The journey which we call life is acceptance of ourself in an external now. Failure to do so, places our lives outside of ourselves. The unhappy person "is always absent, never present to himself" [27, p. 64].

> He cannot become old, for her has never been young; he cannot become young, because he is already old. In one sense of the world he cannot die for he has not really lived; in another sense, he cannot live for he is already dead.

He cannot love, for love is in the present and he has no present, no future, no past. . . . He has no time at all [28, p. 80].

Too often we are so afraid of dying, that we do not find time for living. Fear or terror is an expression of man's spirituality, of his inability to be content with himself.

We must, in Steven Levine's words, die consciously in order to live consciously. "To let go of the last moment and open to the next is to die consciously" [29, p. 68]. Focusing on death is a way of becoming fully alive [29, p. 68]. Perhaps the first recognition in the process of acknowledging, opening, and letting go that I call "conscious dying" is when we begin to see that we are not only the body. We see that we have a body but it is not fully who we are [29, p. 68]. Conscious death is not merely from without; it must also be an act that one personally performs. "More precisely still it must be death itself which is the act and not merely an attitude which man adopts toward death" [24, p. 125].

CONCLUSION

I have attempted to examine the question of meaning in life through the question of the immortality of the person. It is our view that the abstracting power of the mind is an indication that the human person is capable of engaging in an act that cannot be explained by bodily activity. It is our view that the human soul is a spiritual entity which acts in conjunction with the body to gain experience but is not limited to the activity of the body. Since the person is more than a body, the death of the body is not the end of the person's life. Consequently, life takes on a different meaning. The purpose of life is the continual development of the self, a development that will fully occur only after death.

REFERENCES

1. L. Tolstoi, *The Death of Ivan Ilych*, L. Maude and A. Maude (trans.), Health Sciences, New York, 1973.
2. J. Leiber, Is That All There Is? in New York Times, *Greatest Songs of the 60's*, Quadrangle/New York Times Book Company, New York (Originally published 1966), 1970.
3. A. Camus, The Myth of Sisyphus, in *The Myth of Sisyphus and Other Essays*, J. O'Brien (trans.), Vintage, New York, 1960.
4. A. C. Outler, God's Providence and the World's Anguish, in *The Mystery of Suffering and Death*, M. J. Taylor (ed.), Doubleday, Garden City, 1974.
5. C. A. Corr, Reconstructing the Face of Death, in *Dying: Facing the Facts*, H. Wass, R. Neimeyer, and H. Bernado (eds.), Hemisphere, Washington, 1979.
6. Plato, The Apology, in *The Dialogues of Plato*, B. Jowett (trans.), Random House, New York, 1937.

7. Aristotle, The Metaphysics, in *The Basic Works of Aristotle*, R. McKeon (ed.), Random House, New York, 1941.

8. B. Wuellner, *Summary of Scholastic Principles*, Loyola, Chicago, 1956.

9. C. M. Bakewell, *Source Book in Ancient Philosophy*, New York: Scribners, New York, 1939.

10. Plato, The Parmenides, in *The Dialogue of Plato*, R. Demos (ed.), B. Jowett (trans.), Random House, New York, 1937.

11. Aristotle, The Physics, in *The Basic Works of Aristotle*, R. McKeon (ed.), Random House, New York, 1941.

12. Aristotle, On the Soul, in *The Basic Works of Aristotle*, R. McKeon (ed.), Random House, New York, 1941.

13. D. Landy, Death: I. Anthropological Perspective, in *Encyclopedia of Bioethics*, W. T. Reich (ed.), Vol. I, Free Press, New York, 1978.

14. D. M. High, Death, Definition and Determination of: Conceptional Foundations: III Philosophical and Theological Foundations, in *Encyclopedia of Bioethics*, W. T. Reich (ed.), Vol. I, Free Press, New York, 1978.

15. W. L. Reese, *Dictionary of Philosophy and Religion: Eastern and Western Thought*, Humanities Press, Atlantic Highlands, 1980.

16. T. Parsons, Death: V Death in the Western World, in *Encyclopedia of Bioethics*, W. T. Reich (ed.), Vol. I, Free Press, New York, 1978.

17. W. Shakespeare, *Hamlet: Prince of Denmark. Great Books of the Western World*, Volume 27, Encyclopedia Britannica, Chicago, 1956.

18. T. Aquinas, Summa Contra Gentiles, (trans.), [reference to life after death and knowledge of soul], 1945.

19. J. E. Royce, *Man and His Nature*, McGraw Hill, New York, 1961.

20. P. Peay, Back from the Grave, *Common Boundary*, in *Utne Reader*, September/October 1991.

21. R. A. Moody, *Life after Life*, Bantam, New York, 1975.

22. J. Ortega y Gasset, In Search of Goethe from Within, in *Dehumanization of Art and Other Writings on Art and Culture*, Doubleday, Garden City, 1956.

23. J.-P. Sartre, Existentialism as a Humanism, in *Existentialism and Human Emotions*, Philosophical Library, New York, 1985.

24. G. J. Dyer, Recent Developments in the Theory of Death, in *The Mystery of Suffering and Death*, M. J. Taylor (ed.), Doubleday, Garden City, 1974.

25. J. E. Fortunato, *AIDS: The Spiritual Dilemma*, Harper & Row, San Francisco, 1987.

26. R. Troisfontaines, The Mystery of Death, in *The Mystery of Suffering and Death*, M. J. Taylor (ed.), Doubleday, Garden City, 1974.

27. S. Kierkegaard, *Either/Or*, in Hegel and Existentialism: On Unhappiness, A. Lessing (ed.), *The Personalist, 49*:1, 1968.

28. S. Kierkegaard, Sickness unto Death, in *The Denial of Death*, E. Becker (ed.), Free Press, New York, 1973.

29. S. Levine, Conscious Dying: It All Begins with Conscious Living, *Utne Reader*, 1991.

CHAPTER 4

The Idea of "The Glorious Dead": The Conversion of a Uniquely Personal Experience

Bill Warren

A familiar sight in most countries of the world, certainly in most western countries but undoubtedly beyond the west, is that of monuments to those who have died in some war or other ideological struggle. The two Great Wars left widespread markers of loss. From outback Australia to North Yorkshire villages in the United Kingdom, from lonely battlefield cemeteries scattered throughout Europe to the small towns and large cities of America, those who did not die record the names of those who did. More recent conflicts leave similar markers as well as living reminders of the dead in the lives of those who fought but did not die—though they might wish they had.

Indeed, if one does not die there seems to be less honor. Klein criticizes the treatment given to U.S. veterans in the Veterans Administration Hospitals in that country in his provocative book *Wounded Men, Broken Promises*, and there are similar stories of official disinterest and bureaucratic obstructionism in other countries [1]. The "Agent Orange" case after the Vietnam war highlights the gulf between supposed governmental responsibility to not open the floodgates of monetary compensation claims, and the naive beliefs of volunteers and draftees alike that they and their families would be at least looked after if anything happened to them while they were serving their country. We have, then, a situation where to die for one's country—or one's God, or one's ideology—is significant; but to live in a disabled state as a reminder of a conflict is less commendable.

Again, to die for one's personal principles is a different matter to that of dying for the group, marking one out as at least "odd," at worst insane; the taboo on suicide is a case in point. Suicide presents an interesting challenge to social

39

groups. While the phenomenon of the individual taking his or her own life raises many theoretical and practical questions, it is very much a phenomenon in which others seek to intervene. The basis of that intervention is also complex, but a central aspect is that the group does not sanction individuals taking life into their own hands. It is as if there is a "prior claim" made, even to *my own* life. While some groups may sanction suicide, for example, as a means of population control or as a method of dealing with the non-productive elderly, this is still bound up with group norms. It is the group that decides—or, more accurately, the dominant interest within it—when and under what conditions I might take my own life, just as it decides when I may take the life of another.

We see, then, a sentiment running through the individual's social experience and socialization that death in a struggle for one's country, one's God, or for the group ideology, is to be held as a "good," perhaps the ultimate good. This is well captured in antiquity by Horace's Ode in which he notes: "It is sweet and proper to die for one's country" [2, III.2.13]. Yet death is perhaps the most individual of all of life's events, and something an individual might only very reluctantly find "collectivised" and turned to the service of group interests—be they national, ethnic, religious, or otherwise. That is, of course, if the individual was "allowed" to freely reflect on the matter. What is allowed or granted is an increasing *freedom from*; the individual is increasingly free from restraint in more and more areas of life. What is less allowed is *freedom to*; the education and socialization systems combine to create dependence and an inability to think for oneself. Thus, as we will suggest, individuals are discouraged from thinking too deeply about their own death.

Now, these observations set up a tension between the individual and the group, a tension that is exploited in this Chapter for the reflection it generates. That reflection is in relation to death, and in relation to the interventions in the deaths of others in which care-givers engage. The tension has attracted a wide variety of thinkers, some of whom have considered it specifically in relation to death. Two such thinkers who have focused specifically on death, the individual and the group, come to mind: Martin Heidegger [3] and a philosopher much influenced by him, Herbert Marcuse [4]. Further, this problem of the individual and the group is the fundamental problem of social philosophy and of few writers who have addressed it from the perspective of the individual Max Stirner [5] and Soren Keirkegaard [6] are the most forceful. It is useful to begin by noting how these last two see the matter.

Stirner writes of "the One" or "the Unique" [5], Kierkegaard of the problem of "the single one" [6]. Stirner provides the most iconoclastic perspective and this lies in his exposure of the way in which the individual is duped by others. Kierkegaard, draws attention to the "burdens" that the individual carries in respect of self-awareness and provides an indication of how the group can obscure the individual's authentic living.

Stirner focuses on the manner in which we are ruled by *abstractions*. He throws down a gauntlet from the very beginning of his book with the opening line—"I have set my affair on nothing"—from Goethe's poem *Vanitas, Vanitas, Vanitatum*, and begins:

> What is not supposed to be my concern! First and foremost, the Good Cause, the cause of mankind, of truth, of freedom, of humanity, of justice; further, the cause of my people, my prince, my fatherland; finally, even the cause of Mind, and a thousand other causes. Only *my* cause is never to be my concern. Shame on you egoist who thinks only of himself! [5, p. 3].

Kierkegaard also had the courage to raise the problem of "the single one" [6]. For him, the task of human thinking, the reason we had been given the power of individual, meditative, thinking, was to come to an individual understanding of the human predicament. Yet, we too easily succumbed to "group think":

> The more the collective idea comes to dominate even the ordinary consciousness, the more forbidding seems the transition to becoming a particular existing human being instead of losing oneself in the race, and saying "we, our age, the nineteenth century." . . . For what does a mere individual count for? Our age knows only too well how little it is, but here also lies the specific immorality of the age. Each age has its own characteristic depravity. Ours is perhaps not pleasure or indulgence or sensuality, but rather a dissolute pantheistic contempt for the individual man. In the midst of all our exultation over the achievements of the age and the nineteenth century, there sounds a note of poorly conceived contempt for the individual man; in the midst of the self-importance of the contemporary generation, there is revealed a sense of despair over being human [6, p. 317].

The problem of the individual in the group is taken up generally and with specific reference to death by Heidegger and Marcuse. Heidegger was concerned with a number of matters but one aspect of his thought is the question of whether there is anything that lifts us above our trappedness in the "everyday," and thereby allows us a true understanding of the wholeness of our life and the reality of our individuality. His answer is that consciousness of our own personal mortality is such an experience. Such a consciousness lifts us above "particularity"—our lostness in everyday cares, moods, concerns—to a position where we can contemplate the mystery of Being itself.

This broader focus of Heidegger's reflection discloses the manner in which a specific countervailing tendency gets in the way of our individual consciousness of death. This distracting force he refers to as the *they*. The *they* has various features and is related to various outlooks. For example, he talks of the "publicness" and the "ambiguity" of the *they*, our absorption in the *they*, the *they* as determining our state of mind, of our "fleeing" into the *they*. The *they* is related to a lack of authenticity, is plagued by "idle talk" which distracts us from the true conversation that will illuminate the question of Being, and the *they* provides what we take to be "common sense" and the conventional wisdom on all topics. In relation to death, the *they* provides that level of "publicness" in relation to death where "death is 'known' as a mishap which is constantly occurring—a 'case of death' . . . a well known event occurring within the world" [3, p. 296/H253].

Thus, death remains unobtrusive, it remains in the background of our individual life because the *they* provides a ready-made explanation, talking of death as if it was "out there" and not related to *me*, "as if to say 'One of these days one will die too, in the end; but right now it has nothing to do with us' " [3, p. 297/H253]. A matter that is potentially illuminating for the individual is subtly subverted from any radical impact on our consciousness:

> the "they" . . . puts itself in the right and makes itself respectable by tacitly regulating the way in which *one* has to comport oneself towards death. It is already a matter of public acceptance that 'thinking about death' is a cowardly fear, a sign of insecurity on the part of Dasien . . . *The "they" does not permit us the courage for anxiety in the face of death.* . . . In anxiety in the face of death, Dasien is brought face to face with itself . . . The "they" concerns itself with transforming this anxiety into fear in the face of an oncoming event. In addition, the anxiety which has been made ambiguous as fear, is passed off as a weakness with which no self-assured Dasien may have any acquaintance. What is 'fitting' . . . according to the unuttered decree of the "they," is indifferent tranquility as to the 'fact' that one dies [3, p. 298/H254].[1]

Fear, of course, can be overcome through training and reassurance, but anxiety is a different matter. Thus, when one is socialized into the belief that to die for one's country or one's God is a "good," fear of death can be responded to "technically"; for example, skill with weapons, survival training, creation of a culture of obedience and trust in the judgements of those who know better about death, and so forth. This applies also to the need to kill others whose "dissimilarity" to ourselves removes any thought that we are like those whose deaths we effect. Fromm has argued in his criticism of the notion that human beings are naturally or inherently aggressive that in order to be able to kill we must first be taught that the enemy is "inhuman," is not like one of us [7]. Thus we resort to

---

[1] *Dasien* refers to the existence that we can say something "has," though more usually it refers to the existence that *persons* have. *Dasien* refers generally to the everyday existence of an entity, but an entity that as part of its essential nature it raises the question of its own Being. Heidegger distinguishes *Dasien* from "existence," as he distinguishes "ontical" from "ontological." In the first case, existence is what *Dasien* is seeking to understand itself in terms of; *Dasien* seeks to learn from but get beyond the everyday pressures of existence which both illuminate and obscure its self-reflection. *Ontical* refers to facts about the entities or things (including persons) that exist; *ontological* refers to the broader or deeper question of the Being of entities, especially persons.

euphemisms in reference to death; the enemy is a "gook" or a "monkey" that we "waste" or "terminate."

While fear might be combatted, *anxiety* about death is far more personal and touches a deeper area of our being. While anxiety might be addressed through various techniques, there always remains the doubt that perhaps anxiety is "natural" and is telling us something about life, about human existence, about Being. Indeed, the existential and phenomenological perspectives on the human condition commence from the basis of existential anxiety being a fundamental feature of human existence; *not* to be anxious is what is remarkable.

What Heidegger is drawing attention to is the powerful ontological dimension that is masked by our socialization into ready-made answers about, and "comportments" toward, death. Death, in raising the reality of our non-being, potentially provides some insight into the question of Being as such. In colloquial but instructive terms we are led to ask not "Why was I born so beautiful?", but rather "Why was I born *at all*?". At this level of consideration are questions of the meaning not only of *my* existence, but of existence *as such*. However, when death is depersonalized and to be thought of in terms provided by the group, this dimension is lost. The group is more concerned with the question of why I was born "this way" rather than that, and reassures me or "treats" me in order that I might "adjust." It avoids the more difficult but more individually significant question of why I have existence and what this means.

It is the dominance and depth of influence of group concerns that has attracted the criticism of Marcuse [4]. He has asked us to think in terms of the group as a *particular* group. Specifically, Marcuse wants to alert us to the manner in which a particular group masquerades as if its concerns and its priorities where rather universal and of benefit to all human beings, to *civilisation*. This realization that what is said to be good for the group is really what is good for *this particular* group, allows us to reflect on other forms of social arrangement in which there could be much less repression and much more real freedom for the individual.

Marcuse's broader canvas, on which death is but a part of the picture, is a social analysis deriving from the theoretical perspective developed by the Frankfurt School. What the Frankfurt School did, among other things, was to delineate critical or substantive reasoning from instrumental reasoning. Instrumental reasoning is concerned with applying our intelligence to problems in hand. It is an approach to the world that is driven by the motive of *using* that world for some purpose. Moreover, the aim is to achieve the most effective use for the practical end in view, such that the values inherent in, or the morality of the purpose is lost or obscured in the focus on *means*. Instrumental reasoning stays with the "givens" of a situation, it does not consider what questions are being avoided in the particular questions being asked. For substantive or critical reasoning, there is the recognition that what is presented to us as a problem can always be reframed as a different problem and will always mask such alternative reframings.

This distinction between types of reason, or reasoning, draws our attention to the manner in which our thinking is "preempted." In an analogous way, male dominated society perverts women's language and in each case a certain frame of mind is perpetuated that closes off alternative ways of seeing the world. Instrumental reasoning is Heidegger's *calculative* thinking, as contrast with his *meditative* thinking [8]. The latter takes its point of departure from a sense of awe or wonder that is felt by the individual when his or her mind is challenged by something for which there is no immediate or ready to hand solution or explanation. Meditative thinking is *thought-fullness*, it is reflection on the *meaning* of things, a focus on who and what we are.

To return to our specific theme, Marcuse has addressed the issue of death quite specifically, in addition to making various comments throughout his wider writings [9]. In the wider writing he indicts advanced technological society for dehumanizing us. More specific to death, however, was his contribution [9] to Herman Feifel's [10] symposium and volume, arguably the work that launched the significant interest that has been shown in death and dying over the past three decades. Interestingly, in his summing up of the material there gathered, Murphy asked how it is we assume that we have the parameters or the frame of reference for the psychological investigation of death [11]. This question is particularly pertinent to the aims of the present volume, concerned as it is to challenge and broaden parameters and widen the frames of reference.

In his specific contribution to the last volume Marcuse discusses the "ideology of death" [9]. He is curious concerning the inflation of a simple biological fact of life to an ontological status, and he opts for an account of death at the level of the impact of social and historical forces. Here, he notes how it suits "society" to have death seen in more exotic terms which give it the moral dimensions that for him discloses the connection between death and unfreedom in social organization that is repressive. He locates the beginning of the ideological dimension of death in the behavior of Socrates, as discussed by Plato. Socrates' acceptance of death is seen as a tacit acceptance that the *polis* has the *right* to demand his death. Thus, the idea of death as something more than a mere biological fact adds the value dimension by which the individual can be enslaved:

the cohesion of the social order depends to a considerable extent on the effectiveness with which individuals comply with death as more than a natural necessity; on their willingness, even urge, to die many deaths which are not natural; on their agreement to sacrifice themselves and not fight death 'too much'. Life is not to be valued too highly, at least not as the supreme good. The social order demands compliance with toil and resignation, heroism, and punishment for sin. . . . Through death on the field of honour, in the mines and on the highways, from unconquered disease and poverty, by the state and its organs, civilization advances [9, p. 75].

There is ample evidence that the loss of the individual to which Stirner and Kierkegaard, Heidegger and Marcuse are drawing attention has continued and worsened in social life governed by advanced technology. An insistent theme of the writing in philosophy of technology is the reduction of the individual to a mere object for manipulation who has lost the capacity to see what has happened. Marcuse notes how in modern technological society:

> With the decline of consciousness, with the control of information, with the absorption of individual into mass communication, knowledge is administered and confined. The individual does not really know what is going on; the overpowering machine of education and entertainment unites him with all others in a state of anaesthesia from which all detrimental ideas tend to be excluded [4, p. 91].

All of the foregoing observations point to the conversion of death as an individual experience of potentially unlimited significance for self awareness and empowerment, to the service of social organization and of *particular* forms of social organization. In a range of thinkers operating at the very basic level of the social-philosophical question—the relation of the individual to the group—there is an exposure of the impact of the group on individual consciousness. There is, as a corollary, an exposure of the phenomenon of death to a radically critical scrutiny. That scrutiny finds death no less than any other human experience capable of being value laden and then used to limit individual freedom. That limitations is not the limitation of a natural phenomenon—death as a fact of life—but an extension of domination which finds the individual in the "happy consciousness" ready to give up life in the name of this or that honorable cause.

Now, these observations are highly pertinent to the role and functions of care-givers and the manner in which we think about death and dying. In the context of the demands of advanced technology one can look to the education and training, the institutional affiliations, the work expectations and so forth, of psychologists and other helpers within, and beyond, the domain of death and dying. These matters and these professionals will be no less effected by pressures of advanced technology than any other area of human life and conduct. Yet, in a culture described as "anti-man" [12], at what point does the psychologist or other helper become an "agent" for that system? In what ways is the thinking of the helper converted to instrumental reasoning, to calculative thinking?

Indeed, the 1960s saw a powerful attack on "psychology in the service of adjustment" in the development of radical psychology and anti-psychiatry. Brown gathered observations of the manner in which psychology was not just another area of study and practice, but pervaded all areas of life and functioned as an ideology defending the status quo [13]. Further, Warren suggested how the aims of Death Education programs are too easily read conservatively and too easily issue in the "taming" of this last area of human unreason and passion to produce docile consumers—consumers of things and services, and consumers of ideologies [14].

What underpins any intervention—preventive, postventive, and rehabilitative—is a metaphor of the person, a metaphor which expresses the dominant psychological position which, in turn, expresses a group ideology. Two dominant metaphors of the person in the past half-century are those of Psychoanalysis and Behaviorism. The first metaphor is of person as "animal," the second as "machine." These two metaphors constrain or at least narrow our understanding of the human condition, and they issue in and support conservative social ideology and paternalistic interventions. Thus, for Psychoanalysis we are driven by forces we do not understand and have to be "interpreted for" by those who know better. We have to be protected from our basic impulses by strong external controls or internalized commands that become shame and guilt and a conscience. For Behaviorism, schedules of reinforcement have to be arranged in order to secure obedience and social order that has little place for freedom and dignity. As Skinner observes, freedom is escape from aversive stimulation, dignity an outcome of positive reinforcement [15].

The metaphor of the person underlying specific intervention in relation to death and dying is less clear. A general humanistic concern for others appears to be a powerful motivation, coupled to a notion that "there, with the grace of God go I." Yet, whatever the motivation, there will be a metaphor underpinning the particular style of intervention we choose. For example, if we choose to use a behavioral technique of "flooding" in respect of denial operating in a bereavement situation, we will be leaning toward the Behaviorist metaphor. If we choose to try to interpret object cathexis and the difficulty of breaking bonds, in the same situation, we will be leaning toward the Psychoanalytic metaphor. And if we are committed nationalists, or committed to a particular religious position, or upholders of this or that strong viewpoint about the relation of individuals to groups, our practice will reflect this.

In order to respond to the question concerning the metaphor which best captures our practice we need to be open to forces working against this openness. We need to be aware that our whole culture may push us in a particular direction concerning both life and death. In addressing this question we might be again challenged to deeper reflection by Marcuse:

> Whether death is feared as constant threat, or glorified as supreme sacrifice, or accepted as fate, the education for consent to death introduces an element of surrender into life from the beginning—surrender and submission [4, p. 188].

What is required in the face of pressures toward submissiveness is the development of a genuine *freedom to*. In respect of the individual this is the basis of living life in a fashion which accommodates death as the final stages of life. In respect of caregivers, it requires that one's personal-professional values take precedence over institutional demands, and that those personal-professional considerations are themselves under continuous critical reflection.

Freedom to is what in modern terms might be called *empowerment*; yet more than this. It is an ability to make decisions for oneself, an inner strength, a sense of determination, a feeling that one can make a difference. Erich Fromm provided a full account of this idea of *freedom to* in his analysis of authoritarianism [16]. He also referred to it as *positive* freedom, by contrast to the negative freedom that was *freedom from*. He characterized positive freedom in terms of a sense of one's unique selfhood: "the spontaneous activity of the total, integrated personality" [16, p. 222]. Love was for him the significant component of spontaneity, love as affirmation of others, a union with others that did not abolish the individuality of either party. Work, is the other component; not paid wage labor or useless toil, but creative, productive work.

Now, a problem highlighted by two decades of writing in philosophy of technology is the extreme difficulty of developing a *freedom to*; this applies no less to care-givers than it does to anyone else. Tesconi and Morris coined the term "bureautechnocracy" to characterize the environment in which we now live [12]. This is an environment in which the structured, hierarchic organization of decision making is linked to an almost exclusive focus on "means" rather than ends, to produce a state of affairs in which all individuality is lost and we are all used by the system as instruments:

> Our wants are played upon and manipulated. Indeed, most of our needs are artificially created for us, and we easily succumb to the sirens of the marketplace. The system uses us in our work. We are carefully trained for our jobs, but when we perform them, our skills and functions—rather than our personal characteristics—become the defining qualities of our presence in the world; we are known as typists or shoe manufacturers [12, p. 162].

There has, then, been a great deal of concern at the loss of the individual, and this refers to the sense of individuality of both helper and helpee. If each of us is stripped of important aspects of our humanness by life in a society that does not value us *for ourselves*, then we collude in two ways to detract from the significance of death. We lead each other in a blind acceptance of what is taken to be the "fate of the age"; and we share with others not something that is personal and illuminating but which is artificial and constrained as and by the wisdom of the *they*.

With whom, then, shall we, as care-givers and as individual persons who must ourselves die, agree? With Horace when he urges that no death is greater than that in the service of one's country? [2]. With Simone de Bouviour [17] or Dylan Thomas [18] who urge us never to take death as a "mere fact" but rather to curse and rage against it? Or with Plato's Socrates who, while he may too easily accept the right of the state to take his life, urges a *disinterest* in death? [19].

The specific answer to these last questions matters less than the fact that we recognize in asking the questions that we are able to illuminate our own implicit social values, our own ideology, and our own political background choice. In this way, we gain the widest contextual dimension for our interventions. That context is theoretical and it is socio-political. We are irresponsible if we do not critically examine the guiding metaphors of our practice, and equally irresponsible if we ignore the significance of the soci-political pressures of our age.

Yet, professionals seldom find in their professional education and training any opportunity to focus on these wider ideological questions. To be sure, there are various ethical and moral issues that might be canvassed in that education, and these might qualify as representing a philosophical discussion. At its worst, however, such a discussion that occurs within what might be called "applied ethics" might be no more than what Passmore [20] referred to as "lay sermonising." If we are truly professional, then such discussion should bite more deeply.

An interest in death and dying, if it is to be a truly professional interest, must be prepared to address these wider issues. Professionals in any area cannot ignore any dimension of their practice. It is better to know and acknowledge such things as oneself being an agent of the state, or a perpetuator of the status-quo, or an apologist for this or that ideology. In this way, too, we might avoid the charge of a flight from theory, or, especially worse in this domain, of a flight from *thinking*, from *meditative* thinking. The phenomenon of death is arguably unique—akin only to that of the beginning of life—in demanding the deepest and widest level of reflection.

Perhaps in order to ensure that we remain true to the individual—both our individual "charges" and to ourselves—we should heed Stirner's warning and jettison abstractions [5]. Thus, when asked our area of special interest we should not reply that it is the abstract "death and dying." Rather, we should indicate an interest in, a concern for, the *bereaved* individual and the *dying* person. We might then be able to indicate how that interest relates to our own "sense of the world" and our own meaning of life.

Whatever the case, however, we must ask ourselves: "How can I, this *I*, this individual *Self*, adopt a position in relation to dying and bereaved others, until I have seen through those forces and interests that would distract me from my own authentic life and the place of death in that life?"

The perspective advanced in present observations is an insistence that the individual cannot be reduced "without remainder" to being merely a creation of social conditioning. Moreover, it is especially in respect of the phenomenon of death that the "remainder" has its significance. The *I*, the sense of self felt by the individual who struggles for *freedom to*, refuses to be silenced. In meditation on our own personal mortality we are reminded of our individuality, our aloneness, and our consequent responsibility.

CONCLUSION

What we have done in this Chapter is to plunge into a debate concerning the individual and the group, a group now dominated by advanced technology the impacts of which it, and we, little understand. This is a debate of long standing, though with a recent urgency, and one in which the individual "side" is perhaps currently submerged. That submersion lies in the prevailing wisdom that accepts a relativist position that regards each of us as victims, as "constructs" of social forces operating on as at a particular moment in history. It lies also in the fact that technology does not need *me*.

We could not here delve into this debate in a fashion which does the various sides justice and fully defends the stress placed here on the individual; but our purpose is served by the observations made. That is, that a strong and vigorous focus on the individual has been maintained over the centuries and should not be lost. This is important for two reasons. One is that that focus deserves attention in its own right; a tradition of western thought traceable back to the ancient Greeks has addressed the question of the nature of the individual and the by no means obvious reasons behind the fact that individuals form groups. The second is that the idea of the individual—especially in a context which makes the idea problematic—serves as a valuable catalyst for deeper reflection on what we do as care-givers in the domain of death and dying.

Death now appears as something much more than mere biological fact. It has a powerful ideological aspect that permeates all of our thinking in a life dominated by advanced technology. Particular forms of social organization will resort to any means to perpetuate themselves and will use various abstractions to distract the individual. One such abstraction is the idea of a "glorious death," an abstraction that leads us to too easily overlook the particular interests that are urging that abstraction on us. Sacrifice of one's physical self may be necessary to protect the integrity of one's mental self, but in the individual who is *free to* this will flow from an inner strength not from a blind acceptance of the abstraction.

Thus, both as an individual who must die and as "helper," we must remain alert not only to the technical skills of dealing with life and of helping, but to the wider social-ideological context in which those skills are embedded. No matter how well-intentioned our intervention, it ought be placed in context, and the wider context that has been sketched here ought be of some concern to us. The question remains as to our being valued merely for our skills and functions and whether and to what extent we belong to the *they*!

REFERENCES

1. R. Klein, *Wounded Men, Broken Promises*, Macmillan Publishing Co., New York, 1981.

2. Horace, *The Complete Odes and Epodes*, W. G. Shepherd (trans.), Penguin, Harmondsworth, 1983.
3. M. Heidegger, *Being and Time*, J. Macquarrie and E. Robinson (trans.), Basil Blackwell, Oxford, 1978.
4. H. Marcuse, *Eros and Civilization*, Sphere Books, London, 1969, first published 1955.
5. M. Stirner, *The Ego and His Own*, Libertarian Book Club, New York, 1963, first published in 1845.
6. S. Kierkegaard, *Concluding Unscientific Postscript*, D. F. Swenson and W. Lowrie (trans.), Princeton University Press, Princeton, 1941.
7. E. Fromm, *The Anatomy of Human Destructiveness*, Routledge and Kegan Paul, New York, 1973.
8. M. Heidegger, *Discourse on Thinking*, Harper and Row, New York, 1966 (originally published in 1959, in German).
9. H. Marcuse, The Ideology of Death, in *The Meaning of Death*, H. Feifel (ed.), McGraw-Hill Book Co., New York, 1959.
10. H. Feifel, *The Meaning of Death*, McGraw-Hill Book Co., New York, 1959.
11. G. Murphy, Discussion, in *The Meaning of Death*, H. Feifel (ed.), McGraw-Hill Book Co., New York, 1959.
12. C. A. Tesconi and V. C. Morris, *The Anti-Man Culture*, University of Illinois Press, Urbana, 1972.
13. P. Brown, *Radical Psychology*, Tavistock Publications, London, 1973.
14. W. G. Warren, *Death Education and Research: Critical Perspectives*, The Haworth Press, New York, 1989.
15. B. F. Skinner, *Beyond Freedom and Dignity*, Jonathon Cape, London, 1972.
16. E. Fromm, *Fear of Freedom*, Routledge and Kegan Paul, London, 1942.
17. S. De Bouviour, *A Very Easy Death*, Andre Deutsch and Weidenfeld and Nicholson, P. O'Brien (trans.), London, 1966.
18. D. Thomas, Do Not Go Gentle Into That Good Night, in *Miscellany One*, J. M. Dent and Sons Ltd., London, 1963.
19. Plato, *Socratic Dialogues*, W. D. Woodhead (trans. and ed.), Nelson, London.
20. J. Passmore, *Recent Philosophers*, Duckworth, London, 1895.

CHAPTER 5

Suffering and Death:
Eternal Questions in a New Context

Kjell Kallenberg

ETERNAL QUESTIONS

There are eternal questions that have been companions of man as long as he has reflected over himself and the world he lives in. They concern seemingly unchangeable elements of existence and have to do with basic circumstances of life and death. And that could be sufficient.

But it is typical that we do not allow our questions to stop there. We want to understand, sometimes to explain, and find a meaningful pattern in life. The concept "eternal" often implies that there are no final answers. Our knowledge changes and with it the conditions of our understanding. Indeed, the interpretations and answers of earlier generations are important for our knowledge of other cultures and epochs, at the same time as they spread light over our own search around those central questions of life. But the earlier answers are not always ours.

It seems that each era and each generation, even each individual must constantly ask the old questions anew. Neither is any other answer more applicable than one's own. But the dilemma is even greater than that. We have difficulty in finding answers that satisfy requirements of honesty and keenness as well as our inner senses of right, meaning, and coherence. Such requirements apply not least when we talk about the meaning of mortality, especially in connection with suffering.

To be and to suffer is one and the same thing according to Buddha. Suffering exists and must be accepted as part of the reality of life. Death, ceased being, can then put an end to suffering.

We cannot talk about suffering and death as if they were synonymous. Much suffering is not directly related to death. And many people would claim that the good death, which is the exact meaning of euthanasia, is not related to suffering, whether we think of modern hospice care, where the whole person is taken care of, and physical pain is effectively controlled, or of an old person dying in the midst of caring relatives. Still, most people would agree that death often also implies suffering. The two phenomena are independent but overlapping.

The realization itself of the transitoriness of life is part of modern man's existential anguish. The death of a close relative, or someone we love, is always connected with feelings and thoughts that can be difficult or almost impossible to handle. This also holds true when the loss is an elderly relative and whose death is more or less expected. Death is irreversible. What has happened cannot be changed, but it can be worked out and understood. The death of a loved person can also demonstrate the fickleness of my own time on Earth and reveal our fear of loneliness and isolation.

The meaning of death and suffering is maybe the greatest one of those eternal questions to which man constantly seeks an answers. Many assert that death has no meaning. All life is subject to that change in which death is final. Others like the writers of the scriptures, including St. Paul have opened up other dimensions from a Christian perspective: Oh Death where is your victory? Oh Death where is your sting?

Secularization and Death

Empirically, it is certain that the understanding of death in twentieth-century western society has changed radically in relation to previous epochs. This is true of the physical reality, such as the standard of living and the high technological standard in medical care. The change is also considerable in the way people look upon life: what they find valuable and important. Norms and values seem to be certified statements and secular values rather than divine laws and religious beliefs. Health has become an intrinsic value in itself.

Some change in the view of life could be ascribed to secularization [1]. The phenomenon may be understood from a social perspective. Secularization is reflected in ordinary people's view of life and death and actual way of living. It's core is a scientific interpretation of life. The sciences aspire to explain reality as a whole. With such a view of life, many people have lost their sense of wholeness and the deep knowledge that has helped to interpret the difficult periods of life. Maybe it is true that trust in life is being replaced by faith in infallible technology. This change has been going on for a long time but the consequences have been most obvious during the latter part of this century.

At the same time our relationship to death has changed. In the ordered ideal world of the secularized future, chaos has been given no place. Since man first ate the fruit from the tree of knowledge he has tried to understand and order change, not least the final and irreversible change of death. In the great transformation of society, death has been privatized as well as institutionalized. Death has become more and more the concern of a tightly-knit family circle. The funeral service is no longer a public affair but increasingly takes place in silence. And it is not unusual that the obituary appears after the event. The institutionalization of death is supported by the fact that about 80 percent die in hospital and care institutions. All practical activities, from death to burial are carried out by professionals.

The great social changes have affected our relationship to sickness, suffering, and death. In a review of the French historian, Philippe Ariès' great work "L'-Homme devant la mort", a Swedish critic wrote that death in the attitudes of the 1900s continues to take the form of an unbearable scandal [2]. Death is the annoying human factor at the center of super technology.

Death and Suffering: Grief

Death is a trigger that releases grief. Grief is a general human experience of life. It has been compared with working. Freud coined this expression as early as 1917. Like all other forms of work, grief requires time and energy. Grief is also suffering that cuts through the various dimensions of existence.

The loss of a loved person does necessarily mean that one's way of life changes. Grief affects every part of life, our senses and thoughts as well as relationships to others. In that way, bereavement is important to our way of life and for carrying out the many everyday practical tasks. Grief affects our well-being and health. To grieve is to live in a state of tension between presence and absence, with an "attending absence." The inner image of the lost person, with its memories and shared experiences, is constantly present, or, awakened at any time. But the person to whom all this is related is absent. There we find the suffering of grief.

MEANING OF SUFFERING

Understanding the fickleness of life and reality of death is a part of man's existential suffering. Grief at the loss of a loved one is an example of suffering. No matter if we focus on society or the individual, there are a number of ways to act in relation to the suffering in the reality we live, as individuals in a specific culture.

Perhaps the most natural behavior is to try to escape reality, or to protest life as it is. No instinct can be stronger than to evade pain. This also applies to suffering. We feel distaste, sorrow, bitterness and doubt, and our feelings drive us to action. A Job or Camus casts his questions aggressively at the heavens with or without conviction that there is someone responsible for the absurdities of life.

Suffering can also be idealized. It can be seen as a virtue to suffer and endure. At other times, great resources are mobilized to eliminate suffering, which also has been the overall goal of the welfare state.

One may however ask if all suffering can be removed, and if it is desirable to do so? Is not sorrow the price we pay for love? And who would be prepared to give up love only in order not to be stricken later by sorrow? To desire the removal of every form of suffering clears the way for the longing after a reality other than that in which we live in. Each of us has a picture of Eden's pastoral perfection where "the lion lies down with the lamb." As a vision it differs vastly from the artificial world described by Huxley in his famous novel of the future, *Brave New World*, where the total lack of suffering is in itself suffering [3].

The relevant question of meaning in suffering should however be put without reverting to idealization. A relation between suffering and creativity has often been pointed out both in art and science. The multiplicity of art has both an interpretative and therapeutic function. Some of its greatest works have come from these sources whose outflows are called pain and doubt. But how much suffering is art worth? It is possible that the question cannot even be asked without bordering on cynical speculation. Throughout the ages it has been thought that suffering and afflictions in sufficient doses are what we need to mature as persons. But what are sufficient doses, and what do we do with the suffering that stretches beyond comprehensible boundaries and ceases only with death?

Suffering and Death as Central Questions of Life

We all interpret and give meaning to reality. In the humanistic tradition man is regarded as a truth-seeking creature. We have an urge to create meaning and structure in existence. This is dependent on the experience and knowledge of previous generations, but it is also synthesized with the individual's unique experience of what it means to live at a certain time and in a certain culture.

The meaning of suffering and death is certainly a vitally important central issue. But contrary to many scientific problems, there is no unanimity in which direction the answer should be sought. Medical problems are generally solved with the knowledge that is available within the medical and scientific schools. This is natural for most people. The important issues of life are however not only unsolved, there is absolutely no unanimity as to how they should be answered.

With the aid of various *patterns of interpretation* we try to make enigmatic phenomena understandable by placing them in wider contexts [4]. Physics, biology, Christianity and Marxism are examples of such patterns of interpretation. Most often it is rather clear which pattern should be chosen. Medical problems are answered within medicine and astronomy helps us seek the answer to the birth of the universe. For many questions the choice of pattern of interpretation is rather obvious or *closed*.

It is different for questions of vital importance. Why is there so much suffering in the world? The answer can come from many sources. Biology gives an answer. Political ideologies point to basic social and economic factors. Religion points to man's and creation's disunion and the turning away from God. Psychologists investigate man's basic instincts.

Sometimes the various answers complement each other but history has often shown that in authoritarian and reductionist ideologies only one answer from a special pattern of interpretation is acceptable. Nevertheless, this has not altered the fact that choice of pattern of interpretation regarding vital questions, at least theoretically, is *open*. In a democracy which is no longer dominated by a single pattern of interpretation this open-mindedness in the interpretation of central vital issues comes as a challenge to each individual. In which of the patterns of interpretation do I seek an answer to the question of the meaning of death and suffering?

Choices of Meaningfulness

What does it imply that something has a meaning? Primarily it can imply that, whatever I am searching for a meaning in, is possible to interpret and is understandable. Nonsense means non-meaning. A jumble of signs, or a language that does not follow the normal rules is often disregarded by us as meaningless.

To regard something as meaningful we must place our experiences and thoughts in a wider context, a pattern of interpretation. The individual phenomenon is given a meaning when we see it in a greater perspective. In spite of this, each of us has had deep meaningful experiences that cannot readily be explained within any pattern of interpretation. That something has a meaning seems to go beyond the limits of rationality.

There is another dimension that further complicates the problem and that is time. Much of what we do would be meaningless if it were not for the fact that it leads to something else more desirable. Meaning does not need to lie within the boundaries of the act itself. Something we experience, if out of context, can be completely meaningless and trivial. It is first when we see the result of what has happened that it becomes understandable and meaningful and leads to something desirable and good.

This thought is common regarding suffering. Physical pain is a protective element against a greater injury. Suffering which is limited in time is easier to withstand than chronic pain. Pain which is necessary, such as a visit to the dentist is acceptable as the treatment should mean relief from pain.

It is often maintained that suffering can have a meaning, not in itself, but as a step in personal development and maturity. With the common distinction within ethics it can be said that suffering can be instrumental in helping to attain a personal intrinsic value. This line of reasoning continues with one regarding personal development and maturity as something good in itself.

When one talks about suffering and death, it is however important to keep two questions apart. The first question is existential and refers to the individual's quest for the meaning of the suffering that has befallen him. The second question, if suffering and death have any meaning at all, is philosophical and involves many troublesome standpoints. We will come back to that question later.

MEANING AND VIEW OF LIFE OF THE INDIVIDUAL

In search of meaning, the individual must use his own pattern of interpretation, often comprising his entire experience of life. This experience shapes the individual's view of life. The ideas in a view of life are not autonomous. The infant is born into an already existing cultural system of ideologies, religions, and other views of life. All this will have an impact on the infant's experiences from the very beginning and must be internalized in the psyche in order to become a view of life which can create meaning and order in later life. Every person is thus dependent on the knowledge and experience of previous generations.

Religions and ideologies often are vague realities for average people and influence the way they regard life only to a small extent. Then we must ask what it is in a view of life that gives strength and comfort in difficult periods of life. What qualities in the view of life can contribute to a sense of meaning for the individual?

One may suggest that an individual's view of life expresses degrees of totality, meaning, and coherence within a *basic attitude* of trust or mistrust. An individual's basic attitude seems to be one of the essential features of his view of life, as trust and mistrust are established early in life. These concepts have been described by Erik H. Erikson in connection to the first stage in his theory of personality development: the Eight Ages of Man [5]. Trust or mistrust are the basic ingredients in early childhood when identity is being formed. Subsequently, the basic experience of trust or mistrust learned as a child is carried over to all stages in life.

One may further suggest that each individual's view of life contains both trust and mistrust. Even a view of life characterized by basic trust holds some parts of mistrust. An individual who has obtained a basic trust most probably responds to a negative or painful experience as being temporary. Trust is strong enough to endure the presence of mistrust. Trust requires the presence of mistrust to preserve a balance of realism for the individual. Unlimited trust in an individual is often judged as naive and unrealistic. On the other hand, pure mistrust in an individual often leads to depression and despair. A view of life characterized by basic trust has the potential for a confident attitude toward the future even in the face of death and mortality.

It could be said that a view of life is a synthesis of the characteristic words and actions of an individual. This synthesis in turn forms a central system of values and a basic attitude toward life. An individual's view of life rarely conforms to established ideologies in the society. Empirically it seems that the individual's view of life contains bits of ideas and ideological elements which form a very personal pattern. A consequence of this may be that a religious interpretation of life does not necessarily provide a view of life characterized by basic trust. However, when this is the case, the presence of the religious components or faith probably reinforces its interpretative capacity. I contend that the extent to which an individual's view of life interprets difficult life events in a meaningful way is related to resources within the personality, but with a complex interplay with his view of life as a whole.

A difficult experience, e.g., caused by a life-threatening illness, reminds each individual that life has many and varying meanings. A view of life characterized by basic trust can help to hold together reality as a meaningful whole so that also extreme pain and sorrow can be united with it. The most important task of a view of life seems to be to give the individual a framework for interpretation within which the reversals of life can reconcile and the individual ego be given a meaningful place with open-mindedness toward the future.

IS THERE AN OVERALL MEANING IN SUFFERING AND DEATH?

We will now turn to the second question, if suffering and death have an overall meaning. The existential and philosophical questions do not seem to conflict. For the individual, life can be experienced as meaningful without needing to explain its meaning. The reverse is also possible. Faith on a higher level of meaning can be a trust in facing death when the individual feels hopeless and empty.

It can be contented that the meaning of suffering and death presupposes an intentional subject, someone or something to which suffering can be related [6]. Meaning is always meaning *for* someone. That someone can be God, the national will, the world spirit, according to Hegel, or the state, the party or something similar. There can be a conception of a macro-subject, to whom suffering is meaningful.

Many have denied that such a macro-subject exists. That does not necessarily imply that the overall question about the meaning of suffering should definitely be disposed of. A consequence of, e.g., Karl Popper's opposition to idealism, could be that suffering and death in itself have no value [7]. The question is regarded as meaningless and for that reason cannot be answered. No a priori social macro-subject can be defined according to this opinion. There can however be socially and historically varying collectivities, to which individuals can relate meaning of suffering. Thus, relative, subjective, and culture-dependent meanings are asserted in every individual person's interpretation of the meaning of suffering.

One example of this is the way anthropologists can view suffering, as a social answer to a certain situation [8]. The three conceptions illness, disease, and sickness stand for different aspects of affliction. Illness connotes the way the individual, early in life, has learned to show and to communicate an experienced feeling or suffering. Illness is suffering wearing a special, symbolic costume. Disease is an observed and diagnosed condition. Sickness is the socially understandable and sanctioned label or role given to the individual. The patient's pain and the doctor's diagnosis need not necessarily be the same thing. Disease can be a species-universal condition, while illness and sickness are relative and situation specific.

The very core of suffering according to that view is that suffering must be communicated by means of symbols learned early in life in order to be visible to the surrounding world. Suffering demands an "answer" both instrumentally and socially. Consequently, suffering is not something absolute within one and the same culture. Only that which can be felt, experienced and communicated can be called suffering. But suffering as a means of communication gives no guarantee for being understood.

Interpretation of Suffering in Art, Music, and Literature

The skepticism with which modern research regards every attempt to give an overall interpretation of the meaning of suffering and death must be viewed from an idea-historical perspective. The modern technocratic rationality, implying absolute belief in man's ability to create a world worth living in with the help of science and technology has not always been present. Long before our time there existed idealization of suffering, or at least a meaningful interpretation of suffering, as perhaps the only way to withstand conditions of life that could not otherwise be mastered. Exposure to pestilence, poverty and hunger in a world where conditions seemed unchangeable, all that remained was to submit and suffer. If not now, then sometime in heaven "the last shall be first, pain shall be changed to sweetness" [9].

Irrespective of where or when a culture is studied, it appears that people have a need to interpret life and give it meaning in order to strengthen the identity and unity of the culture. Within cultures, the creation of meaning has been preserved in art, rituals, and drama as well as in the views of life that survive the individual as ideologies and religions.

Contributions to the interpretation of suffering and death are done by helping to analyze on intellectual levels, or by giving an outlet and free flow for the emotions. In art, music, and literature both these functions can be discerned: intellectual creation of meaning and therapeutic healing.

In *art*, the meaning of suffering is a theme that seems almost infinite. It is rather difficult to imagine any form of artistic creation lacking some aspect of suffering. Contemporary artists have been inspired by the classical works. Just two examples illustrate the point: Motifs used by Chagall can be traced to Geertgen tot Sint Jan's painting of John the Baptist in the Wilderness, and Golgatha can be found woven into Picasso's Guernica [10].

A similar point can be made about *music*. Sorrow and tears go together. We know that sorrow has its special songs and music. But that tears and song are connected and have a long musical tradition is not well known for many of us. Songs of mourning lead us directly into the house of sorrows with a tone language that helps ease and subdue sorrow with the power of music. In large parts of Europe, it was women, as it still is today, who, with vastly different languages, rituals and social concepts, conveyed songs of mourning as a parallel to—or rather a consequence of—what had happened in the world of men, where heroic songs of battle and great deeds belonged [11].

There is also another music of sorrow that has often a clear connection with Christian circles. Laments and madrigals, such as requiems, are a kind of liturgical organized song of sorrow whose name has been taken from the first line in introitus "Requiem aeternam dona eis, Domine" (Give them O Lord thy eternal peace).

Not only art and music have tried to clarify the meaning of suffering. It is also a basic theme in *literature*. It covers everything from religious documentation through to the Greek tragedies with their consolation and reconciliation as this most sublime type of literary genre which with its world of thought could give the audience confidence. In the middle ages Dante's Comedia is the clearest example. But few texts can compete with Dostoyevsky's The Brothers Karamasov, where the question of the meaning of suffering is mirrored with a depth and intensity that has few counterparts in the history of literature [12].

In our own century, suffering has been industrialized in a way that has displaced all previous degrees of suffering beyond limits of understanding. "After Auschwitz no poetry" were the bitter words of Theodor Adorno. But the writers of our time do not owe him an answer. The reason for suffering as a basic theme of literature naturally depends on the fact that it is a part of life. If the interpreter is silent the stones will shout out. The individual will then have lost his final dignity.

ETHICS AND ACTION IN RELATION TO SUFFERING

As long as the individual via interpretation and with the support of art, music, and literature could integrate suffering and death in a meaningful context, invalidation of suffering did not become the most rational action. This idea has been used by many, for instance Marx, to show the negative power of religion and ideology [13]. He concluded that the failure of philosophers was that they could only interpret the world—it is more important to change it. Action is the opportunity of change.

Action is an inherent imperative of the technocratic rationality. In Western society suffering has been reduced by creating better living conditions and even improving the health of everyone by the year 2000. Science has changed the conditions of life and reduced much of the suffering that was the constant scourge of everyday life. But we are still mortal.

From a practical-clinical perspective modern high technological health care has revolutionized people's health. It has reduced suffering and mainly increased the quality of life to the end. At the same time there is a risk of undermining human dignity and a lack of respect for the individual's integrity. The eternal questions remain unanswered, while modern health care also actualizes new questions. Can all suffering be removed? Has health become the new meaning of life? Do we have the right to die, when medical technology can prolong life beyond every limit? These questions are pertinent, and of course even more the question why so few in the growing world—even fewer and fewer—can receive even the most elementary benefits of this technology.

Perhaps any attempt to theoretically solve the enigma of suffering and death is in vain. Many would say that it is not an interpretation we need but action to prevent the suffering that can be prevented—and consolation when suffering cannot be prevented. Most of all we need to realize that man is still mortal and always will be, and that a realistic awareness of this basic existential fact adds a quality to life. Irrespectively if we believe that we can find a tenable answer or not, we are challenged by life itself to keep to the reality we live in. In everyday life focus is moved from the heights of theories and abstractions to the level of concrete action. What can I do in preparation of my own death? How do I meet others in sorrow?

The answer according to many can only be sought in action supported by love. This was what Dostoyevsky meant and the way that Mother Teresa and many others have formulated their answers in their work with dying people.

An important help in relation to other people is undoubtedly to take seriously those existential questions people have in their hearts. What most people primarily seek is not theoretical answers given by someone else but more a reconciliation with the reality of life in which suffering and death are inevitable parts. As fellow beings it is a most important task to ease the process which can help other people find their own answers to the enigma of suffering and death.

This chapter is based on the book *Lidandets mening*, Individuella och samhälleliga strategier. (The Meaning of Suffering. Individual and Social Strategies) K. Kallenberg (ed.), Natur och Kultur, Stockholm, 1992.

REFERENCES

1. R. Inglehart, *The Silent Revolution. Changing Values and Political Styles among Wester Publics*, Princeton, 1977.
2. C. Rudbeck, *Svenska Dagbladet*, February 12, 1978.
3. A. Huxley, *Brave New World*, 1932.

4. C-R. Bråkenheilm, Suffering as an Existential Quest, in *The Meaning of Suffering*, K. Kallenberg (ed.), Natur och Kultur, Stockholm, pp. 201-215, 1992.
5. E. H. Erikson, Identity and the Life Cycle, *Psychological Issues*, Vol. 1, New York, 1959.
6. B. Söderfeldt, Power and the Meaning of Suffering. History, Care and Ideaology, in *The Meaning of Suffering*, K. Kallenberg (ed.), Natur och Kultur, Stockholm, pp. 58-79, 1992.
7. K. Popper, The Peverty of Historicism, *Economia, 11*:42, New Series, pp. 86-103, 1994. K. Popper, *The Open Society and its Enemies*, Vol. I-II, Routhledge & Sons, London, 1945.
8. L. Sachs, Suffering as Communication—A Human Fenomenon in its Cultural Context, in *The Meaning of Suffering*, K. Kallenberg (ed.), Natur och Kultur, Stockholm, pp. 124-137, 1992. L. Sachs, Misunderstanding as Therapy, *Culture, Medicine and Psychiatry, 13*, pp. 335-349, 1989.
9. K. Johannisson, To Suffer and Endure. Historical Fragments of the Fysical Suffering, in *The Meaning of Suffering*, K. Kallenberg (ed.), Natur och Kultur, Stockholm, pp. 112-123, 1992.
10. A. Ellenius, Suffering in Art, in *The Meaning of Suffering*, K. Kallenberg (ed.), Natur och Kultur, Stockholm, pp. 153-168, 1992.
11. J. Ling, To Overcome Grief and Suffering with Song, in *The Meaning of Suffering*, K. Kallenberg (ed.), Natur och Kultur, pp. 169-183, 1992.
12. I. Johnsson, Suffering in Litterature, in *The Meaning of Suffering*, K. Kallenberg (ed.), Natur och Kultur, Stockholm, pp. 184-200, 1992.
13. K. Marx, *Zur Kritik der hegelschen Rechtsphilosophie*, Recam, Leipzig, 1986.

CHAPTER 6

Meaning and
the Awareness of Death

Galen K. Pletcher

Our awareness of death seems to pose a threat to meaning in our lives, but it is not clear why this should be so. In this chapter, I argue that the attempt to construe life as an intrinsic good is mistaken, and that so to construe life would not relieve the threat of meaninglessness in any case. After showing the contribution to meaning in life of purposeful behavior, I put forward a number of reasons for believing that death and the awareness of our eventual death are necessary conditions for the achievement of meaning in life. I conclude by distinguishing my view from that of two other writers who have maintained a similar thesis.

Cartoons, movies, and folklore commonly reflect a certain element of the history of ideas by linking awareness of the fact of human death with doubts about the meaning of life. The general thought is this: How can the things to which we devote so much effort have any meaning, if one day we shall die and all of it shall be forgotten and without lasting effect? The opening words of *Ecclesiastes* sound this theme in a familiar way:

> Vanity of vanities, saith the Preacher, vanity of vanities; all is vanity. What profit hath a man of all his labor which he taketh under the sun? One generation passeth away, and another generation cometh: but the earth abideth forever. . . . There is no remembrance of former things; neither shall there by any remembrance of things that are to come with those that shall come after [1, Chap. 1:2-4, 11].

At the height of his powers as an author, Tolstoy was stricken with a vivid awareness of death and the seeming pointlessness of life, entering upon a terrible period of depression that he almost did not survive.

Today or tomorrow sickness and death will come (they had come already) to those I love or to me; nothing will remain but stench and worms. Sooner or later my affairs, whatever they may be, will be forgotten, and I shall not exist. Then why go on making any effort? . . . One can only live while one is intoxicated with life; as soon as one is sober it is impossible not to see that it is all a mere fraud and a stupid fraud! [2, pp. 19-20].

This linkage is intuitively understandable to almost all of us, but it is not apparent why it should be. We do not question the worth of many other activities that last only a short time. We do not have the same intuitive understanding of someone who would refuse to eat because of the fact that the enjoyment occasioned by the meal would soon have to come to an end. Nor would we understand any such claims regarding sexual activity, performing or listening to music, and many other activities in which human beings engage. Why then does our awareness of death seem to demonstrate the futility of all that precedes death?

One explanation for the disparity in our views toward, on the one hand, the transience of short-term activities and, on the other, the transience of life as a whole, lies in the fact that the activities that I have mentioned are sometimes thought of as intrinsically good. In this view, some or perhaps all of the goodness of such activities lies within the activities themselves and our attitudes and experiences during them, and not in the fruits of the activities—not in what is sometimes called their extrinsic value. There are differences even here among human beings. One *might* regard eating as good only because it keeps one alive, not because it is intrinsically enjoyable; and one *might* regard sex as good only because it leads to procreation, rather than because of its intrinsic value. But a more usual view is to hold that such activities are both extrinsically and intrinsically good.

If some activity that is intrinsically good were deprived of an extrinsic benefit we thought it would have, we might still console ourselves with its intrinsic goodness. We may have thoroughly enjoyed the challenge of knitting a sweater for Aunt Julie, even though she died just before we could give it to her. On the other hand, there are activities that are primarily only extrinsically useful or good, although these activities are harder to think of than might at first be expected. A very distasteful cleaning job is usually thought to be valuable only because of the more desirable state of affairs that it brings about. A visit to a very unpleasant relative may be desirable only because of the benefits of various kinds that we expect it to have for him or her or for us, such as the satisfaction of a moral responsibility. We can imagine feeling slightly foolish if we did something that was very distasteful only to discover that the benefit we thought we were gaining was not forthcoming. Imagine someone toiling all summer to tuckpoint his house, only to discover that it is about to be seized by eminent domain. Assuming that he found no intrinsic enjoyment in the activity of tuckpointing, we would understand his wishing that he had not spent all that time in fruitless toil.

We began by asking why it is that our confidence in life's meaning or meanings can be so severely shaken by our discovery that life is only temporary. The intervening reflections show that we encounter a similar attitude toward activities that are only extrinsically valuable. The threat that death seems to pose to the meaning of life is very similar to the feeling we have when we discover that all of our effort toward some thoroughly unpleasant task was unnecessary. But is the value of life only extrinsic? If life were conceived of as intrinsically valuable, then we would expect that the knowledge of one's death would have an effect similar to what occurs when an intrinsically valuable experience of some other kind is found to have no extrinsic value. We may have enjoyed ourselves during it, even though the activity did not have the fruits that we hoped it would have. If we had such an attitude, we would not be moved to despair of the whole business by this disappointment. Why is this type of consolation relatively ineffective when we think about life as a whole?

There are at least two considerations involved in our not being consolable in the face of death simply by the intrinsic goodness of much of life. First, life is not an activity comparable to eating. Second, our sense of meaning is not dependent upon enjoyment or lack of it, but upon a justified sense of purpose, of accomplishment, in our lives. I shall discuss each of these in turn.

Life is the necessary condition of every other human condition and activity. If we were not alive, we would not be able to eat, read, listen to music, and engage in all the other intrinsic goods that are open to us. That life ends does not present to us a situation parallel to the ending of one or more of the situations or activities of life. Rather, death presents us with the end of the very condition necessary for any situations or activities—satisfactory or not. Schopenhauer argued that life as such is simply a bore, redeemed only by moments of distraction provided by evanescent pleasures such as eating and sex, or by endeavor toward some goal (which is immediately disappointing when it is reached). For example,

> [W]henever we are not striving for something or are not intellectually occupied, but are thrown back on existence itself, its worthlessness and vanity are brought home to us; and this is what is meant by boredom. Even our inherent and ineradicable tendency to run after what is strange and extraordinary shows how glad we are to see an interruption in the natural course of things which is so tedious [3, p. 287].

But, *contra* Schopenhauer, it is not even sensible to ask if <u>life</u> is pleasant or boring. Life is the condition in which pleasant states are enjoyed and boring states endured.

This is why we cannot expect human beings to be consoled by reference to the enjoyments of life, as they might be consoled at the end of the fair by reflection on how much they have enjoyed the proceedings. The fair will be succeeded by other activities, but the end of life marks the end of conscious states and activities as we know them. Even the firm expectation of some people that life will be succeeded by other conscious states of one kind or another cannot fully console them for the loss of the states they know. (Religions of the East regard the succeeding states as ones that it would be better eventually to avoid altogether!)

The second point raised by our consideration of intrinsic goodness is this: The sense of futility and devaluation that our awareness of death sometimes spreads through our lives does not concern only the quality of our lives and the experiences and states of mind that they make possible. It concerns, as well, the sense of foolishness and futility that arises regarding our consciously undertaken goals and projects when we realize that they do not live on beyond us. Even the author of *Ecclesiastes* finds some consolation, albeit with a touch of bitterness, in thoughts of food, drink and companionship.[1] What he laments is that our human undertakings all come to the same end. The dissatisfaction we feel about the meaning of life upon becoming aware of the fact of human death lies to a large extent in the effects of that awareness upon our natural propensity to view life as an opportunity to accomplish certain purposes.

The service of purposes and projects imparts two related characteristics to life: orientation and integration. When life has meaning, it makes sense, at least much of the time. To some extent, our lives make sense because of social structures that assure us of a place and provide us a perspective. This may be particularly true in traditional societies. However, at the level of the life of the individual, the orientation stemming from our adoption of projects is the primary way in which life makes sense. In the light of our projects, we understand ourselves as working toward certain goals, and this helps remove ambiguity about ourselves and our world. Meaning cannot be gained simply from the enjoyment of intrinsically good states of being. These affect the quality of our lives, but do not assure its meaning. (If they did, despair and suicide would never be found among persons in relatively comfortable circumstances.) The adoption and service of purposes, on the other hand, helps us to define what we are all about, what we *mean*. That we can determine this for ourselves, at least to some extent, is the central feature of human autonomy.

The adoption and service of purposes also help to provide integration in our lives. If life is to make sense, we must be able to see some relationships between

---

[1] E.g., " . . . a man hath no better thing under the sun, than to eat, and to drink, and to be merry: for that shall abide with him of his labor the days of his life, which God giveth him under the sun." "Live joyfully with the wife whom thou lovest all the days of the life of thy vanity, which he hath given thee under the sun, all the days of thy vanity: for that is thy portion in this life, and in thy labor which thou takest under the sun" [1, Chap. 8:15 and Chap. 9:9].

our actions and among our projects and commitments. We choose among possible activities and undertakings partly on the basis of their relationship to our projects. To the extent that actions in life are not integrated in some way, life is correspondingly aimless, pointless, and—I would argue—meaningless. It may be that consolation can be derived from other sources to help compensate for this aimlessness. But ideally, our lives have meaning that results from the deliberate efforts we expend in them.

Although meaning in life is dependent to at least some extent upon patterns that life exhibits, it is not enough that life simply exhibit patterns. The patterns must be at least somewhat of our own devising. If we discovered one day that our lives exhibited some grand design that had hitherto been obscured from our recognition, this would not contribute to meaning in our lives unless the pattern or design were in some way connected with efforts we had been making on its behalf. The undoubted crucial place it occupies in a larger design does not add meaning to the life of a calf being raised in a dark barn for slaughter as veal. There must be some kind of order or purpose to a life with meaning, but it must be order or purpose that has some connection to values that the person has or would agree to if presented with them [4, pp. 585-588].

The connection between the awareness of death and meaning may seem paradoxical. On the one hand, awareness of death is probably more fully responsible than any other feature of our conscious lives for our interest in and pursuit of purposes in our lives. We value pattern in our life partly because we know we will die. We do not have forever. Viktor Frankl asks:

> [W]hat would our lives be like if they were not finite in time, but infinite? If we were immortal, we could legitimately postpone every action forever. It would be of no consequence whether or not we did a thing now; every act might just as well be done tomorrow or the day after or a year from now or ten years hence. But in the face of death as an absolute finis to our future and boundary to our possibilities, we are under the imperative of utilizing our lifetimes to the utmost, not letting the singular opportunities—whose "finite" sum constitutes the whole of life—pass by unused. Finality, temporality, is therefore not only an essential characteristic of human life, but also a real factor in its meaningfulness [5, p. 73].

He concludes that "finiteness must itself constitute something that gives meaning to human existence—not something that robs it of meaning" [5, p. 72].

On the other hand, awareness of death, as we have seen, can effectively enervate our lives, by depriving them of the zest and the motivation that are necessary for life itself. This is what happened with such devastating force to Tolstoy. Awareness of death seems to assure us that all purposes, insofar as they relate to individual efforts, are ultimately frustrated. So death provides the impetus to the creation and recognition of pattern and purpose, yet also shows that the creation of pattern and purpose is ultimately futile. How can we resolve this paradox?

The key to a resolution lies in moving from talk about the psychological effects of the awareness of death to a recognition of the philosophical significance of death *and* of our awareness of it. From this perspective, my thesis is very simple: The meaning that it is possible for human beings to achieve in their lives is dependent partly upon the fact of their mortality. Awareness of death, therefore, is awareness of the possibility that our lives can have meaning. I present several arguments in support of this position.[2]

1. I have argued that meaning derives from the adoption of purposes. Purposes make sense to us only because of the possibility of their being achieved. When purposes are achieved, they are ended. They may be succeeded by other purposes, but the fulfillment of the original purpose intimately involves its cessation. This is true even of purposes that are very unlikely to be achieved in the course of any one lifetime. Insofar, then, as meaning depends upon our working toward purposes, it involves the ending of that toward which we work. Indeed, our own efforts bring about that ending.

2. The hallmark of a life that is concerned with the pursuit of purposes is orientation. Such a life is dynamic; it is going somewhere, by its own values and choices. A dynamic process involves movements through phases—through the beginnings, middles and endings of patterns. If life were static, one would expect that it would not change, and that death would be no part of it. But the dynamism that is the correlate of the possibility of meaning in life insures the successive rising and falling of states of affairs. This series of successions involves cessations of many different kinds, including, as we discover, the end of each life. Death is thus one more manifestation of the very process that makes possible the creation of meaning.

3. An important component of meaning in life is development. Our undertakings in life present us with moving targets, with a series of processes that move

---

[2] In the most basic sense, my reasoning is transcendental, because I accept the following premise as true: *1. It is possible to achieve meaning in life*. I then seek to understand how this can be so. This type of argument may seem to beg the question. But it does not do so any more egregiously than an argument that begins with a contrary or contradictory premise, such as: *not-1. It is not possible to achieve meaning in life*. Some people certainly seem to achieve meaning in their lives, an observation strengthened by the contrast such people form with those who seem not to achieve meaning in their lives. How do they do it? Two other crucial premises inform my argument: *2. Mortality is a defining feature of human beings. 3. The defining features of a thing are necessary to its meaning*. Premise 3., which I think of as Aristotelian because of its reference to defining or essential conditions, stands in need of considerable defense. My partiality to it stems from a conviction that meaning is not a superimposed feature of life, but develops out of the concrete situation of that life. If we accept premises 1. and 3., along with some clarifications, one or two instantiations, and perhaps some waving of hands, it seems to me reasonable to conclude that

A. Death is a necessary condition of meaning in human life. I confess this transcendental turn to my argument at the outset, in the hope that cognizance of it may illuminate my other arguments.

from stage to stage. In many of these, we define the process for ourselves. We aspire to a certain level of competence in some activity, or we hope to break a habit we reject or to acquire a habit we think would be of benefit to us. In cases like this, we define for ourselves an end. We cannot be developing if there is no trajectory to the process, and that trajectory includes within itself a termination of the development.

It may be objected that there can be development without end. One can never run so fast that one cannot run faster, or be so kind that one could not be kinder. Although this is true, our thinking about such processes, and our planning our involvement in them, is always in terms of increments, each defined by an end. If it were not so, involvement in activities that can be developed without end would be guaranteed to fail, since one could always have done better. It is our recognition of endings that marks the increments in such developmental processes and that assures us of the possibility of success.

4. Structure, framework, pattern, are all contributors to meaning in life because of the integration they provide. But structure, framework, and pattern depend on limitation. A limitless expanse, whether of space or of time, is not structured or delineated. Artists, to take one example of this, create the meanings of their works by the way they frame them, give them bounds, and bring them to an end. The limitations are essential conditions of the meaning.

My position on the topic of limitations is opposed to that of some philosophers. For example, Robert Nozick says that

> [T]he problem of meaning is created by limits. We cope with this by . . . transcending these limits. Yet whatever extent we thereby reach in a wider realm also has its own limits . . . This suggests that the problem can be avoided or transcended only by something without limits, only by something that cannot be stood outside of, even in imagination [4, p. 599].

I believe this line of reasoning is mistaken and leads to further mistakes, but I will not be able here to do more than outline my arguments against it.

First, whether or not limitations threaten meaning depends upon individual cases. Someone who confines her activities in such a way as to increase the limitations upon them may enhance the meaning they provide her life. Previously, she may have been spread too thin, too unfocused. Second, limitation would be an enemy of meaning only for something that should not, given its nature, be limited. But we have no idea that that is true of human life. Indeed, it would appear that human life is characterized by limitation; limitations of varying kinds are some of its most distinctive features. If so, the position Nozick takes seems to beg the question against life's having meaning. A more accurate conception of the relationship between limitation and meaning is sketched in 5.

5. Although I have stressed the importance to life's meaning of the selection and service of purposes, there may be an even more basic dimension of meaning

in life: A life that has meaning has value to the person living it. The paradigm of this is Bertrand Russell's moving statement in the "Prologue" to his Autobiography. After delineating three "passions" that have "governed" his life, he says this: "This has been my life. I have found it worth living, and would gladly live it again if the chance were offered me" [6, p. 3]. Russell's willingness, even eagerness, to live his life again bears witness to the high value it had for him.

What makes a life have this kind of value? I have argued that the intrinsically valuable experiences that life makes possible cannot account for our valuing our lives. For one thing, we may not value our lives even in the face of intrinsic goods of many descriptions. For another, we may continue to value life even when its intrinsic enjoyments are reduced or perhaps missing altogether. Here is an alternative suggestion: Value is related to limitation. There is a close connection between something's being scarce, or limited, or impermanent, and its having value. We sometimes dismiss things that do not last long as being of no value, but the value of the bloom of our favorite flower depends partly upon the fact that it does not last long. Freud argued, against a poet of his acquaintance who dismissed the value of beautiful things because of their transience, that the transience of what is beautiful results in an increase in its worth. In general, "[l]imitation in the possibility of an enjoyment raises the value of the enjoyment" [7, p. 305]. Similarly, the value of our lives depends partly upon the fact that they come to an end. Insofar, then, as meaning in life is partly constituted by the value of that life to us, that meaning depends at least partly on the fact of death.

Other authors have maintained the view that death, rather than posing a threat to life's meaning, is a condition of life's having meaning. I shall sketch the views of two other theorists and briefly discuss how my position differs from theirs. I have already quoted Viktor Frankl, who calls attention to the urgency that finitude adds to our lives. He sees two primal elements of human existence: consciousness and responsibility. He believes that finiteness is inescapably present in these two essential factors of human existence. Hence, "finiteness must itself constitute something that gives meaning to human existence—not something that robs it of meaning." After this point he argues, as cited before, that this finiteness puts us "under the imperative of utilizing our lifetimes to the utmost . . . " [5, pp. 72, 73].

The central point of agreement between Frankl and me is that the theory of meaning in life must take full account of the actual nature of life. It must avoid *ad hoc* additions that save human meaning by the operation of some *deus ex machina*. It must deal fully with human life as we experience it. The meaning we seek must be the meaning of this life in all its particularity. The principal difference I have with Frankl is that, having begun in this way, he treats the point before us as if it were one of motivational psychology. He emphasizes that without the knowledge of our finitude (i.e., the awareness of death), we would not be moved to act, could put things off indefinitely, etc. This may be true, but its truth does not guarantee its motivational efficacy; people who realize the importance of their actions may nevertheless not carry them out. Hence, there is no basis for confidence that awareness of death generally has the motivational effect that Frankl attributes to it. Moreover, the point I have emphasized is a philosophical one, rather than a psychological one: Awareness of death is the awareness of the very possibility of structure and accomplishment in our lives. If we did not have this awareness, we could not even formulate the plans and purposes and structures that are responsible for the meaning in our lives. Death and the awareness of death are necessary for the creation of meaning in human life.

Bernard Williams has argued that "[i]mmortality, or a state without death, would be meaningless," and hence that "in a sense, death gives the meaning to life" [8, p. 82]. His basis for this is that "we could have no reason for living eternally a human life," since there is "no desirable or significant property which life would have more of, or have more unqualifiedly, if we lasted for ever" [8, p. 89]. The crucial enemy, he thinks, would be boredom, since one could not expect that continual reiterations of events would have the same effects as the first instance. The resulting boredom, he thinks, would be "a reaction almost perceptual in character to the poverty of one's relation to the environment" [8, p. 95]. Even intense intellectual inquiry will not stave off this boredom, he argues, since fulfilling intellectual inquiries must relate to the inquirer, not just to the inquiry as such. But if someone were immortal, "it seems quite unreasonable to suppose that those [intellectual] activities would have the fulfilling or liberating character that they do have for him, if they were in fact all he could do or conceive of doing."[3] Hence, Williams concludes, one is lucky if one can die "shortly before the horrors of not doing so become evident" [8, p. 100].

There is more to Williams' complex and subtle argument than I can show here. The key difference in our views is that Williams concentrates on an empirical obstacle to the achievement of meaning, rather than on an analysis of the nature of meaning as such. His claim is that if one were to move through an eternity without aging, then deep, palpable, thorough-going boredom would be the result. My point is that without the framework and the limitation provided by our knowledge of the certainty of death, we would not be able to craft meaning in a life of no matter what length.

As might be expected, there are several ways to disagree with the thesis that life would have no meaning if it did not end. One might do so in general, by suggesting that surely, if life did not end, it might nevertheless, *contra* Williams, have meaning of some kind.[4] Or one might do so by referring to one or another religious tradition that prizes a belief in an afterlife and that therefore incorporates this endless sequel to our current life in its conception of human meaning. Or one

---

[3] [8, p. 96] I cite a reply to this argument in note 4.

[4] E.g.: "Persons who are immortal need not be limited to the desires and designs of mortals; they might well think up new plans that, in Parkinsonian fashion, expand to fill the available time" [4, p. 580].

might, as has Nozick, suggest that the view seems to lead to the absurd conclusion that the life of an eternal God would lack meaning [4, p. 580]. Realizing that I cannot fully respond to these objections in this space, I shall sketch the direction a satisfactory response might take.

Our thinking about human meaning must be informed throughout by a sound and adequate philosophical anthropology. The advantage of the view I am suggesting is its incorporating, rather than ignoring or struggling against, two basic features of human beings. First, human beings are members of the animal kingdom. In company with our fellow animals, we die. I have suggested (note 2., premise 2.) that death may even be thought to be one of the defining characteristics of human beings, in the sense that if something did not die, it would not be human. Human meaning must, it would therefore seem, involve death. A feature so basic to our nature must manifest its effects in every principal consideration of our lives, just as do eating and reproduction and respiration. Second, a chief difference from other animals is that we alone are aware of our impending death. Here again, it would be peculiar if such a fundamental feature of our being were not reflected in something so basic as the meaning that our lives have or can acquire. Awareness of death provides both the motivation to live our lives so that they acquire meaning and the conceptual framework that assures the possibility of that meaning.

I conclude that far from being a threat to the meaning of our lives, death is a necessary condition of life's *having* any meaning. Awareness of death calls us to a certain kind of responsibility, as Frankl has noted, and this may be one reason it makes us so uncomfortable. Death is a constant reminder that you cannot proceed endlessly through the projects of your life, and that you cannot wait forever to achieve the happiness that would make you willing "gladly [to] live it again." But death also provides the limitations against which we define ourselves in our projects and in our aspirations, and the limitations that are necessary for the birth of value itself.

Death, like any other constraint and limitation, shapes the nature of our lives. We cannot aim to do things that require superhuman strength, for example, because we do not possess it. Similarly, we cannot aspire to a destiny, the possibility of which is contradicted by the facts of life as we discover them. Death is quite properly construed to be a threat to any type of meaning that requires the facts of life to be other than they are. But it is a mistake to conclude from this that death is a threat to meaning in general. Such a conclusion overlooks the manifold types of meaning that not only are possible within human constraints but that depend upon those constraints for their possibility.

REFERENCES

1. *Holy Bible*, King James Version, *Ecclesiastes*.

2. L. Tolstoy, *A Confession*, Aylmer Maude (trans.), Oxford University Press, London, 1961.
3. A. Schopenhauer, Additional Remarks on the Doctrine of the Vanity of Existence, *Parerga and Paralipomena: Short Philosophical Essays*, E. F. J. Payne (trans.), Vol. II, Clarendon Press, Oxford, 1974.
4. R. Nozick, *Philosophical Explanations*, Harvard University Press, Cambridge, Massachusetts, 1981.
5. V. E. Frankl, *The Doctor and the Soul: An Introduction to Logotherapy*, Alfred A. Knopf, New York, 1957.
6. B. Russell, *The Autobiography of Bertrand Russell: 1872-1914*, Vol. I, Little, Brown & Co., Boston, 1967.
7. S. Freud, On Transience [Vergänglichkeit], *The Standard Edition of the Complete Psychological Works of Sigmund Freud*, James Strachey (ed. and trans.), Vol. XIV, Hogarth Press, London, 1957.
8. B. Williams, The Makropulos Case: Reflections on the Tedium of Immortality, *Problems of the Self*, Cambridge University Press, Cambridge, pp. 82-100, 1973.

CHAPTER 7

Blinkings: A Thanatocentric Theory of Consciousness

Jeffrey Kauffman

> All that we see when we have wakened is death; all that we see while slumbering is sleep.
>
> — Heraclitus

> I have thought for as long as I can remember that the asking of unanswerable questions and the facing of irreparable truths is our only consolation for having to live them.
>
> — Catherine Madsen

Awareness of mortality is the light and the depth of thanatology. Yet the problematics, phenomenology, and discipline of awareness of mortality has been marginalized in thanatology. The thanatocentric theory of consciousness presented here invites the reader to consider the primacy for thanatology of philosophical questions, as well as the primacy for philosophy of thanatological questions. A theory of consciousness is described that is based upon a recognition that human consciousness *hinges* on human mortality. Human consciousness is a virtual but not self-evident expression of mortality.

THE QUESTION OF THANATOLOGY

From Thanatology to Philosophy

We thanatologists are concerned with death. We study social attitudes, psychological processes, anthropological practices, echoes of our mortality in the sciences of man. We seek to understand and to care for the needs of the dying and bereaved. We are attentive to our own attitudes about death and dying, and recognize that the question of our own mortality is key to our work.

Mortality awareness is the spark that initiates thanatological questioning, concern, and research. Awareness of mortality is also the ultimate possibility of thanatological inquiry. From its initial disturbing intrusion into consciousness to its unexpected power of awakening consciousness, awareness of mortality is a quest for meaning in the realm of the unknown.

The entire project of thanatology is built on the foundation of an extraordinary question mark. Thanatology has had a contradictory relationship to this question mark, i.e., our work simultaneously explicates and conceals our mortality. The ultimate mystery of death for human consciousness is a question that goes beyond the confines of scientific research. It goes beyond the stories it prompts us to tell about the meanings of life and death, and beyond our everyday awareness of ourselves in the world. "Going beyond" is characteristic of the sense in which mortality, as the source of consciousness, resides in consciousness. Again and again we find that as mortality defines our very human consciousness, it also dislocates consciousness, and prompts consciousness to go beyond itself.

Consciousness, when it finds itself alive and searching, when it comes back to its starting place—*the presence of death in human life, in one's own life*—may be awakened to the fundamentally radical question of thanatology. Awakened to my questioning *as the question of my mortality*, I am no longer at a distance from my questions. I can no longer look upon data, facts and theories about death without recognizing the presence of my own mortality at the heart of my questioning. The question of our mortality is the question of our being human and of our consciousness. It is I, myself, who is the question.

This is a passageway, a return, from thanatology to the philosophical origins of thanatology. The return is not an awakening *to* our mortality; it is the awakening *of* our mortality. We may retreat from the extraordinary and disturbing consciousness that is awakened in us by the imposition of our mortality on the ordinary consciousness in which we live, as Heraclitus says, slumbering. The retreat from mortality is comforting. Philosophy has long sought to be a palliative for the fear of death. The philosophical thanatology here recognizes the ancestral legacy of the philosopher Heraclitus: "All that we see when we have wakened is death; all that we see while slumbering is sleep."

The mourning process is the way humans seek to bridge death and life, the way we inscribe and integrate death into our living self. It is a human institution in which a repetition of deep psychic forces ambitendently seek expulsion and inclusion of inner representations of a dead person, of the reality of that death, and of our own inexorable mortality. The upsurge of primordial affects makes this inward link between death and life tumultuous. Mourning is the way we live our deaths, realize our capacity to die, create our humanness. Among the psychological aims of the mourning process is the dissolution of the immediate power of death in consciousness.

This tendency is most evident in the very organization of the mourning process. A return to the "normalcy" of consciousness in which mortality awareness has been extinguished is normative. The human being whose eyes have been opened by death is "well" and "healed" when the terrible wakening of death has passed and slumbering consciousness returns.

From Philosophy to Thanatology

Deathspell: Death repels, compels, expels. We flee from death, again and again. We return, unerring in venturing back. Fleeing and returning chronically, never in time, absent-minded, this double motion (repelling/compelling) becomes us, so that *the expulsion of death is our own errancy.*

The possibility of a thanatocentric philosophy has been a defining and elusive script of philosophy since Heidegger. However, the existential-ontological structure of the possibility of death that philosophy has been concerned with and the actual dying and fear of death that we thanatologists have been attending to are different discourses.

The existential-ontological analysis of death, recognizing itself as the analysis of the *possibility* of death, as the analysis of the disclosure of man to himself through this possibility, makes a fatal, if inevitable, error at the very outset of the project. It understands that it is not concerned with *actual death.* The logic of this is compelled by the idealistic traditions of philosophy from Plato's *Ideas* to Husserl's phenomenology.

The knot that philosophy cannot untie or cut through is that *philosophy is the idealization of death.* This is the root of the complex and long history of antipathy of philosophy to awareness of mortality. As it comes toward consciousness of death, philosophy finds itself, and is turned away. Struggling with the deconstruction of its fundamental identity as an idealization of death, it seeks to resymbolize death as a defense against awareness of mortality.

Philosophy replaces death with the matrix of possibility. Does the luminous charismos of the noumenal transcend mortality, or is mortality what compels the logic of transcendence? Can philosophy return to the question of mortality without mourning the ideality of its constructions? The possibility of death as the ground of existential-ontological analysis has force, meaning and vitality only when the possibility of death contains or implies actual death and the horrific pain of the fear of death. Yet, philosophers are prone to devalue actual death and make it *nothing.* Death is the emergent anomaly that defines the continuing crisis of the twentieth-century philosophical thought.

Can we deconstruct the original differentiation between actual and potential death, infuse the meaning of potential death with the concrete, affectively terrifying, deep presence of our mortality within us, and suffuse our attention to actual death with the possibility that it imposes upon us, the possibility of transcendence?

TWO DRAGONS TO BE SLAIN

The two dragons to be slain are two beliefs that are to be called into question. The intent is to find basic assumptions of thanatology and to demonstrate a process of calling them into question.

Two specific basic assumptions constitute thanatology as a natural science. They are 1) that in developing an awareness of mortality, *knowledge* is the mode of consciousness through which we approach death and 2) that by recognizing death to be *natural*, awareness of mortality is advanced. The first task is bringing into question the presupposition that thanatology is, in the first place, a field of knowledge. The liberation of thanatology from the desire to know, from the enchantment and bond of consciousness to the world of objects and its epistemological trappings is examined here in two sections, both in the "Unknowing of Death" that follows and later as the "Objectification of Death." Disempowering the very powerful epistemic illusion is a method of awakening awareness of mortality.

The second dragon to be slain is the belief that death is natural. I do not dispute that death is natural. The problem is, rather, that human nature is mortal; *death defines nature, not nature death*. The nature of consciousness *is* mortality.

Epistemology and the Unknowing of Death

The fear of death is the power which generates the illusions in which we live. The very space and time in which we constitute our experience of reality, through which we navigate, is a projection of our fear of death. Knowledge is a primary navigational instrument. Knowledge is the specific power of consciousness that dissolves the presence of death, and replaces it with known reality. There is no *knowledge* of death. Being awakened to mortality is not an epistemic mode of consciousness. Knowledge about death is, in this basic sense, illusory and an impediment to awareness of mortality.

Listen, for a moment, to Thomas Merton:

> . . . because he is willingly enclosed and limited by the laws and illusions of collective existence he has no more identity than an unborn child in the womb. He is not yet conscious. He is alien to his own truth. He has senses, but cannot use them. He has life, but no identity. To have an identity, he has to be awake and aware. But to be awake, he has to accept vulnerability and death.
>
> *(Raids on the Unspeakable)* [1]

Being awakened to death dislodges consciousness from its enclosure of familiarity and ordinariness. Awareness of mortality dislodges epistemic intentionality. Propelling a radical unknowing, awareness of mortality emerges as an *uncanny consciousness*, a dislocating self-awareness hinged on escalating contradictions. Awareness of mortality emerges as an implosive undoing of knowing. If to have an identity is to be awake and to be awake is to be awakened to death, the riddle of human identity, disclosed in this raid on the unspeakable, is the riddle of our awareness of mortality.

Merton speaks of the "illusions of collective existence." This may be taken to mean that if the enclosure of *social constructs* defines one's identity, one really has no identity. I think that "illusions of collective existence" means not just the social, but the social, psychological, and ontological constructs that constitute virtually the entirety of our experience of human reality. Shedding the illusions of collective existence, through an awareness of mortality, awakens a sense of our being in its most radical or primary sense. Breaking out of the enclosure that our very consciousness projects as reality, recognizing our fear of vulnerability and death as denied in and by these basic projections *is* a spiritual awakening. The mystics' realization of vulnerability and death is not *knowledge* of death.

We do not, however, seem to be able to remain in exile from the enclosure of ordinariness, or to refrain from projecting an experienced and believed world that functions to relieve us of our ontologically and psychologically primal fear of death. We do not seem to be able to stay in a state of unknowing.

Confronted with death we are opened to the extreme limit of the possible: the unlimited. However, when our epistemic and existential ground is undermined, we tend to seek limits to control the unknown: Awakened by death to death, we seek knowledge about death and dying. We seek to foreclose the terrified radiance of being awakened.

Both the inward bearing of death at the core of our existence and the explosion of death into our life experience compel us to create meaning. Death makes us meaning-makers. To refrain from meaning-making, to hang in the balance between death and creation, death and future, to unknow death—is a strange, virtually unendurable enlightenment. While we know that knowing death is impossible, unknowing death is nearly impossible.

What Do We Mean When We Say Death Is Natural?

The death awareness movement has noted that, in our society, death has come to be regarded and experienced as unnatural. Through the work of Lindemann, Gorer, Fiefel, Kubler-Ross and many others who have followed them, we have grown to recognize how we have been alienated as a society and as individuals from the reality of death. Stigmatization and shunning of death and grief impoverishes us and is integral not only to the pathology of our times, but also to the very pathos of human existence. Our new awareness has had social, psychological, and spiritual benefit in helping us to correct some symptoms of the denial of death. The naturalization of death has helped to partially loosen the tight taboo against allowing death to be a subject of social and individual consciousness. One result is more compassionate care for the dying and bereaved. Our acceptance of the naturalness of death is a beacon of social and psychospiritual healing and well-being. The naturalization of death is a core feature of the death awareness movement. However, could our naturalizing death be related to the taming of death in modern social life? [2].

Death is not ever really an ordinary event or a natural part of ordinary reality. Death is extra-ordinary. Death's *naturalness* is a consolation and palliation sanctioning the recognition of death in our lives that also silences a very disturbing realization: Death is unnatural, disruptive and uncontainable by consciousness. The concept of the naturalness of death helps foster the integration of death in the mourning process, but also functions to deny and split off from consciousness the astonishment and terror that death awakens in us.

The unspeakable reality of death is a possibility for awareness. It is an awareness that is difficult and unnatural. The incursion of death into the experienced naturalness of life and the ordinariness of consciousness is a disturbance from which we wish to return to a more *natural* condition.

Yeats in his 1933 poem "Death" writes:

Nor dread nor hope attend
A dying animal
A man awaits his end
Dreading and hoping all
Man creates his death. [3]

Is this not another sense in which death is not natural? *We create our death.* Yet, is it not our nature to create death? So, we might say death is natural, and our creating death raises a question about what human nature is. Our mortality—this most natural/unnatural condition of human life—is our nature. We are compelled to create our death. The poet does not mean the biological fact of death. Our mortality *is* an awareness, a specifically human awareness. Awareness is a reflection of our mortality, and of how things are with our mortality.

The poet says that we create our death in "dreading and hoping all." It is not dreading and hoping that creates death; it is dreading and hoping *all*. The philosopher, Franz Rosenweig, turns the equation around, saying that cognition of the all originates in death. He says, "All cognition of the all originates in death, in the fear of death" [4]. In both accounts awareness of the all is the link to death, i.e., to awareness of mortality. Our relation to the all is anticipatory and affective. The possibility for death realized in "dread and hope" or in "fear" *is* the possibility of awareness of death. Out of the fear of death comes cognition of the all, and in beholding the all or nothing nature of life and death I recognize, I *create* my death. In the power of the all as the mirror of my death, my death creates me, and I create my death. In this possibility of *losing all* (to the all-powerfulness of death), I recognize my inmost and ownmost self to be my omnipotence and helplessness in my all-embracing cognition of death. The way I anticipate my death, the implicit realization of my mortality is awareness of my existence. Beyond all the particulars of my existence, creating my death is self creation. This is my human nature.

The mourning process moves toward restoration of the self, accommodation, reconciliation, integration, acceptance—closure. Death can erupt an intense consciousness, agonizing, catastrophic, impossible—driving us in desperate flights, confusion, hallucination, mania, and despair. The realization of mortality is overwhelming. We are more unconscious than conscious as we awaken to the inner presence and meaning of death in us, as *death awakens us to our existence*. The astonishing awareness present in the terror of death is blinding. Death awakens us, and we yearn for sleep. "If this fear [the fear of death] were as constantly conscious," writes Zilborg,

> we should be unable to function normally. It must be properly repressed to keep us living with any modicum of comfort. We know very well that to repress means more than to put away and to forget that which was put away and the place where we put it. It means also to maintain a constant psychological effort to keep the lid on and inwardly never to relax our watchfulness [5].

We should note that this is not the repression of an experience of death that frightens us. He does not mean that an experience happened, i.e., the death of a loved one, and we repressed the fear of death. It is a fear that is *always already* [6] there. Freud called it "primary," which means that it is not a repression occasioned by experience but a repression that is a condition of experience. Experience itself is conditioned by the repression of the fear of death. When death is experienced, the urge to repress involves effort to put a lid on 1) that experience *and* 2) the fear of death that is the condition of experience, i.e., both primary and secondary repression are called into play. The counter-effort to remain conscious of death aims to retrieve (the fear of) death, to locate and remember death, to take the lid off and inwardly to undo our forbidding watchfulness. This act of remembering death is remembering one's own death. Becoming conscious of death is becoming conscious of oneself. Yet, we now see that *awareness of mortality, when taken as the awareness of the inmost reality of our own mortality, requires confronting the forces of secondary and primary repression.* This is decidedly and profoundly unnatural and most would say that it is simply, by definition, impossible. This impossibility is the radical task of thanatocentric philosophy: the impossible deconstruction of the opposition of actual and possible death, the impossible dwelling in annihilation. While awareness of mortality is our human nature, the impossibility of awareness of mortality is the mystery of human nature.

A PHENOMENOLOGY OF THE AWARENESS
OF MORTALITY: FROM EMBEDDEDNESS
TO AWAKENESS

This phenomenology of the awareness of mortality is divided into four parts. The first part, "The Thanatophobic Dominance of Consciousness," continuing the theme of the previous section on the primary repression of death, asserts the underlying embeddedness of consciousness in the fear of death.

The second part, "The Prereflexive Opacity of Consciousness," describes the fear of death as the original prereflexive crucible out of which awareness of mortality becomes differentiated. This primitive state in which consciousness is permeated with mortality, yet unaware of its mortality is called *mortal consciousness*.

The third part, "Objectification of Death," describes a biphasic process of the emergence of awareness of mortality out of mortal consciousness. The *modus operandi* of consciousness is to negate death and project it as the lived world of human consciousness. The very constitution of object reality is an act of the death disowning nature of consciousness. The development of awareness of mortality is the process of death returning to awareness as the very reality of consciousness. Thus, the biphasic process is 1) consciousness' expelling death and constituting itself as the presence of objects and 2) the return of the reality of death and the possibility of awareness of mortality. Awareness of mortality is consciousness' awareness of itself.

The fourth part, "The Subjective Consciousness of Death and the Problem of Otherness," notes that the return of death from objectification to subjectivity is further riddled with the denial of death. In the subjectivity of consciousness there are aspects of the self that are dissociated [7] from the self's experience of itself and that are not present as part of the self's identity. Subjectivity is nuanced with shadows of otherness within the self. These not-self representations are the locus of mortality disowned within subjective awareness. The otherness within subjectivity, an aspect of our implicit mortal consciousness, marks an abiding limit of awareness of mortality.

Thanatophobic Dominance of Consciousness

"At bottom," Freud writes, "no one believes in his own death, or to put the same thing in another way, in the unconscious every one of us is convinced of his own immortality" [8]. This well-known opinion has become part of the corpus of a modern folk wisdom. It expresses how profound and thorough, how basic to our human nature and capacity for awareness is the repression of death. Even as we mature in our awareness of mortality and integrate awareness of our mortality more fully into our self-awareness, "at bottom, no one believes in his own death."

There is a delusion inherent in increased awareness of mortality. Passion for closure, for closing off the pain of death, reaffirms the belief that I am *not* mortal.

Whenever consciousness is stirred to awaken to mortality, we simultaneously seek efficient refuge in the primary unconscious conviction that we are not mortal. It is a sign of enduring belief in our omnipotence and of the limit of our humility. Belief in omnipotence (denial of death) is the core of the self. Identity is a transformation of infantile omnipotence into a cohesive sense of self. Yet we must also reckon with the consideration that the more that violent, terrible, omnipotent, forbidden Thanatos transforms into autonomy of the self, the more it remains the same. Respect for the recurrence and significance of this originary, primitive power is a touchstone for developing awareness of mortality.

We often use our awareness of death as a palliative: "Now that I know about death, I can feel more at peace. I'm not scared of death anymore." Here death awareness may function in the service of unawareness; the purpose of death awareness is forgetfulness, and perhaps, a conviction, hedged against acknowledgment of the truth, of a mastery over death. Our egos' striving for awareness of mortality may not be an ally of the development of awareness of mortality. The thanatophobic repression of awareness of mortality at the base and growing edge of the development of consciousness, returns as the disruptions, disturbances and dysfunctions of consciousness. Death is not merely absent; its absence is everywhere. The theory of death awareness cannot take its bearings by our relationship to bereavement and anticipatory grief, alone. The theory of death awareness is virtually a general theory of consciousness.

The Pre-Reflexive Opacity of Death

As awareness of death emerges—dispelled, disclaimed, disowned, split off at every turn—initial awareness is *opaque*. The light of awareness is filtered through a diffuse affective cloud. Primitive annihilation anxiety and abandonment anxiety threaten to flood nascent awareness. The phenomenologically early self is a self without differentiated awareness of itself. It is embedded in its inner objects and has no sense of itself *as* conscious. The reflexive luminosity which constitutes consciousness, which constitutes the realm of being awake *is and is not yet*; i.e., in the opacity of consciousness I am unaware of being the source of the cognitive-affective field I live in and of the meanings I live. I do not recognize that I am there mirrored in my experience. In the *virtual immanence* of pre-reflexive consciousness in itself, not yet being for itself an object of awareness—there is, nonetheless, a *virtual reflexivity* of consciousness being for itself; i.e., in the ambiguity of this state of incipient awareness there is a *mortal consciousness* that is not yet a consciousness of mortality. The earliest consciousness is embedded in (its) mortality, yet has no discrete awareness *of* this. Consciousness emerges from pre-reflexive, undifferentiated existence as a subject intending an object, as being conscious *of* something. In this reflexive field there is the emergent possibility for consciousness of mortality. Consciousness awakens toward its being self-conscious, aware of itself. Consciousness is alive to itself as being awareness to which objects are present. Awareness of mortality lives with the awareness of the paradox of the ambitendent significance of self-awareness—that awareness of mortality is awareness of being alive. Awareness of mortality develops from pre-reflexive opacity—through awareness of historically formed attitudes, affects and anxieties about death; through awareness of the deeper significance of these; through self-awareness liberated from these attitudes, affects and anxieties—on a path that comes full circle back to the pre-reflexive opacity and immanence of mortal consciousness. Awareness of mortality may free one from the fear of death and the embeddedness of consciousness in one's own death; yet, this freedom is relative to mortality—which is the condition and the horizon of freedom. Transcendent self-awareness, the apex of consciousness, is indeterminate with mortal consciousness. The possibility of death, as the very condition of consciousness, returns from the heights of transcendent luminosity—*returns* as the realization by consciousness that it lives its mortality.

Another metaphor for the pre-reflexive opacity of consciousness is dreaming. "The dreamer does not realize," writes Erwin Straus,

> that he is the creator of his dreams; he is captive of his own creations. We are all overpowered by the reality of the dream world . . . During sleep, the dream was not mine; I was a part of the dream world which I could not recognize as mine [9].

The difference between sleeping and being awake is in being able to recognize that I (the dreamer who dreams the dream) *create* it and it is *mine*: the difference between sleeping and being awake is in being able to recognize that *I am*. To be awake is to be aware that I am. My self-creating and my mineness that come into perspective in comparing dreaming and waking, highlights that in dreaming there is no reflexive perspective. The luminosity of consciousness is there without reflexivity. The prereflexive opacity of death is a constant state of embeddedness of consciousness in its mortality.

Objectification of Death

Borges writes:

> A man sets himself the task of portraying the world. Through the years he peoples a space with images of provinces, kingdoms, mountains, bays, ships, islands, fishes, rooms, instruments, stars, forces and people. Shortly before his death he discovers that that patient labyrinth of his traces his face [10].

Near death the man discovers that his image of the world is, really, himself. He finds that the task he set himself was never what he thought it to be. He had never, in all the varied space of images he had lived, seen himself before. He created the traces of his existence and he lived them.

In recognizing himself as the creator of images, there is an auspicious freedom from all images; in recognizing himself as portrayed in all images the necessity of inexorable mortality returns. Projected out of an invisible original dreamspace, death-and-creativity, sui generis, yet beyond itself—the human face reveals itself to be the mystery of mortality.

It is inevitable: the task of portraying (and living in) the world is an act of objectification of oneself. We may trace our fears and loves and hates, our night terrors and joyous daybreaks; our truths and lies; objective reality, calendars, natural science and gods—back to our own self. A labyrinth of debts, poems, technologies and politics, a landscape, an imagescape, projected as the world of experience. Like the hallucinations of a person in a sensory deprivation tank, the darkness in us, the primary repressed (fear of) death in us, the affective core of our existence prompts the projection of a lively sensory field. This basic process of projection is the reflexive arc that constitutes the transparency of consciousness. Consciousness originates in the primary repression of death, that prompts projection of the world of lived experience. The objectification of oneself and one's own death is the natural condition of consciousness.

The primacy of the fear of death for consciousness is that consciousness constitutes its objects out of the necessity of distancing and scattering death. Death is everywhere and nowhere because it is the indwelling yet cast out nature of consciousness. Death is projected and dispersed as the world of symbolic, cultural reality which constitutes human experience. Ernest Becker wrote "all culture, all man's creative life-ways, are in some basic part of them a fabricated protest against natural reality [death] . . . " [11].

As image maker and maker of meaning, man cannot see himself, for the images and meanings he creates. His death alone lies outside the fact, defines the act, and compels the act of imagining. The startling circumstance on which the birth of self-awareness pivots is that the image of the self discovered, recovered, uncovered is no image. Recognizing the traces of his face, at first completion, clarity and self-awareness, turns out to be an awareness of the mortal act of object making, an awareness of mortality. The face of man is no trace or image. The face of man is his mortal consciousness.

Mourning cultivates the inwardness of consciousness. Yet, the development of awareness of mortality is, by the very human nature that makes it possible, impeded. Incipient awareness of mortality may be fended off in many ways. Let's consider one. The psychoanalyst and object relations theorist Melanie Klein says:

> The ego is driven by depressive anxieties (anxiety that the loved object as well as itself could be destroyed) to build up omnipotent and violent phantasies, partly for the purpose of controlling and mastering the 'bad', dangerous objects, partly in order to save and restore the loved ones. From the very beginning, these omnipotent phantasies, both destructive and reparative ones,

stimulate and enter into all the activities, interests and sublimations of the child [12].

This defense against inwardness and awareness of mortality is a normal trend in psychological development. The omnipotent phantasies that fend off thanatropic forces are not only defenses. The ego's omnipotent phantasies are also reparative and constructive forces. Omnipotent-based repairs and constructions may underlie a basic sense of goodness in oneself and trust in the world, supporting a disavowal of mortality. Relinquishing omnipotent phantasies in the advancement of awareness of mortality may be declined in favor of the value, protection and power vested in the omnipotent ego.

Death is inscribed in psychic development as "anxiety that the loved object as well as itself could be destroyed." Omnipotent and violent phantasies protect against this thanatropic threat. The developmental process of liberation from the control of omnipotent and violent phantasies and the threat of " 'bad', dangerous objects" is the mourning process. With mourning, the possibility for a subjective awareness of mortality emerges. In the archaic self's face-off between primitive death anxiety and omnipotent phantasy, there can be no awareness of mortality. Awareness of mortality arises out of this matrix through the mourning process.

Objectified, disowned parts of the self, fragments of our denied mortality are also projected onto or into other persons—who then serve as containers of our death anxiety. This is the normal process of objectification in which unawareness of mortality is lived in our experience of other persons—either 1) through dissociated fragments of our death anxiety being experienced as anxiety, conflict, judgment, or injury in relation to another person, or 2) in not regarding the other person as another mortal consciousness, in which case the other is dehumanized. In these every day objectifications of death we escape from the inwardness of our mortality, from the compassion and consciousness wrought by awareness of mortality. The denial and projection of death is the psychogenesis of human experience. Avowing and re-integrating our own death, mourning may awaken our humanity, compassion and self- consciousness.

While Plato and some other mystics say that the recovery of our true self is in recollecting our existence before birth, the thought here is that in becoming aware of the original constitutive presence of death and its ubiquitous expressions in experience, we recollect our true self and the origin of human consciousness.

When a person experiences a trauma, memories tend to be dissociated and fragmented, enacted as lived experience, yet not contained in consciousness [7]. In the process of recovering from a trauma, the lost memories and the lost self may be recovered. When a trauma is experienced, a basic and specific sentient vulnerability is mobilized. Every trauma, every violation of the self, every victimizing act, every loss taps into the awareness of death and vulnerability that is always already there. This underlying vulnerability is the traumatic meaning of death, and part of the normal condition in which experience happens. It is part of the very temporality of experience and the origin of the self. *The recovery of the self is the recovery of the death that is always already there and lost in every moment of experience.* To recollect existence prior to birth is to discover an ideal self that transcends experience. It is to affirm an ideal being that transcends mortality. The recollection of my death, consciousness discovering itself in mortality, (discovery its ideality always already conditioned by its mortality), is the recovery of my mortal awareness.

The Subjective Consciousness of Death and the Problem of Otherness

Sylvan Tomkins noted that shame originates in the differentiation of the mother's face from others [13]. Francis Broucek brings Tomkins' insight closer to home, pointing out that shame, rather, originates when mother herself, the mirror of identity, is felt to be a stranger [14]. When the experience of the self, mirrored in the sacred enclosure of the mother-infant dyad, is distorted or disrupted by an intrusion of a sense of otherness, a deep inhibition of self- experience or a kernel of self-alienation appears. When the mirror of self-experience is disturbed by an intrusion of a sense of otherness into the mirror-space of self-experience, a primitive form of shame occurs. Shame is the return of mortality within consciousness, at the crux of self-experience. Shame is the mortal vulnerability of human awareness [15, 16]. When the nascent self experiences itself to be exposed, experiencing itself to be violated by the consciousness of another, to be in its inmost self not itself—it is horrified and shamed. This mortal vulnerability resembles the violation of sacred prohibitions against the presence of death in consciousness.

While exposure of the self to awareness-inhibiting primitive shaming may seem to be extreme and pathogenic, it is, to some degree, inevitable and normal, a necessary condition for the emergence of the self from the mirror of its birth. Throughout the life history of the self, its otherness from itself, the veil and sign of its mortality, remains at the nexus of self-consciousness; the face of death is inwardly ever present and is covered. In the development of awareness of mortality, deaths that affect us and our own mortality before us come into consciousness interactively with the imminence of death at the core of self-consciousness. Whenever death enters into consciousness with immediacy, it enters like a radical *otherness*, a stranger, an uncanny presence—the most familiar of strangers. As mortality returns from being objectified to being a subjective awareness, it returns, uncanny, as other, as double, as familiar stranger to the subjective identity of consciousness.

This thanatocentric theory of consciousness differs from philosophical and spiritual traditions that celebrate the reflexive identity of self-consciousness. The pure ideality of self-consciousness, a reflection of our divine nature, a transformation of the empirical ego into pure self-consciousness is an enclosure in which death has been cast out. The otherness of the self, the spur of subjective awareness of mortality, the impurity and non-ideality of consciousness, is the site of a mortal wound at the birth of consciousness and an inexorable mystery. Awareness of mortality is the edge, the inner horizon of subjectivity.

AWARENESS OF MORTALITY IS A METABOLIC PROCESS

Awareness is a dynamic state and is always becoming. Whatever I am aware of, I am in the midst of becoming aware of. Awareness is not a term of completion; it is a process. While lightening bolts of awareness present themselves as whole and complete, from the perspective of a life, from birth to death, awareness is always "work in progress." As awareness crystallizes over time, the self is in the process of emerging from being embedded in its mortality. Awareness is a gradual process of metabolizing experience.

The Greek word "metabolic" means change or transition. What is being metabolized in the process of awareness of mortality? What is in transition? Is this process a change in form, i.e., a transformation? The familiar use of the word "metabolize" as a biological term was introduced by Schwan in 1839. Here, "metabolic" means "the process, in an organism or single cell, by which nutrient matter is built up into living matter (constructive metabolism, anabolism), or by which protoplasm is broken down into simpler substances to perform special functions (destructive metabolism, catabolism) [17]. With this example in mind, let us ask again, what is being metabolized in awareness of mortality? If the fear of death is being transformed into awareness of mortality what is changing or transforming in this process? Consciousness itself is transforming through metabolizing the fear of death. And the fear of death is analogous to the biologists' "nutritive material" and "protoplasm."

Awareness is also a way consciousness carries its burdens. If the burdens of human existence are ignored, there is no awareness. When consciousness picks up the burden, there is awareness. Awareness is not merely an internal illumination. Carrying the burden of our mortality is the process of suffering mortality. In suffering its objects, consciousness is a transformative process. Awareness of mortality is a process of self-creating through the anabolic and catabolic work of suffering. Awareness of mortality is a living process of metabolizing mortality. The specifics of my awareness are signs of where I am in the in-between state (i.e., in-between being mortal and the metabolization of mortality) called awareness.

REFERENCES

1. T. Merton, Rain and the Rhinoceros, in *Raids on the Unspeakable*, New Directions, New York, 1964.
2. P. Aries, *The Hour of Our Death*, Alfred A. Knopf, New York, 1981.

3. W. B. Yeats, Death, in *Selected Poems & Three Plays of William Butler Yeats*, Collier, New York, 1962.
4. F. Rosenweig, *The Star of Redemption*, W. W. Hall (trans.), Beacon Press, Boston, 1972.
5. G. Zilborg, Fear of Death, in *The Psychoanalytic Quarterly, 12*, pp. 465-475, 1943.
6. J. Derrida, Freud and the Scene of Writing, in *Writing and Difference*, A. Bass (trans.), University of Chicago Press, Chicago, 1978.
7. J. Kauffman, Dissociative Functions in the Normal Mourning Process, *Omega: Journal of Death and Dying, 28*:1, 1994.
8. S. Freud, Thoughts for the Times on War and Death, in *Collected Papers*, Vol. IV, Basic Books, New York, 1959. (Original work published 1915)
9. E. Straus, *Phenomenological Psychology*, Basic Books, New York, 1966.
10. J. Borges, *Dreamtigers*, University of Texas Press, Austin, 1964.
11. E. Becker, *Denial of Death*, Free Press, New York, 1973.
12. M. Klein, Mourning and Its Relation to Manic Depressive States, in *Love, Guilt and Reparation*, Hogarth Press, London, 1975.
13. S. Tomkins, *Affect, Imagery, Consciousness*, Vol. 2, The Negative Affects, Springer, New York, 1963.
14. F. Broucek, *Shame and the Self*, Guilford Press, New York, 1991.
15. J. Kauffman, Intrapsychic Dimensions of Disenfranchised Grief, in *Disenfranchised Grief*, K. Doka (ed.), Lexington Books, Lexington, Massachusetts, 1989.
16. J. Kauffman, Group Thanatropics, in *Ring of Fire*, V. Shermer and M. Pines (eds.), Routledge, London, 1994.
17. *Oxford English Dictionary*, Oxford University Press, Glasgow, 1971.

CHAPTER 8

Personal Identity and Death Concern—Philosophical and Developmental Perspectives

Adrian Tomer

Most of us are, to some degree, concerned about our eventual death. This concern can be, and has been, empirically and philosophically analyzed and shown to include multiple elements or to come in many varieties [1]. There are two elements that are of particular interest in the present discussion. One element refers to the sharp discontinuity introduced by death in the human existence. The second element is the (prospect of) the annihilation of the self as a conscious, reflective perspective. This is the "fear of ceasing to be," the fear of extinction that was given various expressions in the philosophical belletristic literature [1, 2]. To contemplate my own death is to contemplate my not having a future—this meaning, among other things, the abrupt interruptions of any plans, projects, etc. that I may have in the present. To contemplate my own death also means to contemplate nothingness. From the special perspective that is the perspective of a self vis-a-vis itself, my own death or annihilation seems to be equivalent to the annihilation of the world in its totality. It is perhaps appropriate to point out that this tendency to identify my death with the disappearance of the world is a tendency that I have only in regard with my own death. One strange thing is that, on one hand, death is an extremely common event that does not bother me in the least, unless some special circumstances apply. On the other hand, when it comes to my own death, I have the tendency to perceive this event not only as a profound discontinuity, but as being (my) reduction to nothing which is further interpreted by (my)self as the reduction to nothing of the whole world. I care about my death in a way which is different from the way I care about the death of other people, even about the death of my family members. Interestingly enough, I do not believe that much anxiety revolves around the death of my children (other than by being worried about their possible premature death). It is as if the fact that I am pretty sure that I am not going to survive their deaths makes their death inexistent.

One reason for the empirical study of death, and related concerns and anxieties, is the light this study may shed on the way we construct and determine ourselves as individuals. The opposite of this is also true: The way we construct ourselves as individuals will determine to a great extent our attitudes toward our life *and our death*. The substance of this chapter is this relationship between the concepts of personal identity, the concept of an individual as this is constructed in developmental theories, and death concern.

We start the present discussion from a presentation of some well-known puzzles of personal identity. Next we consider some possible analyses and interpretations of these puzzles—emphasizing the ones provided by Parfit [3, 4] and Nozick [5]. Both of them defend versions of the Psychological Criterion of personal identity. According to this criterion personal identity involves some type of psychological identity over time maintained by the "right kind of cause" [4, p. 210]. Parfit's version of personal identity and of "what matters" in personal identity are especially interesting for our purpose here. The reason for this is that Parfit, based on his analysis, argues for a "liberation of the self." This liberation is obtained, according to Parfit, by realizing that some widely held beliefs about personal identity are, in fact, incorrect. Parfit and Nozick's analyses of personal identity suggest, albeit in different ways, the importance of the notion of transcending a narrow version of our individuality. In a subsequent section we present briefly the concept of "transcending the limits" as this was elaborated by Nozick [5]. This is followed by a presentation of the concept of transcendence as it was incorporated, in one way or another, by several developmental theories, particularly in Erikson's theory of psychosocial development [6] and in Kohlberg's theory of moral development [7]. The main question we want to address here is whether or not a weakening of the concept of an individual makes sense, from a developmental point of view. The next section introduces the notion of being in the world as "being-on-a-mission" as well as the notion of "mystery" as these are present in Albert Einstein's writings and in Gabriel Marcel's existential philosophy. Finally, the last section is an attempt to integrate the analysis of personal identity with the discussion about transcendence of the self. It is suggested that deindividuation, conceived as a "theme" that may appear at different points of development [8] or defined as a final stage reserved to "the old age" is a proper way to deal with the need to transcend our mortality.

PUZZLES OF PERSONAL IDENTITY

Many imaginary scenarios involving puzzles of personal identity have been proposed to advance the philosophical investigation of the topic. This methodology of "thought experiments," although sometimes criticized [9], has been widely used as a tool to reach our basic intuitions concerning beliefs of personal identity and/or types of future changes that we really care about. In this section we will focus on just a few of the numerous puzzles that have been proposed so far. Our main interest is in the possibility that a consideration of these (type of) puzzles, mediated or not by philosophical analysis, may bring about changes in our perception of ourselves and, perhaps, may affect the concerns we have about our own death.

One famous case is the division scenario. In one version [4] the scenario can be presented in the following way. I am one of three identical twins (X, Y and Z). I (X), as well as my brothers (Y and Z) suffer an accident in which my body and their brains are fatally injured. My brain is divided and each hemisphere is transplanted in the body of one of my brothers. Of course each one of the resulting people (A and B) will believe that they are me. How should such a case be described in respect with my (X's) fate? According to Parfit there are four ways: I do not survive; I survive as one of the two people, say A; I survive as the other, B; I survive as both A and B. There are problems with each one of these interpretations. For example, if we decide that the best answer is that I do not survive (on the account that there is no basis to decide between A and B, and I cannot obviously survive as two individuals) then the question should be: what if only one of the two operations had been successful? If I agree that I do survive in this case, it is difficult to understand how I can disagree that I survive when *both* operations are successful.

Another example is the case of teletransportation [4]. In a case of teletransportation a person in place A is being scanned for full information regarding each atom and electron in the body. This information is being transmitted at the speed of light to a place B (say Mars) where, on the basis of it, an identical replica is being created out of matter. At the same time, the original is being destroyed in A. According to the story, the person in A will lose consciousness at the time of the scanning only to wake up several minutes later in B. Of course, the person who wakes up in B identifies himself or herself as the same person who has been a moment ago in A. But is this a correct description? Is it not the case that the person in A has died and a new one was created in B? How can we decide between these two different descriptions. Let us assume, for example, that teletransportation is a common way of transportation and that the people using it, as well as the society at large, consider it as such. What facts can disconfirm this way of conceptualizing? It appears that none. Would we still argue that to be teletransported means dying? What would be the meaning of this? To drive home this point let us imagine that not only is one person teletransported, but a whole family or, perhaps, a whole community. Once they are in their new place, these people resume, in somewhat different conditions, their prior relationships. In what sense can be said that, in fact, they died, and their replicas are different people? Were these people told, perhaps by a philosopher, that they are not the persons that they are supposed to be, they will probably shrug and go about their business. We have here a case in which no additional knowledge about the case may help us to answer the question. Different answers in this case will be only different descriptions of the same facts. Why should it then be important how we decide to answer the question? Such a question is called by Parfit an "empty question" [4, p. 213].

The teletransportation scenario can be modified in different ways. One is Parfit's branch-line case in which the person in A is not being destroyed but his health is irreparably damaged so that death is certain in a few days [3, 4]. Should the person take great comfort from the fact that there is a replica in B? If not, we can say that the modified scenario changes the situation drastically. In this case the identity of the person in B does not depend solely on the past, and on the nature of person in B, but on other events as well, more precisely on whether or not the person in A is destroyed. Since the person in A was not destroyed, and although the teletransported person in B will see himself or herself as the person that was before in A, this will not be the perspective of the person who survived (possibly, for a short while) the teletransportation process in A. We can decide, in this latter case, that personal identity is not preserved by teletransportation. This position will imply that identity of two individuals over time is not completely determined by the nature of these two individuals and by the nature of the process that connects them, but by other extraneous facts, such as the existence of some "competition."

PARFIT'S INTERPRETATION

Parfit's solution to the puzzles posed by the division scenario or by the teletransportation case is to make a distinction between personal identity and "what really matters" in survival. What really matters is psychological connectedness and/or continuity between me, my present experiences, and a future self or future experiences. Psychological connectedness involves direct relationships, such as the relationship between an experience and the memory of that experience. Psychological continuity is based on overlapping chains of direct relationships. Psychological connectedness and/or continuity with the right kind of cause (according to Parfit the right cause is *any* cause) is called by Parfit relation R and relation R is what matters in survival. This relationship depends only on the two terms involved: myself and a future person. Personal identity, on the other hand, depends on additional, extrinsic things: Are there more than one future persons satisfying the psychological criterion? Without uniqueness we do not have the identity, but this does not matter. From this, "reductionist" point of view personal identity does not contain any further, deep fact, distinct from psychological continuity.

Thus, Parfit rejects the thesis according to which whether or not a later individual Y is identical with an earlier individual X, depends only on X and Y. This thesis—"the only X and Y principle" [10] does not apply to personal identity. For example, in the case of teletransportation, the identity of the person on Mars (Y) with the previous person on earth (X) would depend on whether or not X is destroyed on earth. On the other hand, the principle does apply to "what matters" or to what I should care about: It should only matter whether or not a future person is continuous with myself and what is the degree of this continuity, no matter what other facts are. According to this, if I anticipate to live a long life during which I will sustain rather radical changes I should not care too much about my future (old) self.

THE LIBERATION FROM THE SELF
ACCORDING TO PARFIT

Parfit finds his way toward a liberation from the tyranny of the self through a consideration of imagined cases like the teletransportation cases or the fission scenario accompanied by the type of philosophical analysis schematically presented in the prior section. He writes:

> When I believed that my existence was such a further fact, I seemed imprisoned in myself. My life seemed like a glass tunnel, through which I was moving faster every year, and at the end of which there was darkness. When I changed my view, the walls of my glass tunnel disappeared. I now live in the open air. There is still a difference between my life and the life of other people. But the difference is less. Other people are closer. I am less concerned about the rest of my life, and more concerned about the lives of others [4, p. 281].

In the same vein Parfit writes that he is now caring less about his death. After all, this only represents the fact that, after a while, no future experiences will be related to (his) present experience. Thus Parfit "solves" the problem of death in two steps. The first step consists in reducing what matters in survival to psychological continuity. The second step contains the recognition that continuity is a matter of degree. Therefore, death is a matter of degree. Therefore, death is not as frightening as I used to believe.

One can clearly recognize here a basic motive associated with the fear of death—the continuity of my endeavors, perhaps of my character. If only a limited continuity (no connectedness) is involved, then death does not appear so bad. It is pertinent at this point to introduce the second basic motive present in the fear of death—the motive of annihilation of the self/world. This certainly cannot be a matter of degree. According to Parfit's interpretation, this motive or concern has no basis. One problem with this interpretation is that it contradicts basic intuitions about care regarding our future. Consider for example the branch-line teletransportation. The person on earth who is facing death might find some consolation in the thought that a replica of his/her is on Mars. But this sounds like the type of consolation one may find in one's children. The fear of death, of annihilation, is unlikely to disappear or even to be greatly reduced by this thought.

It seems therefore that almost perfect continuity as the one illustrated by the branch-line teletransportation case is not enough to ensure personal identity and to validate the lack of death concern. On the other hand it seems also that personal identity and lack of death concern may exist in cases of very drastic discontinuities. Let us suppose for example that I am destined to have a very long life involving many, let us say rather abrupt, changes, and that *my self* in the remote future is going to be very different from myself (a similar case, the Methuselah case, was considered by Lewis [11]). It seems that in these circumstances I would still care very much about this future self. After all this self of mine is still my "closest continuer" [5]. Considerations of this nature have indeed prompted Nozick to formulate his "closest continuer theory" that takes into considerations which is the best or closest continuer in a determination of "what matters" [5]. According to this theory, although the person on Mars in the Teletransportation case is a continuer, the person on earth may be an even *closer* continuer. Similarly, my distant self, although very different from myself, may be my closest continuer. Therefore, the person on earth or my distant future self are myself.

We can see the importance in Nozick's theory of our basic intuitions regarding concern: Putting ourselves in the situation of the person to be teletransported, we feel much concern about the person on earth, in fact as much as we feel about the person on Mars in the simple case of teletransportation.

LIBERATION OF THE SELF—IS IT ACHIEVED?

Given qualifications of the nature introduced by Nozick is the liberation of the self, a la Parfit, still achieved? On the one hand, the principle of psychological connectedness and/or continuity is still the basic principle determining identity. On the other hand, it is not the amount of psychological continuity that determines the amount of care or concern. Indeed, according to Nozick's theory, we care always in a special way about our closest continuer, no matter what the degree of closeness is. I believe that a possible explanation for Nozick's principle is the second type of concern we have in relation to death—the concern about the disappearance of the world. We tend to link this disappearance to the closest continuer. In other words, from my point of view at t1, it is myself for whom the world will disappear at t2, if the person dying at t2 is my closest continuer. From this point of view, my death, say thirty years from now, is not the death of a (partial) stranger. It is still my closest continuer, I am bound to be extremely concerned about his fate and perhaps nothing can really mitigate this concern.

A probing issue for the "closest continuer hypothesis" is the case of two equally close continuers, the case of a tie. Suppose that I exist at t1 and that I have two equally close continuers at t2 (perhaps via transplantation of my two hemispheres in two very similar bodies). Should we construct this case as one of death or as a case in which I do not die but I continue as two entities at t2? Nozick opts for the first interpretation. On the other hand, my death "is not so very distressing in this case" [5, p. 63]. The reason for this is that, according to Nozick, what I care about is "that there remains something that continues me closely enough to be me if it were my sole continuer."

Perhaps an alternative explanation can be given that uses the disappearance of the world aspect of the death concern. If there is no clear annihilation of the world, in this case, but rather a multiplication by a factor of two, there is no death to be feared. The question whether we should say that my existence came to an end or not becomes a semantic question of preferred ways of expression. We can say, for example, that I ended my existence in its first stage and that I continue my existence as two separate entities in a second stage. This will be indeed pretty close to Nozick's way of expression. On the other hand, it will still allow me to refer to myself as existing in two different stages, so maintaining a personal identity. In any case, since there was no annihilation of the world anticipated, and no special reason for concern, no death, in the traditional sense, was involved.

An analysis of care along the lines provided by Nozick and perhaps with special attention paid to the annihilation issue will thus suggest that, after all, no liberation from the self was achieved by the philosophical analysis. The first step of Parfit's analysis—the reduction of "what matters" to psychological continuity is extremely problematic. This does not mean that we have not accomplished any progress at all in dealing with death concern. Several conclusions may be worth mentioning in this respect. First, we have seen that "what matters in survival" is not necessarily related to the identity of a body or brain (the simple teletransportation case). Second, should we accept an analysis of the type provided by Nozick (or Parfit, for this matter), it would mean that personal identity is not necessarily a function of "X and Y" alone, but may be also a function of the relationship between them and other entities in the universe. For Parfit personal identity is not important, beyond psychological continuity. Our argument here was that personal identity is important beyond continuity, personal identity being the principle that prevents the world from being annihilated. If this is the case, the conclusion that our personal identity, conceived as a relation between X and Y, cannot be completely decided on the basis of X and Y alone is important. It implies that, perhaps in final analysis what we are depends on what other people are. Indeed, it is a conclusion that we might want to keep in mind in our next section that deals with the issue of "transcending the limits of the self."

TRANSCENDING THE LIMITS OF THE SELF— A PHILOSOPHICAL ANALYSIS

It is interesting to consider in this context Nozick's analysis of what means to transcend the limits of the self. Nozick espouses the view that meaning consists in connections. For a life to have meaning it should be connected with things outside itself. From this point of view, the "more intensely you are involved, the more you transcend your limits." This can be done in the area of personal relations by loving another person. It can be done in the intellectual area by achieving an understanding of deep truths about the world. We may want therefore to become as integrated as possible, as widely connected as possible to the world around us. This, however, is not going to solve the problem of meaning or the problem of the threat of death. Finding meaning is a tentative process to which death puts an end. Nozick completely rejects the view advocated by some that death is "what makes life meaningful" [12]. To see this we need only to consider the fact that we desire not only to have things accomplished but also we desire to do things. We could also think about a differently structured life, had our life been much longer than it was.

If meaning is in connections, the unavoidable conclusion seems to be that only an unlimited being has a secure value, in no need of further justifications (connections). However, even assuming the existence of such an unlimited being, it is not easy to solve the problem of meaning of life. Nozick indicates two possible ways. One involves some process through which meaning "flows" from the unlimited being to ourselves. The first seems to correspond to the religious way of communicating with an unlimited entity and it is not discussed in any detail by Nozick. The second way represents the position presented in the Upanishads and the Vedanta school of philosophy. According to this our underlying nature is already the Unlimited (Brahman). The second way presents serious, unsolved, and probably unsolvable problems.

Nozick's discussion seems to indicate that "transcending the limits" as a process of widening one's connections is a process that eventually is bound to fail. If there is at all a way to "save" the meaningfulness of life, this way appears to be the mystic way, in one version or another.

TRANSCENDING THE LIMITS OF THE SELF— DEVELOPMENTAL PERSPECTIVES

Perhaps the dominant developmental motive is the motive of growth. It is true that the view that development is growth has been recently modified to allow it to encompass the whole life span. A life-span perspective makes essential to consider losses that, indeed, become more prominent with increased age [13]. Still the concept of growth is extremely important and a primary task for a gerontologist was, and indeed is to indicate in what respects there is growth in old age in spite of, or as compensations for sustained losses [14]. This approach implies the concept of a growing individual. The general concept of growth encourages a view of development based on self-realization, full expression of the self, maximum integration of the self, etc. This very view may discourage, on the other hand, a direction of "deindividuation" or "liberation" from the self. Notwithstanding this general inclination, the reality of death and of the end of life, puts pressure upon developmentalists to come up with "conceptual inventions" that will reconcile between growth and cessation. The incorporation of losses in theories of development is a step in the right direction. It is doubtful, however, that the concept of loss and of adaptation to losses provides enough intellectual ammunition to cope with the idea of personal death. The very idea of adaptation presupposes an adapting self. The "problem" we face in personal death consists in the fact that there is no self left to adapt to this total loss which is "my death." A different step would consist in an attempt to bridge the gap between, say, a "fully integrated self" and a self that liberates itself from itself. Not surprisingly, developmental theories have borrowed, in this respect, heavily from "philosophical inventions," in particular from the idea of "transcending" oneself. It may be interesting to note that the idea of transcending has a double connotation. It involves the idea of growth or expansion of the self (as the last analysis of "transcending the limits" has made it, hopefully, clear) and it also includes the idea of dissolution or not being oneself. As such the idea of transcending the limits of the self seems to be particularly suited to bridge between the integrated and the liberated self. In this section we briefly review several developmental approaches that deal with old age as a special period of time and/or with the notion of transcending the limits of the self as part of the process of development.

ERIKSON'S PSYCHOSOCIAL THEORY AND THE CONCEPT OF GENERATIVITY

A very influential theory is Erikson's eight stage model of psychosocial development. Especially relevant are the two last stages (7th and 8th) corresponding to adulthood and to old age. The conflict characteristic to adulthood is the conflict between generativity and self-absorption. Generativity may refer directly to rearing children but is extended metaphorically to any other activity on behalf of someone else, individuals, groups, or society at large. In the last stage individuals strive to achieve a sense of integrity. Individuals review their life looking for meaningfulness, for a feeling of having lived up to their potential.

Integrity is the happy resolution whereas despair is the consequence of a negative verdict.

Erikson's idea of generativity is found in other theories of adult development. Thus, Schaie, for example, in his five-stage model of adult cognitive development defined a transition from the individual preoccupied almost exclusively by his personal and career goals in the achieving stage, to an individual who takes responsibility for his family [15]. Further development involves an extension of this responsibility to larger groups—work groups, communities, perhaps nations or even the whole globe (the executive stage). Thus, Schaie's approach involves a successive expansion of the self. The development is somewhat arrested in the last reintegrative stage when, in the face of losses and increasing limitations, the individual has to decide what are the most important, meaningful aspects that he or she wants to attend to.

Another example of Erikson's influence is John Kotre's theory of generativity, which is based on an interpretation of generativity as a "desire" or "wish" that may appear in different forms during the lifespan [8]. Specifically, generativity is "a desire to invest one's substance in forms of life and work that will out-live the self" [8, p. 10]. Kotre distinguishes between four types of generativity: biological, parental, technical, and cultural. Another important distinction is that between the agentic and the communal modes of generativity. The agentic generativity takes as its object the self. It is based on self-assertion and self-expansion. On the other hand communal generativity takes as its object the other and is, in this sense, selfless. It represents the participation of the individual in an interpersonal reality.

OLD AGE AND SELF-ACTUALIZATION IN NORTON'S ANALYSIS OF STAGES OF LIFE

David Norton provides us with a philosopher's description of four "stages of life" from a self-actualization perspective [16]. The principle can be readily applied to a description/analysis of the third stage of life—"maturity." It cannot be readily applied to a characterization of old age as a unique stage with a unique perspective and a unique task to accomplish. The reason for this resides in its lack of future. In Norton's words "qua stage, old age is that stage that has no future, and this self-contained horizon migrates forward to bar the advance of the present by death" [16, p. 204]. This loss of a future implies the loss of the principle of individuation. In other words, the old person cannot choose himself/herself anymore to become what he or she is. The authentic choice is the "re-discovery within the individual of his common humanity" [16, p. 209]. Even more importantly "the work reserved exclusively to old age consists in the recovery of the past as the foundation of present and future living" [16, p. 205]. Here Norton does not talk about the individual past, the one involved for example in the life review process [17]. It is the universal and eternal past that is being recovered.

Norton's description involves a clear realization of the insufficiency of the individuation principle and, in this sense, of the necessity to transcend the limits of the specific self toward a more universal principle. What perhaps the description lacks is an account of what makes this transcending of the self possible at all (and not only "desirable") or with an account about how "the universal past" supplies the (chosen) past with a solid foundation that otherwise this present would lack.

DITTMAN-KOHLI AND BALTES'S NOTION OF WISDOM

According to Dittman-Kohli and Baltes, wisdom is a form of expertise in matters of life (and probably death) achieved through an accumulation of experience [18]. It is typically achieved in adulthood and/or old age. The authors make a distinction between practical wisdom that refers to the praxis of life and philosophical wisdom that refers to concerns beyond one's own self. Practical wisdom seems to involve, similar to Erikson's theory, an increased awareness of one's limitation and an increased ability to function within these limitations. The presentation does not make clear what the relationship is between the two types of wisdom and whether one can be achieved without the other. From our point of view here, the main issue remains the question of acceptance by the self of its death. It seems that there is an important distinction between adapting to losses, and to less than ideal conditions, on the one hand and accepting a complete annihilation, on the other hand. However, this approach reaffirms the basic intuitions that somehow the acceptance of one's death can be achieved only by perceiving oneself in "the context of intergenerational transmission and cultural movement."

KOHLBERG'S SEVENTH STAGE OF ETHICAL DEVELOPMENT

Kohlberg was motivated to add a seventh stage of moral development to the six stages of his classic model by the need to provide an answer to the question: "Why be moral?" [7, p. 192]. Why indeed should someone believe in universal ethical principles? Kohlberg diagnosed this last question (related to "Why live?", etc.) as an ontological question. While admitting that there is purely no rational or logical answer to this question, he argued that a justification of the belief in universal principles implies an acceptance of oneself as part of something much larger (cosmic perspective), a perspective under which "one views things not so much from the standpoint of a distinct individual as from the standpoint of the universe as a whole" [7, p. 207]. Kohlberg's intuitions are similar to Spinoza's theory of natural law. They go beyond Piaget's theory in several respects. As Kohlberg himself points out, a seventh stage of development should be guided by reflective thinking and based upon someone's (possibly) unique life experiences. It is a "soft stage," an optional stage that does not represent a new structural form, but rather a reflective theory providing a new way to experience one's ideas about what is right and one's place in the world.

Kohlberg's presentation strikes us as an important step in the right direction. His deliberations, moreover, are closely related to the issues discussed here. The only way to justify ethical principles is by positing an inherent value of life and human existence. But it seems that death is a formidable obstacle in this path. Eventually each individual will be dead. The only way to salvage humanity, ontologically and psychologically, is via an identification with a larger whole. The weakness of this position, is in its great generality. Can anybody really identify with the cosmos? Is our understanding of the universe and of ourselves advanced enough to allow such an identification?

Kohlberg's identification with cosmos is close to Erikson's identity diffusion (confusion) and to the "selfless self" postulated by Dickstein [19] as a fifth stage of development. In the latter case the self in the fifth stage is described as losing its boundaries, assumably through a process of realization of the fact that it is a part of the whole reality, the whole cosmos. In Dickstein model, the fifth stage is subsequent to the stage of integration and self-realization ("self as-integrated-whole") in which individuation and uniqueness are achieved. Both integration and identity diffusion can be, indeed, seen as different strategies to deal with death threat [20]. Using Kotre's terms we can perceive the fourth, integrative stage as an instantiation (perhaps the best one) of the agentic generativity, whereas the fifth stage is best conceived as an epitome of the communal generativity.

Our (incomplete) review of several developmental perspectives from the point of view of the way they approach old age and death suggests that some form of "transcending the limits of the self" is common to all of them. We still feel the need for a more concrete or specific account regarding the type of experiences and/or reflections that will enable an individual to transcend oneself. The next section Being-on-a-Mission is an account (admittedly schematic and incomplete) of this nature.

BEING-ON-A-MISSION

The term suggests, to us, a soldier who believes that his first priority is fulfilling his mission. His personal welfare, indeed, his life, is of secondary importance. He may fail in his mission or he can get killed. There are others who would go ahead to fulfill the task. The overall design and the final goal is not clear to the soldier. But he has entirely accepted the order of priorities. Acting as being-on-a-mission is acting and behaving out of a general sense of what is good and valuable in general and from a sense of identification with it. The French existentialist philosopher Gabriel Marcel used the example of the complete sacrifice to illustrate the mysterious relationship between myself and my life [21]. He wrote:

> Let us notice that I said giving my life seemed the same as giving myself, not as doing away with myself. Self-sacrifice can be confused with self slaughter by the man who is looking on the hero's or the martyr's act from outside, from the material aspect merely, and who is therefore incapable of associating himself sympathetically with the inner essence of the act. On the other hand, the person who is carrying the act out has, without any doubt at all, the feeling that through self-sacrifice he is reaching self-fulfillment; given his own situation and that of everything dear to him, he realizes his own nature most completely, he most completely *is*, in the act of giving his life away [21, pp. 204-205].

The self-fulfillment is not in dying, in "becoming a corpse" but in the inner significance of the act.

It is not necessary to go to the sphere of the heroic to find examples for living as being-on-a-mission. Pursuing relentlessly a scientific effort across a life span may serve as another illustration. An outstanding example is Albert Einstein whose life was an extraordinarily concentrated effort to understand the nature of reality. In *The world as I see it* speaking about the experience of the mysterious he writes:

> I cannot conceive of a God who rewards and punishes his creatures, or has a will of the type of which we are conscious in ourselves. That an individual should survive his physical death is also beyond my comprehension, nor do I wish it otherwise; such notions are for the fears or absurd egoism of feeble souls. Enough for me are the mystery of the eternity of life and the inkling of the marvelous structure of reality, together with the single-hearted endeavor to comprehend a portion, be it ever so tiny, of the Reason that manifests itself in nature [22, p. 242].

The union of the individual and the cosmos is realized by Einstein in this effort of understanding. It is the encounter of a relatively feeble reasoning power (of the individual, even if this individual is a genius of Einstein's stature) with an extraordinarily beautiful and profound Reason (present in the Cosmos). A key word in the quotation is "inkling." It reflects both the privilege of having a part in this and the limitation of the self. The full sense of the encounter with the reality and with the Reason behind is mysterious: It cannot be fully comprehended and it involves not only the world but also the individual. This heartfelt mystery, based on reflection, is redemptive: my death is as real as it can be. Far from being a tragedy, however, it only sets off "the eternity of life" and its perpetual renewal. At some point any major effort feels the need to start entirely from the very beginning, from zero. We have to die to accomplish this. Untimely death is certainly unfortunate. But not death in general.

To find out the origin of this profound sense of the mysterious in Einstein's thought and to his (unconventional) religious reverence one has to go back to Einstein's childhood and to appreciate the impact of some experiences which remained very vivid in his mind. One example is the sense of wonder experienced by him at the age of four or five when his father showed him a compass. It was a first realization of "something hidden" behind things.

It is interesting to compare the sense of mystery described by Einstein with the description of the "the mystery of being" given, from a different perspective by Gabriel Marcel. In *Being and Having* he presents a mystery "as something in which I myself am involved, and it can therefore only be thought of as "a sphere where the distinction between what is in me and what is before me loses its meaning and its initial validity." While the interaction with a world of physical objects was the origin of Einstein's mystic thought, Gabriel Marcel was brought to his philosophy by "personal experiences" the presence of a loved person or the presence of the past in the present as it is realized in those "Proustian" memories that bring with them an incredible richness of descriptive and affective detail [23].

In spite of differences between Einstein and Marcel, in both cases the origin of the sense of mystery resides in some everyday life experiences that also put the foundation for a sense of "participation," of receiving a precious gift from outside, indeed of one's life constituting a "gift."

LIBERATION OF THE SELF IN PHILOSOPHICAL ANALYSIS AND IN CONCEPTS OF DEVELOPMENT— CONCLUSIONS

Parfit was led by philosophical analysis to conclusions that meant for him a partial liberation of the self. We have expressed doubts about the validity of these conclusions. Notwithstanding these doubts, it is certainly possible that a reflective consideration of hypothetical scenarios of the type considered by Parfit and others can have a psychological influence in a direction of "liberation." It is indeed possible that, beyond their possible contributions to the philosophical analysis of personal identity, these puzzles can make their contribution to a better realization of the fact that personal identity cannot be defined and decided unless the definition and decision are conducted in an interpersonal context. Indeed these thought experiments may make us more receptive to the "mystery" which embraces us and our existence.

An examination of several developmental approaches has shown that more than one scholar has been attracted to the postulation of a stage of development which can be called mystical. The term mystical refers to the fact that a description of this stage has to deal with concepts such as the reunion of the individual and the world, the participation of the individual in the world and with a sense of mystery surrounding them. This stage seems to imply a renunciation of the principle of individuation and is sometimes proposed as a kind of optional stage rather than a stage that is at a higher level than the stage of integration and self-fulfillment [19]. It seems that the logic of "the old age" as the stage of life deprived of future (Norton) does require deindividuation as the final principle characterizing a last stage.

It is also possible to see the principle of deindividuation as another expression of the principle of generativity, as this principle was defined by Kotre: "a desire to invest one's substance in forms of life and work that will outlive the self" [8, p. 10]. In the "communal" form of generativity it is by participating in an interpersonal reality that generativity, as a desire, is being satisfied. As such, deindividuation does not need to be relegated exclusively to the "final stage of development," although old age might be a stage in one's life during which deindividuation has a stronger relevance. An awareness of oneself as one of many possible expressions of underlying, universal principles is a theme that, while perhaps particularly "fitting" old age, should be cultivated at various points or stages of the developmental trajectory.

Our description of being-on-a-mission suggested the importance of developing a sense of mystery about the world and oneself as a way to transcend the limits of the self. Both Einstein and Marcel derived this sense of mystery from the world around, although in one case that was the world of the objects and in another the intersubjective reality, the world of the other. The realization of the presence of a beloved one or the realization of the depth and beauty of the Reason in nature are mystical experiences that help us to conceive of our own life as a gift (although the terms of this—the conferrer and recipient are mysterious). The person in the stage of "the old age" may want to devote oneself more to this type of experiences. Much has been written about the older person devoting much of the time to the process of remembering or reviewing the past [6, 17]. For Marcel remembering is a type of incantation. The past that is being invoked has a real and mysterious presence and my being able to invoke it is a mystery about a mystery [24]. By recalling my past I do not only engage in the operation of examining and possibly "reconstructing" my life. I also engage in a (mystical) experience which allows me to transcend the limits of myself.

Transcending the limits of the self is an important developmental "task," perhaps the most demanding of all tasks. It is our awareness of death that gives this task its urgency and poignancy. It is also a task that is never completely "mastered." The efforts toward its accomplishment need to be renewed again and again. As I hope this chapter has showed, these efforts need not be hopeless.

REFERENCES

1. J. Choron, *Death and Modern Man*, Collier Books, New York, 1964.
2. J. Choron, *Death and Western Thought*, Collier Books, New York, 1963.
3. D. Parfit, Personal Identity, *Philosophical Review, 80*, pp. 3-27, 1971.
4. D. Parfit, *Reasons and Persons*, Oxford University Press, New York, 1984.
5. R. Nozik, *Philosophical Explanations*, Harvard University Press, Cambridge, Massachusetts, 1981.
6. E. H. Erikson, *The Life Cycle Completed*, Norton, New York, 1982.
7. L. W. Kohlberg and R. A. Ryncarz, Beyond Justice Reasoning: Moral Development and Consideration of a Seventh Stage, in *Higher Stages of Human Development*, C. N. Alexander and E. J. Langer (eds.), Oxford University Press, New York, pp. 191-207, 1990.
8. J. Kotre, *Outliving the Self*, The Johns Hopkins University Press, Baltimore, 1984.
9. M. Johnston, Human Beings, *The Journal of Philosophy, 2*, pp. 59-83, 1987.
10. H. W. Noonan, *Personal Identity*, Routledge, London, 1990.
11. D. K. Lewis, Survival and Identity, in *The Identity of Persons*, A. Rorty (ed.), University of California Press, Berkeley, 1976.
12. V. E. Frankl, *The Doctor and the Soul: From Psychotherapy to Logotherapy*, Bantam, New York, 1955.
13. P. B. Baltes, Theoretical Propositions of Life-span Developmental Psychology: On the Dynamics between Growth and Decline, *Developmental Psychology, 23*, pp. 611-626, 1987.
14. D. H. Utall and M. Perlmutter, Toward a Broader Conceptualization of Development. The Role of Gains and Loses Across the Life Span, *Developmental Review, 9*, pp. 101-132, 1989.
15. K. W. Schaie, Toward a Stage Theory of Adult Cognitive Development, *International Journal of Aging and Human Development, 8*, pp. 129-138, 1977-78.
16. D. L. Norton, *Personal Destinies*, Princeton, New Jersey, 1976.
17. R. N. Butler, *Why Survive? Being Old in America*, Row, New York, 1975.
18. F. Dittmann-Kohli and P. B. Baltes, Toward a Neofunctionalist Conception of Adult Intellectual Development: Wisdom as a Prototypical Case of Intellectual Growth, in *Higher Stages of Human Development*, C. N. Alexander and E. J. Langer (eds.), Oxford University Press, New York, pp. 54-78, 1990.
19. E. Dickstein, Self and Self-esteem: Theoretical Foundations and their Implications for Research, *Human Development, 20*, pp. 129-140, 1977.
20. A. Tomer, Death Anxiety in Adult Life: Theoretical Perspectives, *Death Studies, 16*, pp. 475-506, 1992.
21. G. Marcel, *The Mystery of Being*, G. S. Fraser—Vol. 1 (trans.), and Rene Hague—Vol. 2 (trans.), Henry Regnery, Co., Chicago, 1950.
22. A. Einstein, *The World as I See It*, A. Harris (trans.), Covici & Friede, New York, 1934.

23. G. Reeves, The Idea of Mystery in the Philosophy of Gabriel Marcel, in *The Philosophy of Gabriel Marcel* (Ch. 8), P. A. Schilpp and L. E. Hahn (eds.), La Salle, Illinois, 1984.
24. J. V. Vigorito, On Time in the Philosophy of Marcel, in *The Philosophy of Gabriel Marcel* (Ch. 15), P. A. Schilpp and L. E. Hahn (eds.), La Salle, Illinois, 1984.

PART III

Humanistic Reflections on Mortality Awareness

Philosophical thanatology has a broader scope than the more strictly philosophical topics of the previous chapters. The reflective discipline born of awareness of mortality is not in principle nor in practice restricted to abstract meditations, but includes a broad range of reflections on the human condition. Awareness of mortality mediates and is mediated through our theoretical perspectives, life experiences, beliefs, projects, and dreams. Death is universal. Whatsoever comes into being passes away. Even the universe shall die. But only humans are mortal, i.e., are aware of death as defining our very own existence. Human development, science and humanities, culture, social order, values and projects, all the human world is replete with signifiers of mortality. The field of philosophical thanatology is virtually coextensive with the human world. The range of topics in this section gives the reader a sampling of the many directions in which awareness of mortality may reflect itself.

Doka describes the development of awareness of mortality through the life cycle. He highlights the specific dawning of the more salient and personal awareness of mortality that occurs in mid-life.

Schermer provides the reader with a history of the place of death in psychoanalytic theory. He traces the development of Freud's death instinct theory to Melanie Klein, who builds it into a theory of an awareness of death. Schermer takes Bions' concept or preconception (". . . an implicit structural principle and potential which guides and informs energizing experience and links the unknown to the known.") to develop a new psychoanalytic construct, death as preconception. He further develops the psychoanalytic theory of death, describing four ways in which death appears in the psyche—absence, merger, place, and decay. His psychoanalytic epistemology proposes that all knowledge is impregnated with death.

Lamers approaches the awareness of mortality by tracing the history of attitudes about death reflected in fairy tales. She examines changes over time in the story of *Little Red Riding Hood* and correlates sociocultural attitudes toward death.

Corless takes the AIDS-crisis as a touchstone for reflection upon mortality. She examines the mortality awareness of individuals and groups experiencing multiple AIDS related losses. The experienced broken continuity of the assumptive world is analyzed as a key feature of the mortality awareness for these individuals and groups.

Leviton presents a personal account of the transformation of awareness of horrendous death (HD) into a life philosophy of affirmation and of action aimed at nurturing global health and well being. "Assuming," he writes, "that my wife and children could die at any time, HD serves as a stimulus to action." He proposes an agenda of social values intended to eliminate HD.

Mathur, in the wake of personal loss, reflects upon her traditional Hindu beliefs. Focusing beliefs such as that death is a moment in the continuum of the endless process of life, she considers how Hindu philosophy helps to make death less painful.

CHAPTER 9

The Awareness of Mortality in Midlife: Implications for Later Life

Kenneth J. Doka[1]

> "Doctor, Doctor, Will I die?
> Yes, my child, and so will I."
>
> Nursery Rhyme

Between these two lines of the old nursery rhyme lies a complex developmental process. Most research has indicated that the very young child cannot comprehend either the finality or inevitability of death. Gradually, as the child ages to about eight or nine, the child begins to recognize that death is personal, universal, and inevitable [1, 2]. As these researchers have indicated, this knowledge of death accrues in various stages consistent with the overall theories of Piaget [3] and Kohlberg [4] on the development of abstract thought.

Yet, while the older child is aware that death is personal, universal, and inevitable, the concept of death is often not personalized. The child recognized that he or she, like all living creatures, will die, but that thought is pushed into a very abstract future. The issue of the inevitability of one's own death is simply not cogent unless provoked by a life threatening illness [5]. The cognitive comprehension of death does not necessarily entail the recognition of personal mortality. There is a great gap between the statements "people die" and "I, too will die."

While this recognition of death may begin in childhood as the understanding of the inevitability and universality of death increases, developmental issues which arise in adolescence tend to make the awareness of mortality (that is the personal recognition that one is mortal and at some future time will die) more of a cogent concern. The adolescent is struggling with a number of issues that intersect with death. Primarily, the adolescent is striving to create an individual identity. As the

[1] This chapter draws from previous work of the author published in *Gerontology Review* 1(2):19-20.

adolescent struggles with this individuality there can be a growing awareness that death, nonexistence, represents a great threat to that emerging identity. In some cases, perhaps, this may lead to extensive denial of death or challenges to death evident in dangerous behaviors found in this stage of life.

The threat of death can also be accentuated by the stress and isolation that the adolescent experiences. In this time of critical reflection and reassessment, previous sources of support, such as religion, may no longer be as viable. With an emerging sense of individuality, may come a growing sense of aloneness [6]. "There is no one like me" easily becomes "there is no one who fully understands me." There may be a sense of separation from parents. There may be a mourning for the loss of childhood [7]. As Alexander, Colby and Alderstein assert, death may become a more significant issue at times in which one's identity experiences psychological and social stress [8]. Their projective testing techniques indicated that death is affect-laden for adolescents, albeit on a less conscious level.

While the awareness of mortality may begin to sharpen in adolescence, it is well defended against. One of the major defenses is simply adolescents are very present-oriented. This is clear in Kastenbaum's work on the meaning of death in adolescence [9]. Kastenbaum found that most of his adolescent participants had little sense of futility. In their present-oriented world, death was simply not a major issue. Only a small minority of his participants thought about death. These results were similar to a much earlier study that found college students relatively unconcerned about death [10]. Similarly Newman in a review of literature found that while adolescents were fearful of nuclear war and environmental devastation, they had comparatively few concerns about personal death [11]. Perhaps there is an illusion of invulnerability, emerging from this intense present-orientation, that contributes to that earlier mentioned tendency to challenge death. In summary then, while adolescents may begin, albeit perhaps subconsciously, to recognize their own mortality, their intense present-orientation makes it unlikely that this awareness of mortality will become a significant issue for them.

This awareness of mortality can also be ignored in early adulthood. Erikson for example, sees young adults consumed by a quest to establish identity [12]. The young adult is concerned with the external world—establishing intimate relationships, beginning a family, starting a career.

While some psychoanalytic theorists such as Freud [13] or Weisman [14] assert that humans can never imagine their own deaths, other developmental theorists have implied that the full awareness of mortality begins to emerge in middle adulthood. This awareness of mortality is the recognition that one will die, although not necessarily in the immediate future. It is the understanding that there is an end to one's time that is inexorably drawing closer. In short, it is the increasing perception that one has one life to live and that it is being lived. To many theorists it is in middle adulthood that the concerns become more internal and introspective. Erikson characterizes this stage of life a "generativity vs. stagnation" [12]. Implicit in his discussion of this stage is an increasing awareness of personal mortality that creates a desire in these adults to "pass on the torch" to a newer generation. The middle adult wants to develop a legacy, a contribution that can be left to establish the significance of one's life. That desire is fueled by the increasing understanding that there are limits to one's time. Hence, if the person does not use this time productively, there might not be future opportunity. Other theorists have seen middle adulthood similarly. For example, although the universality of a midlife crisis is debated, its adherents claim it is the knowledge of future death that provides the impetus for a major re-evaluation of one's life [6, 15-20]. Research by Rothstein supports the view that death becomes more of a cogent concern in midlife [21]. He interviewed thirty-six adults, aged thirty to forty-eight. His older respondents (43-48) tended to personalize death more than those in the thirty to forty-two age groups. Death becomes a more salient issue in midlife, responded to first by shock and then resigned accommodation.

This chapter seeks to further synthesize and develop this concept. It is the thesis of this chapter that the awareness of mortality develops in middle adulthood and has both positive and negative impacts on adult development. The remainder of this chapter seeks to fulfill two objectives. First, it describes the particular conditions of midlife that lead adults to become aware of their own mortality. Second, it explores the implications of the awareness of mortality for other aspects of adult life.

DEVELOPING THE AWARENESS OF MORTALITY

There are a number of conditions and circumstances that contribute to the development of an awareness of mortality in middle adulthood. First, as adults reach into their thirties, forties, and fifties, they begin to experience varied physiological and sensory declines. The recognition of these declines reminds one of the inevitability of aging and eventual death.

> In the late thirties and early forties a man falls well below his earlier peak levels of functioning. He cannot run as fast, live as much, do with as little sleep as before. His vision and hearing are less acute, he remembers less well and finds it harder to learn masses of specific information [17, p. 213].

Women experience menopause and both men and women may experience a gradual diminution of sexual prowess. This, too, is a vivid reminder of loss and aging. And, as Kastenbaum and Aisenberg suggest, there may be an inverse relationship between reproductive capability and a sense of terminus [6].

Second, there is a dramatic increase in the mortality rate, particularly for those in their forties. For example, the male mortality rate for men forty-five to sixty-four is six times that for those twenty-five to forty-four [22]. As one enters midlife, then, one begins to regularly experience the death of peers from causes other than accident or suicide. Stephenson notes that when a loss is experienced, there may be both reactive and existential grief [23]. Reactive grief is a response to the loss of a person. Existential grief is the recognition, often prompted by the loss of another, that one will suffer and die. Thus, the loss of others in one's cohort is a vivid reminder of personal vulnerability.

A third factor is that one begins to see one's own parents and their cohort aging and dying. The previously omnipotent parent increasingly is seen as weak and vulnerable. To Blenkner this is a significant factor in adult development [24]. Not only does it create a new relationship with an aging parent, it reinforces one's own aging and death. This is further underlined by the fact that one's own children are at the point of establishing their own families and careers, reinforcing the reality that one's own cohort is advancing in age toward distant but inescapable death. As Moss and Moss state:

> The loss of a parent represents the removal of a buffer against death. As long as the parent was alive the child could feel protected, since the parent by the rational order of things was expected to die first. Without this buffer there is a strong reminder that the child is now the older generation and cannot easily deny his or her own mortality [25].

Other factors in midlife may also increase awareness of mortality. Grandparenthood, which is a midlife experience, is often interpreted by grandparents as a mark of age [26]. Preparation and consideration of retirement, albeit somewhat distant, reiterates the passage of time. The approach of what is perceived as a significant birthday (e.g., 40, 50, etc.) may also be understood as a mark of age. A serious operation, health crisis, or onset of chronic illness may increase the awareness of mortality.

It would seem, then that given the differing conditions and circumstances that lead to the awareness of mortality in adults, this awareness can develop gradually, over time, as a person slowly becomes aware of physical declines and personal vulnerability. In other cases, this awareness may be a sudden insight in response to a crisis. And though it seems that events in the early age when any given individual will achieve this recognition will also vary depending on the situations and circumstances of life.

IMPLICATIONS OF THE AWARENESS
OF MORTALITY

No matter how the awareness of mortality develops, it has certain implications for adult life. First, the middle age person's sense of time is modified. The child primarily looks toward the future. Time is measured from birth. The elderly person may be more oriented toward the past. The "time remaining" is considered both cogent and short. Neugarten theorizes that this restructuring of time occurs in middle age where the increasing awareness of finiteness leads middle agers to think both in terms of time since birth as well as time left to live [19, 27]. Gould found empirical support for this concept [28]. In that study, the middle age group (35-43 years) had a sense of timelessness. They recognized the past and present and looked toward the future. Subjects in the next group (45-50 years) have a sense of life's limits. While they still felt they could accomplish their goals, they had a recognition of the immediacy of time. The oldest group was more concerned with the past.

As the recognition of time shifts, there are profound implications for the sense of self. As stated earlier, the recognition of personal mortality leads to a reassessment of one's own self identity. The middle age person must consider what one has been, what one wished to be, and what one still can become. In essence, one begins to consider what one could leave behind. To use Lifton and Olson's terminology, there is a search for symbolic immortality in creations or progeny that will remain [29]. As Erikson states, generativity becomes a central issue.

> Generativity . . . is primarily the concern in establishing and guiding the next generation . . . And, indeed, the concept 'generativity' is meant to include such more popular synonyms as productivity and creativity . . . [12].

Levinson describes a similar concern:

> Knowing that his own death is not far off, he is eager to affirm life for himself and for generations to come. He wants to be more creative. The creative impulse is not merely to "make" something. It is to bring something into being. To give birth to generate life [17, p. 222].

This illustrates that there is not a morbid preoccupation with death in midlife. The middle age person recognizes that one is in the prime of life with death likely to be decades away. The recognition that it will come can create a desire to see that the remaining years are well spent.

Thus aspects of the awareness of mortality have been identified as life enhancing. Neugarten for example, sees the awareness of mortality acting as a prod, adding zest to life [27]. Koestenbaum sees the knowledge of finiteness as contributing to a renewed sense of vitality [30]. In understanding one's personal mortality, there is a greater appreciation for the tedious and common tasks that contribute to the completion of goals. Life takes on a new perspective. Zacks, too, feels the recognition of limited time creates an intensified search for self actualization [20]. In addition, these processes may make the person more inner directed. Faced with finiteness, the constraints placed by others may seem to be less significant.

While this reassessment represents a symbolic, long-term preparation for death, other forms of preparation may take more mundane forms. The middle age person will become concerned with the more practical aspects of death such as obtaining insurance, providing for trusts, and writing his wills. This preparation continues to increase with age [31].

While the awareness of mortality may in some ways enhance the quality of life or ease the impact of a future death, there can be negative aspects as well. The awareness of mortality strikes at a time when that recognition can be quite problematic. Family responsibilities and financial constraints may be at their peak. Career commitments may be at their apex. Life goals, even as reassessed, are likely to be incomplete. Under such conditions, the knowledge that one will die is likely to provoke great anxiety. It could be expected then that death anxiety would be at its highest in midlife as the adult becomes increasingly cognizant of the paradox of both heightened responsibility and limited time.

There is research to support this view. Neimeyer and Chapman found more fear of death among those whose central life projects were incomplete and those who reported a disparity between perceptions of ideal vs. real self [32]. Research among young adults found death anxiety to be inversely related to subjective life expectancy [33, 34]. While some researchers have found no relationship between age and death fears [35, 36], other researchers have found that middle age populations exhibited greater fear of death than older populations [37-42].

The relationship between age and death anxiety is a complex one that may have different explanations. It may be a statistical artifact, simply reflecting the greater religiosity of older cohorts that seems to reduce death anxiety [31]. Kalish and Reynolds speculate on other reasons [31]. Perhaps the aged, suffering varied losses, disabilities, and pain, see life as having less value. Or perhaps they have lived their lives and recognize that now, according to the natural state of the world, they are approaching death. Or finally, Kalish and Reynolds suggest the elderly may be anticipating and preparing for their own eventual death which may reduce their overt anxiety [31].

Middle aged persons, though, have different concerns. They become aware of death when their commitments and opportunities are extensive. Death becomes the haunting specter that may yet rob them of the opportunity to achieve their goals and enjoy the fruits of their efforts. Death perhaps is the great terror, stalking midlife, threatening goals and plans, heralding incompleteness, and even, for some suggesting the futility and meaningless of existence.

But perhaps then this crisis creates a process of concession to eventual death. This process may entail a reevaluation of life, renewed commitment to the achievement of critical goals, increased focus on health so as to forestall death, and attempts to reduce the uncertainty and impact of death by prudent preparation. There may also be an increased concern with spirituality. While the issues of spirituality, religiosity, age, and death anxiety are too complex and debated to consider here, it would not be inconsistent with developmental approaches [4] to posit that it may be that the recognition of eventual death encourage spirituality, if not religiosity, in older cohorts. Perhaps this crisis forces midlife adults to confront life to find or to construct meaning so as to avoid the terror of death. And perhaps, the longer one lives side by side with now recognized death, the less terrifying it becomes.

To summarize, the awareness of mortality may be the most significant psychological event in middle life. As described earlier in the chapter, the awareness of mortality has two major implications for adult life.

First, it changes the nature of time. Aware of their mortality, midlife adults constantly struggle with the issue of time remaining. One now sees both the finish and starting line of one's life. One's sense of future is now bounded.

This leads to a second implication. An awareness of morality leads to a quest for finding meaning in one's life. Aware of limited time, even if it is measured in decades, a midlife adult becomes deeply concerned that one's life has meaning.

There is a reassessment of where one is in one's life. If one is generally content with one's past present life, and content with the direction life seems to be taking, this concern with meaning may not be overly troublesome. One simply needs to reaffirm the meaning one has already found and perhaps commit to one's current goals. Perhaps such persons may reprioritize their goals and themes, for example, deciding to spend more time with family.

But others may not face the future with such equanimity. If one's past is problematic, there may be a concern to begin closure, perhaps expressed by entering therapy or confronting past issues and demons. If one views the present as troubling or the future as unresolved. This awareness of mortality can engender a sense of panic of terror. Perceiving the boundaries of life, one becomes aware of the fact that the time to construct and to live a meaningful life may no longer seem possible. There may simply not be enough time to find meaning in a here to fore meaningless existence. Perhaps the "midlife" crisis is a manifestation of this frantic concern to achieve meaning by rearranging one's present and future.

Not everyone, of course, struggles with the issue of meaning. To some, the awareness of mortality is simply too terrifying to confront or the quest to find meaning too difficult to pursue. Such persons may select varied coping mechanisms, such as escapist or denial strategies to avoid confronting one's mortality. In discussing the fear of nuclear holocaust, Lifton and Olson described a process of "psychic numbing," where the threat is so terrible yet pervasive that one becomes psychologically incapable of considering it [29]. Perhaps, for some, the threat of death holds so much terror that it can never truly be faced.

The awareness of mortality becomes the critical defining moment in adult life. It forces individuals to find or to construct significance and meaning in life, or to surrender to terror.

CONCLUSION

It has been the thesis of this chapter that midlife is characterized by an increased awareness of personal mortality. This means that the person recognized the inevitability of one's own death. This awareness is part of a long developmental process. The process begins in childhood with the cognitive conceptualization of death as natural and inevitable. By eight or nine, the child is able to cognitively recognize that people die. In middle adulthood this recognition is personalized. The adult is able to understand that he or she will die. Finally in later life, this is a recognition that death will come soon. As Erikson notes, this knowledge may be greeted with acceptance or despair [12]. Perhaps another way to perceive this is to recognize that at different phases in the life cycles, understandings and perceptions of what death is and what it means change.

There may, then, be three overlapping and related processes that occur as humans struggle with death. In the first process, conceptualization, the child must cognitively comprehend the reality of death. The second process, beginning in late childhood and culminating in middle adulthood, is one of personalization. In this process, the person becomes aware of his/her own individual mortality. In the final process, the individual concedes that death will occur soon, that life is near end.

It is evident that the awareness of mortality is affected by a number of variables. Certainly life events such as parents' deaths, health crises, and the like seem to have impact on the timing of the awareness of mortality. The effect of other variables such as race, gender, ethnicity, social class, religiosity, educational level, and residence on the awareness of mortality ought to be investigated. Many of these variables do seem related to general attitudes toward death [19, 31, 36, 38, 43].

Additionally, further research of adult orientations toward death is necessary to develop the thesis that awareness of mortality occurs at midlife. If an awareness of mortality is found, what factors impact upon it? Do off-time life events (i.e., and out-of-order death, the early departure of children, etc.) increase awareness? Are particular sets of these event such as the sudden death of a peer more likely to increase awareness of mortality?

Research on the effect of the awareness of mortality on other variable also needs to be considered. Are there adults who do not experience an awareness of mortality in adult life? How is this related to their subsequent aging and dying? How are they affected by loss? How do they grieve? Do other individuals use strategies such as substance abuse or endless diversion to escape or avoid a confrontation with one's mortality? In what ways do those coping mechanisms affect later orientations to loss and death?

These are only examples of the significant work yet to be accomplished in comprehending adult orientations toward death. In advancing such work, we will extend exploration of midlife perceptions of mortality, heretofore only marginally studied. The awareness of mortality may represent a significant process in adult life. And while such awareness increases anxiety at first, as we learn to live with the specter of death in midlife, death becomes less foreboding as we near it. As Frank Herbert states in his epic novel Children of Dune:

To suspect your own mortality is the beginning of terror; to learn irrefutably that you are mortal is to know the end of terror [44, pp. 133-134].

REFERENCES

1. M. Nagy, The Child's Theories Concerning Death, *Journal of Genetic Psychology, 73*, pp. 3-27, 1948.
2. B. Kane, Children's Concepts of Death, *The Journal of Genetic Psychology, 134*, pp. 141-153, 1979.
3. J. Piaget, *The Language and Thought of the Child*, Harcourt, Brace, & Jovanovich, New York, 1926.
4. L. Kohlberg, Stage and Sequence: The Cognitive-developmental Approach to Socialization, in *Handbook of Socialization Research and Theory*, D. Goslin (ed.), Rand McNally, Chicago, 1969.
5. M. Bluebond-Langner, *The Private Worlds of Dying Children*, Princeton University Press, New Jersey, 1965.
6. R. Kastenbaum and R. Aisenberg, *The Psychology of Death*, Springer, New York, 1976.
7. B. Raphael, *The Anatomy of Bereavement*, Basic Books, New York, 1984.
8. I. Alexander, R. Colby, and A. Alderstein, Is Death a Matter of Indifference? *Journal of Psychology, 43*, pp. 277-283, 1957.
9. R. Kastenbaum, Time and Death in Adolescence, in *The Meaning of Death*, H. Fiefel, (ed.) McGraw-Hill, New York, 1965.
10. W. Middleton, Some Reactions toward Death among College Students, *Journal of Abnormal and Social Psychology, 31*, pp. 155-173, 1936.
11. A. Newman, Planetary Death, *Death Studies, 11*, pp. 131-135, 1987.
12. E. Erikson, *Childhood and Society*, MacMillan, New York, 1963.
13. S. Freud, *Thoughts for the Times on War and Death*, in collected papers, (IV) Hogarth Press, London, 1925.
14. A. Weisman, *On Dying and Denying: A Psychiatric Study of Terminality*, Behavioral Publications, New York, 1972.
15. O. Brim, Theories of the Male Mid-life Crisis, *Counseling Psychologist, 6*, pp. 2-9, 1976.
16. E. Jacques, Death and the Mid-life Crisis, *International Journal of Psychoanalysis, 46*, pp. 502-514, 1965.
17. D. J. Levinson, *The Seasons of a Man's Life*, Alfred A. Knopf, New York, 1978.
18. R. J. Lifton, On Death and the Continuity of Life: A Psychohistorical Perspective, *Omega, 6*, pp. 143-159, 1975.
19. B. Neugarten, Adaptation and the Life Cycle, *Counseling Psychologist, 6*, pp. 16-20, 1972.
20. H. Zacks, Self-actualization: A Midlife Problem, *Social Casework, 61*, pp. 223-233, 1980.
21. S. H. Rothstein, *Aging Awareness and Personalization of Death in the Young and Middle Adult Years*, Ph.D. Dissertation, University of Chicago, 1967.

22. L. Tamir, *Men in Their Forties: The Transition to Middle Age*, Springer, New York, 1982.
23. J. Stephenson, Death, *Grief and Mourning: Individual and Social Realities*, Free Press, New York, 1985.
24. M. Blenkner, Social Work and Family Relationships in Late Life, with Some Thoughts on Filial Maturity, in *Social Structure and the Family: Generational Relations*, E. Shanas and G. Streib (eds.), Prentice-Hall, New Jersey, 1965.
25. M. Moss and S. Moss, The Impact of Parental Death on Middle Aged Children, *Omega, 14*, pp. 65-76, 1983.
26. B. Neugarten and K. Weinstein, The Changing American Grandparent, in *Middle Age and Aging*, B. Neugarten (eds.), University of Chicago Press, Chicago, 1968.
27. B. Neugarten, The Awareness of Middle Age, in *Middle Age and Aging*, B. Neugarten (ed.), University of Chicago Press, Chicago, 1968.
28. R. Gould, The Phases of Adult Life: A Study in Developmental Psychology, *American Journal of Psychiatry, 129*, pp. 521-531, 1972.
29. R. Lifton and E. Olson, *Living and Dying*, Bantam Books, New York, 1974.
30. P. Koestenbaum, The Vitality of Death, *Omega, 2*, pp. 253-271, 1971.
31. R. Kalish and D. Reynolds, *Death and Ethnicity: A Psychocultural Study*, Baywood, New York, 1981.
32. R. Neimeyer and K. Chapman, Self/ideal Discrepancy and Fear of Death: The Test of an Existential Hypothesis, *Omega, 11*, pp. 233-240, 1980.
33. L. S. Dickerson and S. J. Blatt, Death Concerns, Futurity and Anticipation, *Journal of Consulting Psychology, 30*, pp. 11-17, 1966.
34. P. Handel, The Relationship between Subjective Life Expectancy, Death Anxiety, and General Anxiety, *Journal of Clinical Psychology, 25*, pp. 39-42, 1969.
35. D. Templet, C. Ruff, and C. Franks, Death Anxiety: Age, Sex and Parental Resemblance in Diverse Populations, *Developmental Psychology, 4*, p. 108, 1971.
36. H. Wass, M. Christian, J. Myers, and M. Murphy, Similarities and Dissimilarities in Attitudes toward Death in a Population of Older Persons, *Omega, 9*, pp. 337-354, 1979.
37. N. Kogan and F. Shelton, Beliefs about Old People: A Comparative Study of Older and Younger Samples, *Journal of Genetic Psychology, 100*, pp. 93-111, 1962.
38. D. Martin and L. Wrightsman, The Relationship between Religious Behavior and Concern about Death, *Journal of Social Psychology, 65*, pp. 317-325, 1965.
39. K. Sharma and V. C. Jain, Religiosity and Fear of Death in Young and Retired Persons, *Indian Journal of Gerontology, 1*, pp. 110-114, 1969.
40. R. Kalish and A. Johnson, Value Similarities and Differences in Three Generations of Women, *Journal of Marriage and the Family, 34*, pp. 49-54, 1972.
41. B. Kahana, Attitudes of Young Men and Women toward Awareness of Death, *Omega, 3*, pp. 37-44, 1972.
42. R. Kalish, Death and Dying in a Social Context, in *The Handbook of Aging in the Social Sciences*, R. Binstock and G. Shara (eds.), Van Nostrand, New York, 1976.
43. V. Bengstom, J. Cuellar, and P. Ragan, Stratum Contrasts and Similarities in Attitudes toward Death, *Journal of Gerontology, 32*, pp. 76-88, 1977.
44. F. Herbert, *Children of Dune*, Berkeley Books, New York, 1977.

CHAPTER 10

Intimations of Mortality from Recollections of Early Childhood: Death Awareness, Knowledge, and the Unconscious

Victor L. Schermer

"Our birth is but a sleep and a forgetting"—William Wordsworth, "Ode: Intimations of Immortality from Recollections of Early Childhood"

"As soon as a man is born, he begins to die."—Proverb

The universal dynamics of death and dying, mortality, loss, and grief, are significant not only in bereavement counseling, but also in the psychotherapy of a wide variety of emotional disorders. As counselors and psychotherapists, we encounter the awareness of death in the words and silences of our patients as they experience and express the vicissitudes of life. These strangers who come to our consulting room have recently or long ago lost a loved one. They express fantasies and fears about death: about coffins, death masks, judgments, black holes, underworlds, unfinished business, goodbyes, and so on. Death pervades life, and as the above proverb suggests, death is a felt presence from the very beginning of life, "and from the first declension of the flesh . . . " [1, p. 25].

A PREFATORY NOTE

When my friend and colleague, Jeffrey Kauffman, as editor of this volume, asked me to elaborate upon the connections between psychoanalysis, the unconscious, and death, I realized that there are aspects of the psychoanalytic frame of reference which may trouble some readers who work in the fields of bereavement counseling and related disciplines. Psychoanalysis, with its emphasis on the unconscious as a dark realm wherein we try to shed the light of consciousness and truth, often appears to omit from consideration the nurturing elements of compassion, empathy, existential concern, the "here and now," and the spiritual life. Although such criticism is not without merit and needs to be addressed by psychoanalysts, I sincerely hope that my efforts to address the relationship between death and the unconscious do not devalue the nurturing and healing features of counseling and psychotherapy. I do indeed genuinely believe in the leaven of love in the treatment process and agree with the philosopher Unamono, who once said that "We die of cold, not of darkness." Today, with the work of Winnicott [2], Kohut [3, 4], Stern [5], and others who have focused on the impact of deficits in early nurturance and "attunedness," we are seeing the psychoanalytic pendulum swing toward warmth, "holding," and empathy as curative factors. Regarding religious and spiritual perspectives, psychoanalysts and psychologists such as Meissner [6, 7] and others have recently attempted to integrate "mainstream" psychoanalysis with concepts from religion and spiritual healing.

Although I am largely supportive of these developments, I agree too with the psychoanalyst Wilfred Bion's emphasis on self knowledge as the nutriment of the human mind and soul. Self awareness, the end and aim of psychoanalytic psychotherapy, is important not only in treating mental illness, it is also a source of growth and solace in facing life, the human condition, mortality, death, and dying. The search for meaning, perspective, and inner growth is a path chosen by some for coping with the wearing and yielding of "this mortal coil." So I ask that the reader join me on this journey remembering that, although we hope to find light in darkness, we also know that without warmth, love, and compassion, we die before we die.

THE DOMAIN AND SCOPE OF PSYCHOANALYSIS VIS-A-VIS DEATH AND DYING

Psychoanalysis sets out to explore death as an ongoing, shifting awareness with unconscious and developmental determinants. Consciousness of death and loss develops early in childhood and with import in virtually every human being, and, as we know, when it is repressed, makes itself felt in symptoms, characterological problems, and prolonged or "masked" grief. Exploring the relationship between death and the unconscious is an ambitious endeavor, and all I can hope to do is to point out a few historical factors and contemporary lines of thought on the matter. Freud himself approached the problem of death with great tentativeness and his own "death consciousness" appears to have emerged almost against his will [8, pp. 97-105].

I will begin by briefly recalling and elaborating the place of death within psychoanalysis and in particular Freud's emergent understanding of the relationship between death and the unconscious. Expectably, the alliance between the "life instinct" and psychoanalysis has always proved harmonious, while consideration of the "death instinct" has always been an unwelcome visitor. Thus, there is the paradox that, while images of death occur frequently in parapraxes (mental slips), dreams, myths, and other "roads to the unconscious," Freudian psychoanalysis (with the notable exception of a minority of writers such as Brown [9], Eissler [10], Jacques [11], Menninger [12], and Zilboorg [13]) continues to disavow even to this date Freud's thesis, formulated relatively late in his career, that death is a central motif in the development of the psyche.

The fact that Freud used the phrase "death *instinct*" did not help matters. As I shall try to show, Freud, biological reductionist that he was, could not see that death is not so much an instinct which drives man as a predisposition and "preconception" which confronts him with a dialectic of paradoxes and dilemmas which may promote *either* growth *or* destructiveness. It was a vast oversimplification on Freud's part to resolve this dialectic as a desire or motive. In this respect, I cite the Lacanian thesis that the unconscious is not purely a biological matrix as Freud believed, but is equally embedded in language and speech [14, pp. 44-46]. I also invoke the anthropologist Levi-Strauss' position that large scale concerns of the species, such as life and death, occur across cultures as pairs of dialectical opposites or "mythemes" [15]. For Levi-Strauss, such "mythemes" are pre-given cognitive-emotional structural elements, not biological drives.

Next, I will turn to contemporary object relations theory to suggest that Melanie Klein and her student, Wilfred Bion paved the way for a psychoanalytic psychology which accords to death key status in the mental life. Klein, *via* her theory of projective identification, and her profound awareness of bodily phantasy, gave us a means to comprehend how a concept so complex as death and relegated to occur at the end point of the life cycle, can yet have a representation in the minds of infants and young children [16, pp. 330-331, 394, 395]. Klein, retaining Freud's drive/instinct frame, saw evidence of a death instinct in the power of destructiveness, early splitting mechanisms, and the harshness of the primitive superego. Bion, by shaking loose the entire underpinnings of psychoanalysis and replacing it with the Kantian notion of the thing-in-itself and with the further idea of transformation, retained what was important in Freud's idea of "instincts" while defusing and desaturating its erroneous implications ([17], introduction, for a discussion). Through the intermediary of a "preconception," which facilitates movement from the realm of the biological into the psychological, Bion allowed us to think of death as innately "known," yet not necessarily as an instinctual self-destructive "urge" [18]. Such a shift in conceptualization is I think a key to unlocking a richer dynamic psychology of death and dying.

I will then explore, if only tentatively and briefly, how "thanatology" and "epistemology" are related disciplines, how the philosophy and psychology of death and of knowledge are intimately intertwined. I will connect epistemology, the theory of knowledge, to the early curiosity of the child, what Klein initially termed the "epistemophilic instinct" [19, p. 65]. I will exemplify how curiosity comes into play in the development of death awareness and how knowledge is impregnated with the awareness and/or denial and repression of death.

Finally, I will discuss a timely topic for a period in history dominated by self-consciousness and self-preoccupation [20]: the relationship of death to narcissism and the self, an area of convergence which has far from received the full attention it deserves.

FREUD, DEATH, AND THE UNCONSCIOUS

Only the barest outline of the historical connection between psychoanalysis and death awareness can be given here. A thorough investigation of this relationship has yet to be completed, although Edward Becker made an important beginning in *The Denial of Death*, where he focused on the character traits and defenses which ward off the profound fear of death and argued for the centrality of death awareness in human development [8]. It is my opinion that Becker's courageous formulations cry out for a far more detailed understanding of the ideation, structures, and developmental processes associated with the awareness and knowledge of death. For example, Becker did not elaborate on the critically important question of how mental representations of death are formed in the earliest experiences of attachment and loss, in the child's processing the presence and absence of significant others.

While Freud, as a youth, experienced within himself an abundance of the "life instinct," i.e., intense and vital daydreams, world conquest ambitions, romantic attachments, and an intense personal investment in and enthusiasm for life, he conceived of psychoanalysis when, commencing his career as a physician, he suffered a mental depression which included feelings of guilt, illness, and a fear that his life would end in middle age [21, pp. 58-59]. Psychologically speaking, Freud's depression was part and parcel of the birth of psychoanalysis and is reflected in fragments of Freud's own mental life which he reported and analyzed in *The Interpretation of Dreams* ([22, esp. pp. 138-154], on the famous dream of "Irma's injection") and also disclosed in his letters to Wilhelm Fliess [23].

The myth of Oedipus, which became the cornerstone of Freud's theory, has as much to do with death as with incest: the Plague, the devouring Sphinx, attempted infanticide (the young Oedipus abandoned by his parents to die on Mount Citheron), parricide, and Oedipus' death at Colonnus are elements which lend both the myth and Sophocles' drama a pervasive air of the presence of mortal danger and of death in life. Thus, by making the death-infused legend of Oedipus the central feature of his psychology, Freud, although he emphasized the incest theme, revealed that *death was present as the "shadow" or dissociated side of psychoanalysis as its point of origin.* Furthermore, in his understanding of the Oedipus complex in children and in neurosis, Freud posited his first theory of the fear of origins of death, linking it to the fear of castration, the imagined threat the father holds over the son, perhaps most poignantly illustrated by Freud in the child analysis of Little Hans [21, pp. 258-260; 24].

The death motif appears as well in the pervasive morbidity of the decadent and hypocritical Viennese cultural life, manifest, for example, in the case of Dora [25], who was enveloped in a deadly interpersonal matrix of seductions, manipulations, and ensorcellments carried out *sub rosa* by her own father and one Herr K. Many of Freud's first patients suffered from a mental disorder, namely hysteria, which communicated in private, secretive symbolism the strangulating effect of a culture whose underpinnings were increasingly infused with a death drive.

The composer, Gustav Mahler, who had a brief consultation with Freud [26], was preoccupied with death, manifest, for instance, in the song cycle, *Kindertotenlieder*. Within two years of his fateful encounter with Freud, Mahler was to die of a cardiac condition which Garcia has viewed as psychosomatically related to Mahler's passionate marital disputes with his wife Alma [26]. During his meeting with Freud, Mahler recalled that, as a child, he heard an organ grinder's song outside the window of his home. Later relating the image of an organ grinder to his own premonition of death, Mahler wrote:

> Now the pale figures of my life pass before me like shadows of a long-lost happiness . . . And once more we are wandering together in that familiar countryside, and there we see the organ grinder standing, his hat proffered with his fleshless hands . . . " [26, p. 25].

Mahler related the childhood incident of the organ grinder's song, which he recalled having heard in the background at the moment when his parents were engaged in a hostile argument, to difficulties with musical composition in which a common melody intruded upon the "noblest passages" of his music. The organ grinder is a personification of death. Graves has pointed out the word pun relation of "organ grinder" and *vagina dentata*, the "vagina with teeth," re-evoking Freud's linkage of death and castration anxiety [27].

Mahler's *Kindertoten Lieder*, Thomas Mann's novels *Magic Mountain* and *Death in Venice*, the haunting, suicidal poetry of Georg Trakl [28], and other literary and artistic expressions of Freud's Vienna explored the death theme from vantage points of grief, awakening, artistic creation, and sexuality. Death was thus represented prominently in the culture and was absorbed within psychoanalysis as an unconscious motif waiting to be made explicit in theory and in clinical work.

It was only following the violent horrors of World War I, however, and as a consequence of his studies of war neuroses, not to mention his own aging process and the pervasive warlike atmosphere in Europe, that Freud elevated the death motif to a central feature of his metapsychology.

When Freud, in *Beyond the Pleasure Principle*, finally addressed death as a basic theme of the unconscious, it was as if the profound awareness of the bio-psychological centrality of death emerged almost against his will [29]. Freud, the evolutionary "biologist of the mind" [30], and with a long-standing Lamarckian teleological bent, held that life strives to live, grow and change (adapt to its surroundings), and transform, not die: death in this scheme of things is clearly not the result of a "motive" but rather of the legacy of the inanimate matrix, of entropy, the tendency towards randomness, towards "winding down," a law of thermodynamics which life somehow, against all odds, briefly contravenes. From this standpoint, life itself strives toward higher organizations of matter and energy, survival and growth. Death is an inanimate state which is, if anything, contrary to the telos of the living organism.

However, as a result of his analyses of war neuroses, Freud was compelled to acknowledge that psychic trauma creates a paradoxical state of affairs regarding the life instinct: Freud held that the traumatized psyche, rather than seeking pleasure and adaptation, endlessly repeats an unpleasurable experience, as if there is present within an actual force pressing toward the inanimate, toward earlier stages of development, toward death. He suggested that this movement toward death may be seen even at an early age, and offered the example of how his grandson, in the absence of his mother, engaged in a form of repetitive behavior, playing a game with a spool of thread, in which he repeatedly recovered the spool and then threw it back. In response to separation from his mother, the child reverted to a primitive, repetitive mode of behavior, an observation which anyone who observes the mourning process would confirm as present in grief at all stages of the life cycle. For grief is a process of repetitive focus on the lost love object, calling it back until the image is incorporated in the psyche as a part of the self.

Freud speculated that all biological organisms have a fundamental organic tendency toward death. (Arnold Toynbee much later articulated a similar view of a biologically rooted death motif. Toynbee said, "Death is the price paid by life for an enhancement of the complexity of a live organism's structure" [31].) Freud saw an analogy between his Eros/Thanatos instinct theory and the biologist Weissman's notion that the potential for death evolved with the process of sexual reproduction.

Thus, in a systematic, if highly speculative way, Freud argued for the presence of a biological impulse toward death. For the most part, however, the generation of analysts following Freud rejected this thesis, which they correctly felt lacked sufficient confirming evidence to earn the status of a scientific law.

Following his early formulations of dreams and hysteria, and prior to the above described theory of the death instinct, Freud had addressed the ego's relationship to death in terms of the mourner's response to the loss of a loved one, which constitutes the focus of present day bereavement therapy [32]. Within the life cycle, grief and trauma are the processes which most clearly relate libidinal attachments to loss and death and through which the individual becomes most aware of the presence of death in life.

Freud noted the resistance of the ego, in its narcissistic delusion of immortality, to accepting his own demise or that of a significant other, whose memory is equated with the self and hence kept "alive" [32, 33]. Even the mature and individuated ego is able to detach from the lost one only partially, and only by keeping the deceased "alive" in phantasy, sometimes punishing the lost person out of guilt and anger, and finally assuring that he or she will live on in memory by idealizing and memorializing this person who, in life, was regarded with much greater ambivalence. In "Mourning and Melancholia," Freud first noted the connections between loss, death awareness, internalized object relations, and the development of the unconscious portions of the ego and superego [32]. As a result of these early observations of Freud, it has been in the sphere of object relations, ego, and superego development that most psychoanalytic work on death and dying has focused.

MELANIE KLEIN ON THE INFANT'S MENTAL DEVELOPMENT

Melanie Klein was a psychoanalyst who, starting out as an analysand and student of Karl Abraham and of Sandor Ferenczi, became one of the pioneering figures in the "widening scope" of psychoanalysis in treating severe psychotic and borderline disorders, as well as a founder of "object relations theory." Grosskurth's biography of Klein portrays both the astounding achievements and tragic nature of her life and career [16]. Hanna Segal has written a readable and accurate exposition of Klein's theory [19].

Klein believed that the infant developed a formative and elaborate mental life even in the first weeks and months of life, well earlier than Freud placed his estimates of the beginnings of significant mental conflict. Unlike most of her peers, she accepted Freud's formulation of a death instinct, equating it with the aggressive drive.

Klein held that the infant is not only preoccupied with pleasure, satisfaction, and satiation, but also with fears of its own fragmentation, death, and annihilation at the hands of phantasmagorical figures, the so called "bad objects," creations and projections of its own mind in response to the demands and vulnerabilities of the soma, the physical body, and the self. In this way, her perspective suggests that the infant has an intimation of death from the very beginning. This intimation is not equivalent to an adult's more highly evolved fear of death but is a primal awareness of a threat to organismic safety, as well as to the continuance of the infant's essential relationship to the primary caregiver. It is true, in Melanie Klein's view of the infant's "cosmos," that "as soon as a man is born, he begins to die." Klein contended that the infant's primary preoccupation is with the self and that it experiences danger and "death" as attacks on the self from "bad objects," i.e., phantasic threatening images from its own primitive "unconscious." Guntrip (1969) subsequently termed this primal fear, "annihilation anxiety" [34].

Parallel to Ms. Klein's contributions, the notion that the infant has a primal awareness of danger acquired credence within psychoanalytic ego psychology. Margaret Mahler, pioneering psychoanalyst, investigator of child psycho- pathology, and astute observer of the mother-infant symbiosis/separation- individual process, noted an annihilatory fear in infants which she termed "organismic panic" [35]. Such panic and its expression represents a desperate emergency call for help in response to an internal experience "sensed" by the infant to be profoundly life endangering (the trigger for this panic reaction may be mental, physical, or both). More recently, Shengold connected these early anxiety states to the infant's experience of "nothing" as opposed to an omnipotently satisfying "everything" [36, pp. 1-7]. If mother nature abhors a vacuum, so too does the infant abhor "nothing," which signifies a profound danger to its being. Grotstein has referred to this state of "nothing" as a black hole, and endowed it, like the astronomical black hole, with intense forces and paradoxes [37]. Neither Mahler nor Shengold make reference to a death instinct, but Grotstein does view his black hole concept as the "bottom line" dread associated with the fear of death. He regards death as a signifier of the ultimate psychic catastrophe, the black hole. He speaks of a "death instinct," but considers it, in a manner consistent with the point of view of the present chapter, to be more of a Lacanian "signifier," i.e., a set of meanings [37, pp. 35-36]. Grotstein holds that it is not death which is feared in the unconscious, but the "hole" of which death is but a symbol. Yet, for Grotstein, the "black hole" of which death is but a symbol. Yet, for Grotstein, the "black hole" is not castration, but rather the dreaded catastrophe of mental collapse, of psychosis. Just as the astronomical black hole results from the death of a star, so the psychological black hole results from an emotional death, chaos, and abandon- ment.

As has been mentioned, Melanie Klein revised and extended Freud's theory to include the vicissitudes of the infant's preoccupation first with its own survival against the onslaughts of persecutory objects and then with the mother's capacity to tolerate the child's aggressive wishes and actions. Thus death is associated with feelings and phantasies of being attacked by persecutory objects which reverse passive "death" into active "murder." The originary infantile experience of death is thereby represented in the persona of an external bad object, such as the adult might see in the image of the "grim reaper."

At a somewhat later point in development, in the "depressive position" [19, pp. 135-140], death, according to Klein, becomes connected with the problem of guilt. At a stage in infant development which Ms. Klein called the "depressive position," the child begins to fear that its aggression may damage or kill the mother. This so-called "depressive anxiety" explains in part the origin of what gives death its ominous quality of retribution and judgement, for the child fears that the mother will exact revenge. Such a complex of aggression, guilt, and reparation is carried over into adult life in the ambivalent feelings and wish to make restitution that often follow the loss of a loved one.

It is a subtle but perhaps important point that Klein never implied, as did Freud, that the infant has a death "wish" as part of his or her inner nature, but rather that the child's inherent aggression and states of unpleasure set up conflicts with which he or she copes by defensive maneuvers of the consequent mental representations of the conflict. She considered that, if the infant, with the assistance of the mother's ministrations, could not successfully manage the intense impingements from its own aggressive drive as well as from environmental disruptions, then a strong "death wish" might emerge as a derivative of intense conflict.

In retrospect it thus appears that Freud was indeed premature in formulating a death wish or death instinct rather than investigating how such a wish or impulsion might arise or be exacerbated in early life experience and relationships. In other words, it can be said that a death "wish" is a derivative of an early death "awareness" converted by early experience into an attitude toward the self. Death is initially an intimation or awareness, not a wish or an instinct.

BION: THE THEORY OF THINKING AND THE "PRECONCEPTION"

W. R. Bion[1] a student of Melanie Klein, evolved a psychological framework which minimized outworn biological constructs and permitted an openness to new meanings such that terms like "life" and "death" would be unsaturated with old ideas and receptive to new understandings and possibilities. Bion expanded and modified Freudian and Kleinian theory into a general framework based in the philosophies of Plato and Kant [17]. Best known for his work on groups, Bion subsequently focused on the analysis of severe borderline and schizophrenic patients [38]. In his efforts to understand the catastrophic changes in the personalities of such individuals, Bion believed he needed to go to the very heart of the formation of mental processes and to look at them from a new theoretical perspective.

Bion's work provides a framework whereby we can rectify Freud's use of an outmoded instinct theory without rejecting the notion of inherent "wired-in" structure. Rather than speaking about "instincts," Bion evolved a theory of thinking which began with biological stimuli, called "beta elements," through dream images ("alpha elements") to preconceptions, conceptions, and abstract thought [39]. The preconception is pivotal because it allows the transition from incohate phantasies to coherent ideas. The preconception suggests both a world of images and also a world beyond images, that which Grotstein has termed "non-sensory

---

[1] Wilfred Bion was a member (and past president) of the British Psycho-analytical Society who subsequently came to Los Angeles where he trained, supervised, and inspired psychoanalysts from all over the world. Bion died in 1979. His own response to learning that he had a terminal illness seems to have been of a stoical nature. He said to a friend, "Life is full of surprises, most of them not very pleasant."

experience" [40]. Preconceptions originate in the biological/ somatic strata and substrate of the senses, the erogenous zones, intense need states, and so on, but rather than simply being carbon copies of these elements, what Freud called "mental representations," preconceptions facilitate *transformations* from the physical to the mental domain.

(It is important to emphasize that by the term "preconception," Bion meant "prior to a conception or idea," not a "fixed attitude, belief or conviction," which is implied in the everyday usage.)

Ogden aptly exemplifies a preconception of infancy with respect to the mother's breast as a need-satisfying object. Consistent with the present viewpoint, Ogden prefers to speak of "deep psychological structures" rather than instincts when referring to the infant's seeking of a need-satisfying external object such as the mother's breast. Illustrating the "preconception" of the breast, Ogden says:

> The infant does not anticipate the actual breast in the sense of having a mental picture of it . . . ; on the other hand, he 'recognizes' it when he encounters it, because it is part of his biologically structured internal order that was silently available to be given representational form (italics mine/VLS) [41, pp. 192-193].

Bion's use of the notion of "thoughts without a thinker" derives from Plato's belief that beyond the senses there exists a world of "ideal forms" of which, following the famous "cave analogy" we perceive only the shades, i.e., sensations, percepts, images "representing" the forms (e.g., the appearance of a particular triangle evokes but is not the same as the "pure" idea of a triangle.) Kant went a step further to suggest that the mind functioned as a "net" which had axiomatic givens which captured certain aspects of the reality "beyond" the senses. "Preconceptions" are Kantian axiomatic givens or structures capturing *inner* reality.

The "preconception" is the pre-given pattern of mind which informs the ideational and affective complex that emerges from what initially are bodily changes and sensations "without a thinker." The preconception is a template which seeks out sensations, images, and ideas and gives them form. The pre-conception then seeks to mate with a "conception" or object representation which the person may then experience, feel, and cogitate upon. The preconception is analogous to "messenger RNA" which carries the pattern from the "DNA" ("thoughts without a thinker") in order to build actual structures (complexes of ideas, feelings, content).

Following this line of reasoning, we may say that death is a preconception, a way of anticipating, interpreting, and incorporating a particular set of biological, psychological, and cultural experiences which would otherwise remain ineffable or "unthought." Death as a preconception is a special way of organizing a particular set of otherwise incohate and incomprehensible experiences into a coherent whole. Had Freud phrased Eros and Thanatos as "preconceptions" rather than "instincts," the door might have been opened to a general investigation of the vicissitudes of death awareness throughout the life cycle, parelleling the vicissitudes of sexuality, identity, and so on. Rather than prejudging the nature of human impulses and motivational tendencies, the "preconception" encourages us to articulate the relationship between 1) the psychobiological basis or *anlage* of experience, which can range from the adrenaline "rush" of aggression to womblike and sleep states, etc. (the somatic core, the "thing-in-itself"); 2) death as an intimation of loss and non-being; and 3) the higher level subjective and intersubjective ideas and associations about death and dying which occur throughout the life cycle. Our interest is focused on how ideas and emotions take place, in movement from the body on through to the affective, cognitive, and spiritual levels.

DEATH AS PRECONCEPTION

If we view death as a "preconception" rather than an "instinct," a sounder foundation can be built for an understanding of the role of death in psychological development. Let me reiterate that what Bion meant by a preconception is an implicit structure, principle, and potential which guides and informs emerging experience and links the unknown to the known. As Ogden has suggested, *there exist inherent structures which guide and inform primal experience* [41]. I am asserting that one of these structures is that which we call Death. Death is a template and filter which conditions all mental life.

To provide an example from animal behavior, we know that primates react with horror and avoidance to a deceased body of their own species, even if they have never seen one before. It is as if they have a preconception of "dead primate" which matches with the actual experience to induce a state of fear and avoidance. Similarly, a child learns early in life to discriminate animate and inanimate matter and to know that an insect or a small animal, for example, is dead. Of course, for humans, this discrimination is never perfect, and as a result of such ambiguity, we sometimes become fearful when someone is asleep, or when wind rustles the trees or a window pane, etc. The imperfection of our discrimination only further highlights the intimation of death and is part of what evokes a sense of the "uncanny," the presence of those who have died, etc.

It is both the credit and the eternal suffering of human beings that death is a felt presence of *pervasive* and *ultimate* significance. This sense of the power of death is not, however, experienced without sleep ambivalence and defendedness.

For instance, in Tennessee Williams' play, *Cat on a Hot Tin Roof*, Big Daddy, a wealthy southern patriarch whose anal and phallic character traits prevent him from acknowledging his vulnerability and loss, is afflicted with a terminal cancer which is concealed from him by his physician and family [42]. Says Big Daddy, "Ignorance of mortality—that's a comfort. Man don't have that comfort—he's the only living being that conceives of death and knows what it is. The others go without knowin', without any knowledge of it. That's the only way any living being should go, go without knowin' it." No matter how much Big Daddy pretends, some part of him does know he is going to die, which makes him human, and, to the extent that he denies and avoids his death, to that extent he is unable to complete his life.

Such central preoccupation with death, which Becker considered to be definitional of human experience and being, is a genuine spiritual consciousness which derives from a reflexive self-awareness cognizant of its existence within a time-space continuum. (It is also an additional reason why an "instinct" theory of death fails at the human level: the preoccupation with death stems as much from man's self-consciousness as from his animal nature.) Lacan noted that the birth of the reflexive self is demarcated by the child's self-recognition in the mirror, a developmental milestone which he called the "mirror stage," the *stade du miroir* [14, pp. 62-66]. "Reflection" in this context has the double meaning of a mirror image and the ability to think. It is the interaction of the reflexive self with the preconception of death which brings into intense focus the concerns with mortality which are so much a part of our inner life and of culture.

Lacan's depiction of the "mirror stage," in which the self is captured and lost in its own illusory, external image, combined with the awareness that the mythical Narcissus' death is a result of "falling in love" with his mirror image, suggests an essential relationship between death and self-love, a subject to which we will return later. In the work of the modern French artist, Rene Magritte, a surrealist artist who influenced Lacan [14, p. 22] the self-consciousness of death and nothingness is portrayed by juxtaposing and condensing images of the living and the dead, the animate and the inanimate. Magritte's mother died suicidally by drowning, and an image of her body described by his governess haunted him throughout his life [43]. Each person has within him an "image of death" which emerged in early childhood, an image which derives from a set of preconceptions and structures which constitute a part of the child's idiomatic nature as well as his fundamental humanness.

THE FOURFOLD PRECONCEPTION OF DEATH

We can never know death directly, as a "thing in itself" because, by definition, death is non-experience or beyond experience, but we can infer something about the preconception of death from the experiences and ideas we do have, and especially from our reconstructions of the earliest and most primitive infantile experience. I believe that the preconception of death has four structural themes or motifs from which the spectrum of death awareness emanates. These thematic aspects of the preconception of death are:

1. *Absence* (non-being, annihilation)

2. *Merger* (oneness; symbiosis; loss of identity; transcendence)
3. *Place* (location, container)
4. *Decay* (entropy, the abhorrent, the unclean, the sick and diseased)

These motifs bring into focus what we struggle with when we encounter our own mortality and that of others. The four motifs are asymptotically close to death, but death remains mysterious even when these have been elaborated. Nevertheless, I would suggest that many experiences relating to death and dying consist in various syntheses of these developmental themes. Such a method of analysis parallels the ideas of Levi-Strauss concerning "mythemes" which pervade all cultures [15]. It also relates to the Lacan/Saussure relationship of signifier to signified which pervades all language and thought [14, pp. 46-49].

Death as Absence, Annihilation, and Non-Being

The characteristic of death which is most central to its universal meaning is that of absence or non-being. In the symbolic logic of the "unconscious as infinite sets," death as absence and non-being is the null state, the zero, the cipher [44]. The death of the self is the zero state of the subjective; the loss of another is the cipher of the object.

A dichotomy of being and non-being appears to be a prefigured category of experience. Life and death are intertwined from the very beginning of thought, embodying the paradoxes and dualities of everything versus nothing (omnipotent hallucination versus helplessness and negative hallucination); dichotomous logic; the expression of all cultural myths in terms of paired opposites [15]; sleep and oblivion versus wakefulness and alertness; being versus non-being.

The meaning of death as negation and nothing was expressed by the modern American poet, James Wright, in a poem entitled "For the Marsh's Birthday":

> The not were nothing then
> Now let the not become
> Nothing, and so remain,
> Till the bright grassbirds come
> Home to the singing tree.
> Then, let them be [45].

In Wright's poem, death is a calling and a homecoming. There is present an injunction that we not awaken the dead: "Then, let them be." In a clinical example to be discussed later, birds also play a role in a patient's symbolization of death and dying. In terms of early experience, birds perhaps represent the mother's voice, the arrival of nurturance and hope to comfort the aggrieved, and also rebirth, which justifies death and transforms nothing into everything.

Psychoanalysts have noted various sources and derivatives of infantile experiences of absence, nothingness, and loss. Spitz and, in a radically different way, Bowlby,[2] emphasized the relational element of attachment and loss, the binding and breaking of an original object relation [46, 47]. Spitz used the term "anaclitic," ("leaning on," "clinging to," "dependent upon") to refer to a form of depression occurring in infancy which he believed resulted from a lack of actual physical contact between baby and caregiver [48]. In more recent discussions the early need for contact has been called "adhesive identification" by Bick and Meltzer, an early form of attachment and identification in which the infant presses against the mother, establishing skin contact [49]. Thus "nothing" implies lack of contact, isolation, and a vastness without the mothers' support, an element which is often feared in death.

Freud stressed the loss of narcissism and omnipotence as the major loss of childhood, viz. the loss of the primary illusion of power and self-sufficiency in an infant who is in fact highly dependent on a caretaker [33]. Thus, later on, the anticipation of death challenges our self-sufficiency and awakens primordial feelings of helplessness and dependency.

Winnicott, emphasizing the mother's provision of a facilitating and holding environment, noted the importance of absence *in time*: the delay between the infant's awareness of need and the arrival of the mother to meet that need [50]. If the delay is neither too short nor too long, but sensitively timed, then the infant develops a sense of "going on being," of the continuity of existence. Winnicott presciently observed that in the context of "good enough mothering" there also evolves a "potential space" wherein the infant begins to think, imagine, and sustain "illusion." Absence (the non-presence of the other and of our world as we know it) is an aspect of the unbearable death we all fear. Winnicott, unlike Freud, who emphasized that illusions were falsehoods, believed that illusion consisted of imaginative creations which sustained the child and contained the magical and metaphorical stimulation necessary for living. Illusions and creations fill the space of absence and provide a sense of intensified life, birth and creation as an antidote to death. Art provides an excellent example of such sustaining of illusion in its highest form.

Winnicott held that the infant's own breath (think of the biblical "breath of life") gave him or her a primal awareness of aliveness. He inferred from clinical material of adult patients that excessive or ill-timed maternal deprivations and intrusions may lead to a "deadness" in the form of depression, despair, and the withdrawal of the true self from interaction with others.

---

[2] Bowlby's perspective on loss and mourning in childhood utilizes the ethological perspective of animal behavior *in vivo*. His emphasis on the primacy of attachment and loss in child development has had a strong impact on the investigation of grief and bereavement, while not receiving the attention it deserves within psychoanalysis. The latter perhaps is an example of how the investment in a theory leads to ignoring data which may contradict the theory.

In Winnicott's view, suicide was sometimes the outcome of the self's feeling endangered by life itself and by interaction with others. In such instances, death paradoxically preserves the life of the self. Aliveness is the commitment of the self to "going on being," and the perception the deeper layers of connectedness of the mind and experience to the biological, the sensual and sensuous, the body. Death, on the other hand is the cessation of being and the experience of being dis-embodied, of having no body, of being cut off from ones living body.

Guntrip, a student of Winnicott, and participant in the ferment of British object relations theory, held that the most fundamental human anxiety was that of being annihilated as a self [34]. There is increasing evidence from psychoanalytically based infant research that the self is the fundamental, axiomatic basis of experience and interpersonal relatedness. It appears that newborns are endowed with a primordial "sense of self" whereby they initiate activity with significant others [5]. In this respect, the devastating "nothing" or "absence" is the loss or annihilation of the sense of self. (As mentioned earlier, Freud originally interpreted the fear of death as a repressed fear of castration, but it appears that "castration anxiety" is itself a derivative of an earlier and more primitive fear of annihilation.) As Beebe and Stern observed, such a devastating experience can occur when the mother averts her gaze as the infant attempts to establish eye (= I?) contact [51].

At the extreme, the broken "mirroring" causes the self to pine away, be consumed, and die in madness, as with Shakespeare's Lear and in Oscar Wilde's *A Picture of Dorian Grey*. Kohut referred to a loss of self "cohesion," and spoke of fragmentation of the self as the primal source of anxiety [3, p. 119]. The empathetic death of the self in response to a loss entails such "brokenness," as portrayed by a young woman borderline schizophrenic patient who, reflecting on the death of a beloved grandparent, drew a picture of a flower with a broken stem from which dripped a drop of blood. For her, the loss of her grandparent was experienced as an active attack on her own "budding" self and its fragile "stem."

To reiterate a point made previously, Grotstein, by analogy to the astronomical phenomenon, postulated a "black hole," a region of the mind in which aspects of self and mentation are absorbed into oblivion and are inaccessible to consciousness and experience [37]. The "gravitational" pull of the black hole is so strong that one something is pulled into it, it is trapped. Grotstein found that many patients report such a "black hole" experience in connection with clinical depression, psychotic regression, and borderline splitting. "Black holes" can also be found represented in the imagery and fantasy life of dreams, creative works of art and literature, and so on.

Individuals who have had spiritual transformations report going through a black hole "purgatory" or a "cloud of unknowing" [52]. An experience of entering a long tunnel is frequently reported in connection with near death experiences [53]. To some extent, Jesus' spiritual principle that we have to die in order to fully live implies experiencing the black hole of existence.

Grotstein drew a connection between the black hole and death. Grotstein, like the present author, critiqued the "death instinct" concept: death is not an instinct but a signifier, a linguistic sign or symbol, in the Lacanian sense [37]. "Death," in this view, is a component of experience and language that incorporates annihilation and the black hole, the ultimate absence and nothingness.

The astronomical black hole has an "event horizon," a point beyond which no contact can be made. Death also has an event horizon. Once someone dies, the living can have no "real time" contact with him or her. (While many people believe they can contact the dead through a medium or extrasensory perception, this contact is considered extraordinary and supernatural.) The terrible thing about the death of a loved one is that we can no longer touch them, talk to them, be with them. The status quo can never be restored. We obtain some solace from their "echo" coming to us in hallucination, visitation, memory, and their inspiring achievements and ideals. An "echo," important symbolically and developmentally on account of its relation to the mother's voice, is, however, a conjuring of her voice no longer present and its ethereal and incorporeal qualities are similar to that of a ghost. Death is an absence, but it always implies too an echo of a former presence.

Death as Oneness or Merger

Once, in the process of early development, a degree of differentiation and individuation has taken place, the self seems to experience the loss of its boundary as a "death." In some instances, this death of the differentiated self may in fact be toned with positive emotions, a reviving of a blissful symbiosis with the mother, as in an oceanic experience of oneness with the universe, God, or a cosmic force, or, sexually, in the moment of orgasm (un petit mort, "a little death"). Conversely, the fusion and loss of boundary may be dreaded, as in fusion or possession by a demoniacal object, psychotic regression and "re-engulfment," or feelings of helplessness related to a serious illness or severe loss.

The poet Anne Sexton expressed a death wish for a merger experience with the primal mother in a poem called "In Excelsis," written not long before this long-suffering woman committed suicide. Having portrayed the ocean as a primal "mother," with all her primitive power and moods, she writes:

> I wish to enter her like a dream,
> leaving my roots here on the beach
> like a pan of knives . . .
> and walk into the ocean,
> . . . where I would drink the moon
> and my clothes would slip away,
> and I would sink into the great mother arms I never had . . .
> [54, pp. 265-266].

Death is for Sexton a return to the mother ocean, providing release from her "knives," her anger and pain, her fate, and offering her a symbiotic maternal experience she felt was never hers.

In her work with AIDS patients, Elisabeth Kubler-Ross emphasized the importance of "letting go," both in terms of making peace with and detaching from significant others, and also surrendering to death [55]. Such surrender to the merger experience restores an early "presence," that of the mother and her love. It also signifies the "absence" of the boundary and of a separate but soothing contact or warmth. If the early parental object abandoned the infant at the point of symbiosis, the death merger will be filled with the horrifying abandonment. This experience would be akin to what one patient showed me in an art reproduction she brought to a session. The painting showed a large door behind which there was nothing but blackness. It is as if the perception of reality itself can become punctuated or even filled by death, nothingness, abandonment.

In the symbolic logic of numbers, or, as Bion called it, algebraic notation, if absence is the cipher, the individual is one, the mother-infant dyad is two, and the mother/father/child family structure is three, then the merger experience is infinity (or, temporally, eternity) [18]. Infinity and eternity may be experienced as either an empty, absurd vastness, as in some versions of existential philosophy, or as a metaphysical infinity of love, bliss, and interdependence, as in aspects of Christianity and Hinduism. Thus it is typical that during intense "fusion" or merger experiences, whether in meditation, sexual climax or orgasm, moments of "agape," I-Thou relatedness, near death experiences, and so on, the sense of the infinite, the eternal, the Creator and creation, may take place.

The absoluteness of death as both nothing and everything gives to death an awesomeness, especially in its anticipation as it closes in on our life projects. This gripping quality was expressed by Henry Wadsworth Longfellow in a poem called "Mezzo Cammin" as, in midlife, he contemplated the limitations of his past and future as he, "half-way up the hill" heard, "above me on the autumnal blast, the cataract of Death far thundering from the heights" [56].

Death as Place, Location, and Container

A paradoxical aspect of the preconception of death is its association with a designated place to which the dead go. The idea that death has a place or location (the "land of the dead," heaven and hell) may be accounted for by the nature of perceived reality and the principle of conservation of matter and energy: since *all* things have continuity and occupy space, the dead too must continue to exist some*where*.

In Piaget's stages of cognitive development, there is a time in the early sensorimotor phases when the infant discovers that things continue to exist even when they are not visible or present; prior to that, the infant thinks that when something is hidden from view, it no longer exists [57]. Similarly, in Mahler's stages of separation and individuation, the attainment of "emotional object constancy" signifies the child's ability to retain a "constant" image of mother even in her absence [35].

Such early acquired sense of the continuity in space of things as well as persons generalizes to our preconception of death: we feel that the dead exist somewhere. For the ancient Greeks, the dead departed to an underworld. In western religion, the dead go to purgatory, heaven, or hell. In Hinduism, the dead repeat the cycle of life and death by reincarnation in another form, or, interestingly, if self-realization is attained, the soul transcends ordinary space/time and merges with God and the universe.

In cultural and community relations, the notion of death as a place is related to the need to dispose of the dead in a place apart from that of the living, in order to prevent visitations by predators or infectious contamination of the living. In the motion picture, *Little Big Man*, the aged Indian retreats to an isolated mountain to die [58]. Elderly Eskimos may drift away on an iceberg when they are ready to die [59]. Such a place where people go to die is akin to the "sacred space," a place invested with special spiritual significance, where people may be "resurrected."

Death's connotation as a place or location endows it with the psychological function of a "container" for projective identifications. According to Melanie Klein (see [60]), the child "translocates" and projectively identifies aspects of its self and object world into the mother's "body" (more precisely, the fantasy elaboration of the mother's body). In effect, the infant has the "belief" that some of its own experience, contents, and processes are now "inside" the mother. The mother thus functions as a "container" for what the infant deposits in her. The infant later learns that it can rid or void unwanted content into father, siblings, and eventually the cultural matrix.

In a like manner, death provides a place where disavowed, unwanted, or desired but taboo aspects of self, object, and experience reside. Milton's *Paradise Lost* and Dante's *Inferno*, for example, depict with enormous power and detail many of the fearful and desired experiences supposed to reside in the realm of the dead, further suggesting a connection between death and the unconscious in which both form repositories of disavowed, prohibited experiences. Of course, these elaborate, uncanny, and profoundly disturbing scenarios are a catalogue of the fears, wishes, and symbolic experiences of the *living* projectively identified into the realm of the dead where they are sufficiently removed to be contained and experienced in dissociated and distorted forms which are safer to contemplate on account of their distance. Death is thus a harbour for many of the castaways of thought.

In such a way, the dying carry with them the "badness" of the self and the group, so that there is a connection between the dead and the scapegoat. The scapegoat is the punishment emissary who contains the badness of the social group and is sent to the wilderness with the shame and guilt of the group. Perrera points out that, in the wilderness, the mythic scapegoat finds another god to the one worshipped by the group, and so is not entirely without redemption [61]. Similarly to the scapegoat complex, much of the shame and guilt we feel around death and dying results from our own and the group's "badness," which has been projected for containment into the dying and deceased person. There then follows the further defense of the idealization of the deceased, which further seals off the badness from contaminating the living. For example,

> A patient who had for years experienced anger and rage towards his father for abandoning him when he, the patient, was a youth, only to return and then to abandon him again by dying, had a severe anxiety attack upon his father's death. Not long after his father died, he was often "certain" he saw him on the street or coming around a corner. The patient's own anger and guilt, projected into his father as the latter was dying, came back to haunt him as a potential retribution in the form of his father reappearing. That the father was thought of as so powerful in death was indeed a denial of the father's actual fear, helplessness, and weakness during a prolonged terminal illness. At the same time, the patient overidealized the therapist as a "good father" as a way of preserving the wished-for love between his father and himself. The deceased father contained the badness, while the therapist retained the goodness. This was how the patient, in light of his anger at his father, managed his grief in its early stages.

Mourning helps us to bury not only the deceased, but also a part of our own "badness" which we project into them in death.

Death is all at once a container of zero, finite, and infinite dimensionality! In the null, zero dimension, death is the black hole, absence of all sensation, nothing, the corresponding symptom of which is claustrophobia. This "minimalist" spatial representation of death leads in part to the burial of the dead in tombs, crypts, caskets which represent a narcissistic preservation of the self with the minimal object relations of whatever symbolic objects are placed there. A tomb is a "way station" to the other world. It is a confining narrow space something like a womb and birth canal. Its narrowness acknowledges the shrinking of space in the dying process (cf. the near-death "tunnel" experience described earlier).

Death as a finite dimensional container seems to have manifold connotations and possibilities regarding death as human existence beyond "this mortal coil," what Hamlet means when he says, "To die, perchance to *dream*" (italics mine/VLS; again the connection between death and the unconscious). First of all, death is an incorporation of the parental imagos, becoming like them a container of the child's dialectical opposition of omnipotence versus helplessness. In addition, death is a container for the unwanted, abandoned, lost, and mourned persons and aspects of our lives. In that respect, from the standpoint of Melanie Klein's theory, death represents a breast and a womb wherein are housed past, projected, and discarded object relations. (Consider the object relation quality of "whiteness" of milk, ghosts, and dead bodies: ghosts are often white, like milk and embalmed persons who are "white as a sheet," often at first covered by a sheet.) Indeed, if we extend this idea through the child's development, death as a container may at various times connote aspects of the various erogenous zones and psychosexual phases: oral, anal, phallic. In other words, as the child explores the intimate body environment, he or she endows all experiences and parts of body and self with the significance of both life and death.

> For example, a suicidal adolescent girl sought death (fortunately without success) through a valium overdose. She perceived dying as a way of achieving reunion with her deceased grandparents who had given her, in sharp contrast to her profoundly distressing adolescent upheaval, a warm, caring experience.
>
> As another example, the imagos of the so-called "vagina dentata" as well as "castration anxiety" suggest that the death container is sometimes housed in the genitals, represented by the scythe of the "grim reaper." This connection of death with the genitals further interrelates death with its opposites, copulation and birth.

Death can powerfully emerge as a container of infinite dimensionality [50]. In this context of death as the infinite eternal is to be found the messages of salvation of Jesus and other prophets. Death is everything that has not been possible in this earthly, bodily, temporal, spatial prison. It is expansiveness, eternity, oneness with God. Thus, people in deep meditation may have encounters with death. The infinity of death relates to the infinity of the unconscious, its "symmetrical logic" [44], which encompasses all possibilities as distinct from the confining "either/or" of the superego and the reality principle. The death container is the universe, the cosmos. In psychosis, the remnants of object relations destroyed in the psychotic regression and by "attacks on linking" are projected into this vastness experienced as cold and empty. On the creative side, the infinitude of the death container may be a vehicle for self-transformation, revolution, and artistic and scientific productions. In the infinite moment, a door is open to powerful, innovative change.

The relationship between death and containment is reciprocal: death is both container and contained, and in this respect is a paradoxical, non-commonsensical, container object like the Mobius Strip (a strip of paper fastened together with one twist which makes its two sides one). Death (eventually) contains everything or nearly everything, like a gigantic suction machine. To be assimilated, death itself must be contained, by good, supportive, nurturing objects, by ideas and meaning, by comfort and solace. Containing death is, of course, one of the primary functions of religion.

Death as Decay, Entropy, the Abhorrent,
the Unclean, the Diseased

Finally, and what is conspicuously repugnant in our everyday conceptions of death and why conversation about death is so typically avoided, because it evokes disgust, is the visible way in which death and dying represent a biological decay process, the outflow and loss of life, *rigor mortis*, the entropic tendency toward randomness which Freud emphasized in *Beyond the Pleasure Principle*. Death and dying remind us of the decaying insides of our body. Death signifies and is signified by violence to the body, the amorphousness of the body, and the rotting of the body.

Becker relates bodily death and decay to the human's awareness of his/her "creatureliness," being housed in a body which is frail and time limited [8, pp. 25-30]. The decay "products" of the dead are associated with urine and feces. (According to Catholic liturgy, "Entretat faeces et urinas, nascimur"; we are born between urine and feces.) We are endowed, as Becker says, with the potential to be perfect, omnipotent, divine, but for our anal "hole" which is a constant reminder of our imperfect, mortal nature [8, pp. 30-34].

Thomas Mann, in *The Magic Mountain* and in *Death in Venice*, struggled with the implications of death and decay for the personal quest and for art. Hans Castorp, suffering from tuberculosis, undergoes a spiritual transformation in a sanitorium high in the Alps. In *Death in Venice*, Gustav Aschenbach experiences the irony of death via the plague in Venice, where he sojourns for the purposes of rest and revival of the spirit. His homosexually tinged fascination with the beautiful adolescent boy, Tadzio, who symbolizes aesthetic beauty and is a mirror for the artist's self, is also colored with the pain of the "death" which pervades the artist's life work.

To return briefly to the impact of European culture on Freud, the intensification of the awareness of death at the end of the nineteenth and in the early decades of the twentieth century seems to have in part resulted from the deconstruction of modernity with its illusions of perfection, continuity, coherence, and meaning [62]. Death appears to be the ultimate deconstructionist.

To review, I have suggested that, instead of regarding death as a biological instinct, as Freud had done, a deeper and richer understanding of the dynamics of death awareness in its relation to mental development and the unconscious may be gained by regarding death as a set of preconceptions, i.e., predispositions to encode and structure incohate images and thoughts into ideation about death and dying. The four central aspects of death as preconception are posited here as absence, merger, place/containment, and decay/entropy. Death both organizes and is organized by these basic thought dispositions, which emerge in infancy and childhood and evolve throughout the life cycle. Death imparts special qualities to these dispositions and, in turn our ideas about death are conditioned in these specific ways. In addition, preconceptions may play an important role in helping us to anticipate and prepare for actual death. At the same time, preconceptions, like myths, hover somewhere in the space between truth and illusion, and, as Bion emphasized so often, we must be prepared to find out something entirely unexpected and new. We must face death with tolerance for what is unknown and mysterious in order that we may learn from and be transformed by our mortality. Such an ultimate ridding of the mind of preconceptions is perhaps related to the Zen Buddhist notion of "no mind."

DEATH AND THE QUEST FOR KNOWLEDGE: THE "EPISTEMOPHILIC INSTINCT"

In psychoanalysis, Thanatos and Eros together form the basis of the "matrix of the mind" [41]. Death and sexuality are vast and universal preconceptions which shape and drive all mentation, all ideation. Death and sexuality condition the very nature of thought, as well as our ideas about ideas, what philosophers call epistemology, the theory of knowledge.

Bion's perspective, elaborated above, wherein we understand death to be a "preconception," itself presupposes a theory of knowledge which is structuralist and "idealist" in nature and related to the Kantian philosophy of the "thing-in-itself" which is filtered through a perceptual/cognitive "net" in order thus to be thought about. As Bion says, until someone thinks the thought, it remains a "thought without a thinker," or, as Bollas has called it, the "unthought known" [63].

Indeed, there is a profound inseparability between death and such idealist knowledge, because it is death itself which, by its implication of constituting something unknowable and wholly other, leads to a philosophy in which there is a world beyond appearances (Plato), a world of pure ideas (Hegel), a world of ideas in the mind of God (Berkeley), a world of demonstrable truths and "things in themselves" (Kant). (See Bertrand Russell's classic *A History of Western Philosophy*, for a readable, if somewhat biased, discussion of the theories of these and other "epistemologists" [64].)

Conversely, theories of knowledge which do *not* advocate or postulate pregiven or innate ideas, for instance, empiricism (Locke, Hume), positivism (Russell, and in a different vein, Wittgenstein and the "Vienna Circle" of philosophers), and, more recently, and in a radically different perspective from either empiricism or positivism, deconstructionism [65], attribute the totality of human knowledge to experience and deny that which lies outside of experience, thereby also excluding from consideration the intangible, pre-given, intuitive elements of death, "intimations of mortality."

In retrospect, we can say that Freud was grounded philosophically in the empiricist view, put forth by his scientific mentors [66]. Yet Freud's empirical understanding of the unconscious mind is paradoxically imbued with his preoccupation with the uncanny and with the "unthought known." These mysterious elements were alien to Freud's conscious intent, yet they penetrated and influenced his thinking.

Melanie Klein gave primary importance in the motivational hierarchy to the child's curiosity drive, which she called the "epistemophilic instinct," literally the "instinct of the love of knowledge" [67]. For Ms. Klein, not only does each child have an innate desire to know, but he or she is in fact a "mini-philosopher" and is possessed of an implicit—if primitive—theory of knowledge, an epistemology. For example, since their early cosmos consists of the body, the family, and the home, children in their early "investigations" want to know, among other things, what mother and father do in the bedroom, and where babies come from. Children find answers in their own imagination, as well as in fairy tales and folklore. These sources often seem to provide better—certainly more believable—explanations than what their parents tell them!

Pursuing the matter more deeply, children find that most important, desired, and feared form of knowledge, the forbidden kind, is to be found in cavities such as the vagina (Pandora's Box), or something eaten, as in the biblical Adam and Eve biting into the forbidden fruit. Such "theories of knowledge" become more elaborate, abstracted, and "reality oriented" as children mature, but the infantile roots are always present in adult mentation.

The earliest human curiosity is about the body, for as Klein said, "The child is an intensely embodied person" [68]. She noted that the external world and the interpersonal milieu which subsequently become the center of the child's interest, unconsciously symbolizes the body.

Two of the most "embodied" and puzzling foci of interest for the child, as for all ages, are of course sexuality and death. Thus, the search for knowledge becomes intertwined with bodily, erotic, and "thanatological" interests.

Curiosity and the desire to have explanations lead the child to form mental linkages, which Bion termed L, H, and K links, mental connections formed via Love, Hate, and the quest for Knowledge respectively [69]. These early linkages and explanations are impregnated with magical thinking, illusion, and what Jung called the "numinous," i.e., the supernatural, mysterious, divine. Such linkages in effect form the child's earliest philosophical, scientific, and theological systems.

Freud and most analysts have given only limited attention to their patients' curiosity about death, simplistically viewing such curiosity as a derivative of sexual interest. Curiosity appears to be an inherent motivating force of its own. The present chapter articulates a view that death, like sexuality, is of central import in the child's world, and that the child strives to assess its meaning and significance. The following is a clinical example from an adult psychotherapy patient of dreams and recollections reflecting childhood curiosity about death:

> Carla (pseudonym) came to therapy with unresolved mourning of the loss of her father, a grief which had generalized to several other personages: her

husband (from whom she was divorced), her lover (she impulsively ended the relationship after two years), and her brother (whom she nursed and cared for throughout his protracted and ultimately terminal illness).

Several weeks into treatment, Carla recalled, from early childhood, a memory of discovering a dead bird in her backyard, an experience which shaped her later mental development. Important for the patient's interest in death and her subsequent difficulties, she remembered that her mother deceived her about it. (The patient's recollection was that her mother lied about what kind of bird it was rather than about its being dead.) This experience set the stage for later difficulties regarding death, separation, and loss.

In a subsequent session, Carla associated the bird to her father's pet parakeet, which for her father symbolized hope and life, and which eventually flew away (separation, loss, loss of hope).

Carla said that her father was emotionally dead in the midst of life, having become severely depressed and incapacitated as a result of a war induced post-traumatic stress syndrome. She recalled that when he finally died of a heart attack, she could not fully mourn, but instead suppressed her anger, guilt, and grief for many years. The disruption of Carla's grief was attributed not only to intense guilt surrounding her incestuous and aggressive feelings toward him, but also because she had already internalized his living death as well as his absence during much of her childhood.

In treatment, Carla, related a dream in which:

> I was renting a room. When I walked in, the room was filled with all kinds of bird cages and multi-colored parakeets. Some were scraggly, molting, pecking each other, it was too much! I said to the landlord, "I like the room, with its big walk-in closet, but I can't deal with these birds." I was left with this dilemma: it's difficult to live with some of these birds.

Renting the room very likely symbolizes being in psychotherapy, and, in the transference, the landlord is the therapist. The obvious sexual and Oedipal implications of a dream in which the birds represent the male genitals are evident from the vulgarism of the penis as a "bird" and a "pecker." Unconscious phantasies of courtship, copulation, and birth are suggested by birds who are molting and pecking at each other. Indeed, as suggested by the quality of the dream (the overwhelming multiplicity of birds and the intense activity), the patient was in fact at times overwhelmed and flooded by real and imagined sexual/romantic overtures of men. We can also suppose that the "closet" is the "primal scene" setting, the "closeted" intercourse of mother and father, and perhaps the patient herself coming "out of the closet" sexually.

From another perspective, one can see the connection of the birds to the dead bird of childhood, as well as the relationship between the father's pet parakeet and his life before the War. The patient was told by family members that her father was a vital, exciting, vibrant person prior to his war trauma. Such associative links lead us to believe that the birds in the dream also represent the father's emotional dying, fears of which are now overwhelming the patient and encroaching on her "life space." In this motif, the closet represents the father's coffin, which is more spacious and peaceful than the space left for the patient in her current life, in which she constantly experiences the intrusion of incessant reminders of loss, grief, and death.

Regarding Carla's implicit theory of knowledge, we can further hypothesize that the birds represent repetitive obsessional ideas (of sex, of the father, of death). These ideas emerged in treatment and were bursting out of containment (the cages). The patients' theory of knowledge, deriving from her childhood experience, is that the pieces ought to fit together in a logical system (L, H, K links), but these linkages have been disrupted [70], partly because of the mother's lie, and so both life and death continually burst out of containment. In this respect, the Hegelian syntheses of thesis and antithesis cannot be formed in this patient's epistemology, and her view of reality is very "post-modern" in that it contains unresolvable paradoxes and contradictions. The patient did indeed have great difficulty forming a coherent picture of herself and her world.

The dead bird cage in Carla's childhood memory is a messenger of knowledge who becomes the mother's prey. The bird died, and then the mother lied, killing the knowledge, and the patient, years later, "knows but does not know," and feels overwhelmed by the return of repressed awareness. The childhood experience also presaged and conditioned a subsequent preoccupation with death and loss and an intense need to nurture her dying brother, her father, and her husband.

Thus, death, like sexuality, is an object of the desire to know. Within Lacan's "symbolic order" [14, pp. 103-107], death, like sexuality becomes absorbed in "word presentations." Words, language, social rules and boundaries, which constitute the symbolic order, are impregnated with death and dying. Objects can "die," family and kinship ties can "die," relationships can "die," parts of the past, parts of the self can "die." Therefore, our knowledge of all things, living and dying, animate and inanimate, is impregnated with death, just as Freud had articulated the pervasiveness of sexuality in human affairs.

DEATH, THE SELF, AND NARCISSISM

As a result the work of Kohut and others, the nature and dynamics of the self has become a focus of interest in psychoanalysis. The relationship between death and the self is "reflected" (pun fully intended) in the myth of Narcissus, who pined, faded away, and was transformed into a flower when he became infatuated with his mirror image in a pool of water. There are two sides to this myth: one is that vanity and self-love are ignorant and dangerous; the other, that directly beholding the shortcomings of the self is unbearable. We must first see "as through a glass darkly," and only then, "face to face." Indeed the very process of psychotherapy is intended to slow the process of self-knowing down so that we may see ourselves through the darkened glass of interpretation in a way that prevents an emotional catastrophe. A far more tragic figure than Narcissus, Oedipus, blinded himself as the catastrophic result of too direct an apprehension of himself.

In contrast with Oedipus, whose self-blinding led to great *in*-sight, Narcissus dies on seeing his image without seeing the deeper truth: that it is death and dying which shows us who we are, that death is a true mirror of the self. Death gives us the humility and finality to see our creatureliness, our temporality, our vanity and grandiosity, our unconscious motivations.

The power of death in transforming our lives poses a great mystery, yet it is a mystery which, in our insatiable Faustian curiosity, we persistently strive to understand, even if, like Sisyphus, our curiosity becomes a stone which rolls down the hill every time we push it to the top. Death is a puzzle without a solution.

There are two foundations for the epistemic and obsessional power of death in life. The first is a logical paradox: the self can conceive of the death of the objectified "other," but it cannot conceive of itself in death because in its own death it would not be present as an observer to perceive and conceive death. (Thus, in psychotic patients, the "death" of the *self* which occurs in the decompensation process is experienced as "world destruction fantasies," i.e., the destruction of external *objects*, rather than the death of self as such.)

A further reason for the power of death is the reflexive nature of the self. Early in its development, the self objectifies and externalizes itself and enters into dialogue with itself. Lacan depicted the emergence of the reflexive self in the *stade du miroir*, the "mirror stage" [14, pp. 62-66], the time when the child recognizes his own image in the mirror, establishing an alienated double. Only through the mirror image can the self can then achieve the subject-object duality which is essential to all language. Yet this very duality sets up the condition for the self's alienation from itself.

Internalizing the mirror image permits the self to be in dialogue with itself. At this point the self can love itself. Only when the self can love itself can it mourn its own loss. The self has to make of itself an image, a "self-representation" in order to grieve for itself. Therefore, the reflexive self is a precondition for the anticipation and mourning of one's own death. Again, this possibility of mourning is infused with narcissism, but a narcissism whose power has been broken by loss.

The narcissistic personality, on the other hand, transforms the wish for immortality into hallucinated "reality" by virtue of a delusion of invulnerability consonant with an omnipotent and vain self-image. The narcissist cannot mourn because loss is not consonant with the vanity of the self. If the narcissist is faced with real loss, he or she merely reassures himself by a look in the mirror of adulation, beauty, fantasy. However, it is inevitable that the illusion breaks down, leading to fragmentation of the self. Pathologically distorted narcissism is thus death in life, the price of vanity, and the denial of death as experience, the "negative hallucination" of death.

A NOTE ABOUT DEATH AND THE FORMATION OF THE UNCONSCIOUS

I have by the tenor of my arguments tried to suggest that death is a fundamental aspect of the unconscious mind. The awareness of death is omnipresent and hovers around us: death informs all aspects of our being. Georg Groddeck, a contemporary of Freud who also articulated a view of unconscious motivation, said, "We are lived by the It" [21, p. 410]. One could say, "We are lived by our death."

The convergence of death and the unconscious may be made clear by the following argument. For something to be remembered it first has to "die" (be repressed) into the unconscious. The unconscious is filled and saturated with "dead" objects and experiences (repressed memories). However, the unconscious also denies death and gives the appearance of an immortal narcissism and gratification of desire. This is the side of the unconscious which Freud so insightfully conceptualized as a wish-fulfilling id. He then incorporated death in the superego, with its prohibitive shame and guilt. However, death is prior to the formation of the superego, as there can be no life without death. Indeed, death is unconscious itself, and once again we are faced with the fact that consciousness and life are the true mysteries, the true miracles. Death and the unconscious, despite their fascination for modern minds, are banal. Consciousness, the "tip of the iceberg," is awesome. As the mathematician and philosopher Henri Poincare (undated reference) said, "Thought is only a flash between two long nights, but this flash is everything" [71].

It is in this last sense that we might speak of death as the omnipresence of unconsciousness hovering around the conscious mind. It is this condition which makes life sometimes appear absurd and which makes every man and woman very much the fool. At the limit of experience, *the impossibility, negation, and denial of the death of the subject is coequivalent with the development of the unconscious, with the loss and mourning of the memory trace itself.*

REVIEW AND POSTSCRIPT

At the end of our journey, we return to the beginning to affirm that there is something "beyond the pleasure principle" which is present in the unconscious. Following Derrida, this "something" is the "trace" of death which pervades yet is beyond experience [63, pp. 196-231]. By studying the varied manifestations of death as potentially transformative sets [44] of preconceptions, we are in a position to enhance the ways in which we achieve emotional growth and renewed hope within the mourning process and the awareness of mortality.

My venue in this chapter has been to explore a broadened psychoanalytic investigation of the role of death and dying in human development and unconscious processes. The ideological key which I have invoked to open this door is a shift from a "death instinct" to a "death preconception" or an intimation of mortality which is present in every human being from the time of birth. I have cited four preconceptions: nothingness, merger, place, and decay which pervade our thoughts about death and dying.

In my view, for the present at least, we should be less concerned about exact theoretical formulations and more to seek ways in which the range of psychological processes surrounding death and dying can be explored. With the much needed tolerance for alternative schools of thought which Wallerstein termed "psychoanalytic pluralism," we should be able to allow for multiple conceptual schema for grasping the role of death in the mental life [72]. Grief, bereavement, and loss is certainly one area in need of further formulation, but, as I have suggested, the psychology of death has implications for emotional development as a whole and especially for the theory of knowledge and the development of mind. This is a largely uncharted territory.

Starting points to entering this territory may reside in object relations theory as well as the complementary study of narcissism and the self. It is no accident that Freud's seminal essay on object relations was "Mourning and Melancholia," where he said, with the beauty of literary expression which won him the Goethe Award for Literature [21, pp. 571-572], "The shadow of the object fell upon the ego" [32]. This remarkable phrase, capturing the powerful impact of early relationships on the emerging self, echoes in its tone and image the psalmist's words, "Nay, though I walk through the Valley of the Shadow of Death, I will fear no evil." (Similarly, Jung had used the image of the "shadow" to depict the darker and split off realms of the self.) The shadow of the object, like the shadow cast by light over the human form, is both an image of the self and a separate entity, similar to and different from a mirror image. The shadow object or shadow *of the* object reminds us of our death. Thus, object relations theory and death came together for Freud in "Mourning and Melancholia," and we may perhaps take a cue from him in pursuing the matter further.

To conclude, when a person is dying (and to some extent each of us is ever and always in that condition), (s)he faces the duality that (s)he a) will bring to the door of death all the baggage of his or her life (the ego investments, object relations, and anxieties which psychoanalysis has so assiduously studied), and b) must face the impelling necessity yield all of that in the phrase of grief and loss which Kubler-Ross termed "acceptance" [73, pp. 112-137]. When the inevitability of one's own death is faced, nothing else is important, yet everything is of enormous importance, and we are faced with the need to see our lives in a radically different light. It is this crucial psychology of emptying and filling, and of inner transformation, which a study of the relationship between death awareness and the unconscious can help to elucidate.

REFERENCES

1. D. Thomas (1953), *Collected Poems*, New Directions, paperbound, New York, 1971.
2. P. L. Giovacchini (ed.), *Tactics and Techniques in Psychoanalytic Therapy III: The Implications of Winnicott's Contributions*, Aronson, Northvale, 1990.
3. H. Kohut, *Analysis of the Self*, International Universities Press, New York, 1971.
4. H. Kohut, *Restoration of the Self*, International Universities Press, New York, 1977.
5. D. Stern, *The Interpersonal World of the Infant*, Basic Books, New York, 1984.
6. W. W. Meissner, *Psychoanalysis and Religious Experience*, Yale University Press, New Haven, 1984.
7. W. W. Meissner, *Life and Faith: Psychological Perspectives on Religious Experience*, Georgetown University Press, Washington, D.C., 1987.
8. E. Becker, *The Denial of Death*, The Free Press, New York, 1973.
9. N. O. Brown, *Life Against Death*, Viking, New York, 1959.
10. K. R. Eissler, *The Psychiatrist and the Dying Patient*, International Universities Press, New York, 1955.
11. E. Jacques, Death and the Mid-life Crisis, in *Death: Interpretations*, M. M. Ruitenbeek (ed.), Delta, New York, 1969.
12. K. Menninger (1938), *Man Against Himself*, Republished in paperback, Harcourt, Brace, and World, New York, 1962.
13. G. Zilboorg, Fear of Death, *Psychoanalytic Quarterly, 12*, pp. 465-575, 1943.
14. M. Sarup, *Jacques Lacan*, University of Toronto Press, Toronto, 1992.
15. C. Levi-Strauss, The Structural Study of Myth, in *The Structuralists from Marx to Levi-Strauss*, R. De George and F. De George (eds.), Anchor, New York, pp. 169-193, 1972.
16. P. Grosskurth, *Melanie Klein: Her World and Her Work*, Knopf, New York, 1986.
17. J. S. Grotstein (ed.), *Do I Dare Disturb the Universe: A Memorial to Wilfred Bion*, Maresfield Reprints, London, 1983.
18. W. R. Bion, *Two Papers: The Grid and Caesura*, Imago Editora, Rio de Janeiro, 1977.
19. H. Segal, *Melanie Klein*, Viking, New York, 1979.
20. C. Lasch, *The Culture of Narcissism*, Norton, New York, 1978.
21. P. Gay, *Freud: A Life for Our Time*, Norton, New York, 1988.
22. S. Freud (1900), *The Interpretation of Dreams*, Paperback Edition of the Strachey translation, Avon, New York, 1965.
23. J. M. Masson (ed. and trans.), *The Complete Letters of Sigmund Freud to Wilhelm Fleiss 1887-1904*, Belknap Press of Harvard University Press, Cambridge, 1985.
24. S. Freud, Analysis of a Phobia in a Five-year-old Boy, *The Standard Edition of the Complete Psychological Works of Sigmund Freud, 10*, Hogarth, London, pp. 3-152, 1909.
25. C. Bernheimer and C. Kahane (eds.), *In Dora's Case: Freud, Hysteria, Feminism*, Columbia, New York, 1985.
26. E. E. Garcia, A New Look at Gustav Mahler's Fateful Encounter with Sigmund Freud, *Journal of the Conductors' Guild, 12*, pp. 1-2, 16-30, 1991.
27. M. Graves, Personal communication, 1993.
28. F. Graziano, *Georg Trakl: A Profile*, Logbridge-Rhodes, Durango, 1983.

29. S. Freud, Beyond the Pleasure Principle, *The Standard Edition of the Complete Psychological Works of Sigmund Freud, 18*, Hogarth, London, pp. 3-66, 1920.

30. F. Sulloway, *Freud: Biologist of the Mind*, Basic Books, New York, 1979.

31. A. Toynbee, *Life After Death*, Weiderfelds and Nicolson, London, 1976.

32. S. Freud, Mourning and Melancholia, *The Standard Edition of the Complete Psychological Works of Sigmund Freud, 14*, Hogarth, London, pp. 237-260, 1917.

33. S. Freud, On Narcissism, *The Standard Edition of the Complete Psychological Works of Sigmund Freud, 14*, Hogarth, London, pp. 67-104, 1914.

34. H. Guntrip, *Object Relations and the Self*, International Universities Press, New York, 1969.

35. M. S. Mahler, F. Pine, and A. Bergmann, *The Psychological Birth of the Human Infant*, Basic Books, New York, 1975.

36. L. Shengold, *"Father, Don't You See I'm Burning?"* Yale, New Haven, 1991.

37. J. S. Grotstein, The "Black Hole" as the Basic Psychotic Experience: Some Newer Psychoanalytic and Neuroscience Perspectives on Psychosis, *Journal of the American Academy of Psychoanalysis, 18*:1, pp. 29-46, 1990.

38. W. Bion, *Experiences in Groups*, Basic Books, New York, 1959.

39. W. R. Bion, *Seven Servants—Four Works by W. R. Bion*, Aronson, New York, 1977.

40. J. S. Grotstein, Inner Space: Its Dimensions and Coordinates, *International Journal of Psychoanalysis, 59*, Part I, pp. 55-61, 1978.

41. T. Ogden, *The Matrix of the Mind*, Aronson, Northvale, New Jersey, 1990.

42. T. Williams, *Cat on a Hot Tin Roof*, New Directions, New York, 1992.

43. D. Sylvester, *Magritte: The Silence of the World*, Abrams, New York, 1992.

44. I. Matte-Blanco, *The Unconscious as Infinite Sets*, Duckworth, London, 1975.

45. J. Wright, *Above the River: The Complete Poems*, Farrar, Straus, and Giroux, New York, 1990.

46. J. Bowlby, *Attachment and Loss*, Basic Books, New York, 1969.

47. J. Bowlby, *The Making and Breaking of Affectional Bonds*, Tavistock, London, 1979.

48. R. Spitz, Anaclitic Depression, *The Psychoanalytic Study of the Child, 2*, pp. 213-242, 1946.

49. E. Bick, The Experience of the Skin in Early Object Relations, *International Journal of Psychoanalysis, 49*, pp. 484-456, 1968.

50. D. W. Winnicott, *Maturational Processes and the Facilitating Environment*, International Universities Press, New York, 1965.

51. B. Beebe and D. Stern, Engagement-disengagement and Early Object Experiences, in *Communicative Structures and Psychic Structures*, M. Freedman and S. Grand (eds.), Plenum, New York, pp. 33-55, 1977.

52. W. James (1902), *The Varieties of Religious Experience*, Republished, Mentor, New York, 1958.

53. S. J. Blackmore and T. S. Troscianko, The Physiology of the Tunnel, *Journal of Near-Death Studies, 8*:1, pp. 15-28, 1989.

54. D. W. Middlebrook and D. H. George (eds.), *Selected Poems of Anne Sexton*, Houghton Mifflin, New York, 1988.

55. E. Kubler-Ross, *AIDS: The Ultimate Challenge*, Collier, New York, 1989.

56. H. W. Longfellow, *Favorite Poems: The Complete Poetical Works of Henry Wadsworth Longfellow*, Dover, New York, 1992.

57. M. A. Boden, *Jean Piaget*, Penguin, New York, 1980.
58. A. Penn (Dir.), *Little Big Man*, Film, Hiller Productions, 1971.
59. V. Morford, Personal communication, 1970.
60. J. S. Grotstein, *Splitting and Projective Identification*, Aronson, New York, 1981.
61. S. B. Perera, *The Scapegoat Complex: Toward a Mythology of Shadow and Guilt*, Inner City Books, Toronto, 1986.
62. P. M. Rosenau, *Post-Modernism and the Social Sciences: Insights, Inroads, and Intrusions*, Princeton University Press, Princeton, 1992.
63. C. Bollas, *The Shadow of the Object*, Columbia University Press, 1987.
64. B. Russell (1945), *A History of Western Civilization*, Simon and Schuster, New York, reprinted 1972.
65. J. Derrida, *Writing and Difference*, University of Chicago Press, Chicago, 1978.
66. P. Amacher, Freud's Neurological Education and Its Influence on Psychoanalytic Theory, *Psychological Issues, 4*, 4, Monograph 16, International Universities Press, New York, 1965.
67. M. Klein, Early Analysis, in *Love, Guilt, and Reparation and Other Works: 1921-1945*, M. Klein, Delta, New York, pp. 77-106, 1977.
68. H. Guntrip, *Personality Structure and Human Interaction*, International Universities Press, New York, 1961.
69. W. Bion, *Learning from Experience*, William Heinemann, London, Second reprinting, 1988, Maresfield Reprints, London, 1962.
70. W. R. Bion, Attacks on Linking, *International Journal of Psycho-Analysis, 40*, pp. 308-315, Republished in W. R. Bion (1967), *Second Thoughts*, William Heinemann, London, 1959.
71. H. Poincare, *Science and Method*, Dover, New York, n.d.
72. R. S. Wallerstein, *The Common Ground of Psychoanalysis*, Jason Aronson, Northvale, New Jersey, 1992.
73. E. Kubler-Ross (1969), *On Death and Dying*, Macmillan, paperback edition, New York, 1972.

CHAPTER 11

Children, Death, and Fairy Tales

Elizabeth P. Lamers

"Children, Death and Fairy Tales" examines the evolution and transformation of themes relating to death and dying in children's literature, using illuminating parallels from historical demographics of mortality and the development of housing. The classic fairy tale "Little Red Riding Hood" is used to draw these trends together.

HISTORICAL BACKGROUND

There is a history behind each of the familiar stories that parents read at their children's bedsides. Many of what have now become common fairy tales had their origin in an oral tradition intended as adult entertainment, replete with ribald humor and sensational events. As these tales began to be transcribed and considered more specifically as material intended for children, they began to contain incidents and behavior that reflected the customs of the place and period in which they were written down and that were intended to provide children with a moral education. Especially in the earliest versions, death had a place in children's stories because of its ubiquity and drama. There have been significant transformations to fairy tales, and to the content of children's stories in general, since a literature for children first appeared. Until recently, topics that have come to be considered disturbing to young people, concerning issues that adults would wish to protect them from, have been diluted, softened, and removed from the literature for children. In our modern generations, children have been insulated from an awareness of mortality.

Particularly in the last hundred years, a significant movement away from issues of morality and mortality has taken place. This has reflected the tremendous changes in attitudes concerning children and death over the last century. These changes have coincided with the shifting of the demographics of death in this time period and with the changing of attitudes toward children and their upbringing.

Up to the end of the nineteenth century, the highest mortality rate was to be found in children under the age of fifteen; today the highest rate is found in adults of far more advanced years. In the past, children were exposed to dying because it occurred almost exclusively at home after a short illness; death now occurs almost exclusively in some sort of health care institution following a prolonged illness. Although in recent years hospice programs have sought to return dying to the home, the majority of elderly persons still die either in a rest home or a hospital. As a result, children and even young adults today are commonly separated from the reality of death [1]. This isolation is reinforced by a scarcity of material that would introduce children to the universal experiences of dying and death.

The changing composition and structure of the modern family has also had an isolating effect on the young person's awareness of mortality. At the end of the last century, it was common for children to grow up as a member of an extended family, consisting of parents, grandparents, aunts and uncles, who all lived in the same rural area. A child today is more likely a member of a "nuclear" or one parent family, living in an urban area, often separated from relatives by hundreds of miles. Children in rural areas once were exposed to dying and death in their families, in their communities, and among farm animals. They had repeated opportunities to be close to death, to ask questions about death, and to participate in healing religious and social bereavement ceremonies and rituals.

While once the loss of a relative was an occasion for ceremonies that emphasized and reinforced family coherence, today the death of a relative, especially an elderly or distant one, may pass with little or no observance. Many parents have come to believe that children should be shielded from dying and the facts of death, and it is common today for children not to attend funeral services [2].

Although children may be exposed to literally hundreds of deaths in television programs and cartoons, these are a different kind of death, typically of a "bad" person, who because of some evil actions "deserved" to die. Children's cartoons consistently present a distorted view of mortality to children, even fostering the especially erroneous conclusion that death is somehow "reversible." With little contradiction, beliefs like these can continue to influence and pervade perceptions of death [2]. They come to stand in place of substantial experiences with dying and death, giving rise to difficulties and misunderstandings in later years when the child, as an adult, has real experiences with mortality. Beliefs like these have been fostered by the isolation of the child from the experience of death as a part of life, an isolation that can be traced in the transformation that has occurred to the stories and fairy tales that have been read to children since such tales first appeared in written form in the early 1700s.

BOOKS ABOUT DEATH FOR CHILDREN

The removal and glossing over of incidents of dying and death from material that children are exposed to has been occurring regularly since about the 1920s. At the same time religion was being removed from school books. It is only in the last twenty years that this tendency has begun to be reversed, and children's books now often contain topics that were previously taboo, including feelings, divorce, sex, and even death. Religion is still taboo in school books.

From the early 1800s until the 1920s, American children were commonly taught to read with a series of textbooks, such as those by Lyman Cobb, Worcester, Town, Russell, Swan or McGuffey. In *McGuffey's Eclectic Readers*, the subject of many of the selections and poems was the death of a mother or child [3]. These deaths were typically presented as a tragic but an inevitable part of life. The manner in which death was portrayed can be found in such representative examples as William Wordsworth's poem "We Are Seven," in which a little girl describes her family as having seven children, even though two are dead and buried in the church yard near their house. The experience of the death of an older sister is also described in this poem [4, p. 163]. Other selections from the Readers in which death is a theme are: "Old Age and Death" by Edmund Waller [5], "The Death of Little Nell" by Charles Dickens [6], "Elegy in a Country Courtyard," by Thomas Gray [7], and "He Giveth His Beloved Sleep," by Elizabeth Barrett Browning [8].

A selection in the Fourth Reader by an anonymous author, entitled "My Mother's Grave," provides an emotional account of a young girl's experience with her dying mother [9]. The story aims to make children polite and obedient to their parents, by giving the example of a young girl who didn't realize how fleeting life can be. The author of the story recaptures her thoughts while revisiting the grave of her mother, who had died thirteen years previously. She remembers how she had been unkind to her mortally ill mother after coming home from a trying day at school. Realizing her lapse in manners later in the evening, she returns to her mother's room to ask forgiveness, to find her mother asleep. The little girl vows to awaken early to "tell how sorry I was for my conduct," yet when she rushes to her mother's room in the brightness of morning she finds her mother dead, with a hand so cold "it made me start." The author relates how even thirteen years later, her remorse and pain are almost overwhelming. This is not the type of subject matter and emotional content that is generally considered appropriate for today's basal readers.[1] The basal readers commonly used today in classrooms rarely contain any references to death or dying. They might contain a chapter from a book such as *Charlotte's Web*, by E. B. White [10], but the chapter would not be the one in which Charlotte dies.

---

[1] A basal reader is a text with which reading is taught. There are many different series, each usually having one book per grade level.

Insight into the fashion in which scenes of death and dying were typically portrayed in the nineteenth century can be found in the book *Little Women*, written by Louisa May Alcott in 1869 and still widely read by young readers today. Alcott wrote of the death of young Beth in a straight-forward manner that was especially uncommon for her day. Recognizing that her depiction was at odds with the melodramatic scenes that were current in more romantic literature, Alcott added in the paragraph following Beth's death: "Seldom, except in books, do the dying utter memorable words, see visions, or depart with beatified countenances . . . " [11].

The elements that Alcott took exception to were all common in death scenes in the literature of 1830 to 1880, where they reflected the expectations of an audience that was accustomed to being given a romanticized picture of death and its consequent "final reward" in what was known as "consolation literature." A preoccupation with death and a glorification of the afterlife was evident in the popular literature from both England and America in this period. Much of this literature was written either by Protestant clergy (especially Congregationalists and Unitarians), their wives, or pious women of the congregation [12].

Between 1940 and 1970 only a few children's books contained references to death. Two that have become classics are *The Dead Bird*, by Margaret W. Brown [18] and *Charlotte's Web*, by E. B. White [10]. White's publisher initially refused to publish *Charlotte's Web* unless the ending was modified to allow Charlotte to live. White refused [14, p. 531]. The book was criticized by reviewers who said that death was not "an appropriate subject for children." *Charlotte's Web* is still a best seller, and often is one of the books which second or third grade teachers choose to read to their classes.

The separation of children from death has diminished somewhat in the last twenty years. Elisabeth Kubler-Ross' early work helped make death a subject that could be discussed and studied [15]. Children's books in the late sixties began to discuss subjects that had previously been neglected, such as death and divorce. During the nineteen-seventies and eighties over 200 fiction books were written for children with death as a major theme. Unfortunately very few measured up to the standard set by *Charlotte's Web, Little Women, The Yearling*, or *The Dead Bird*. During the same period some very good non-fiction books about death were written for children of various ages. (See resource list at end of chapter.)

This cornucopia of books on death has helped to begin to make death a more acceptable topic for discussion. The hospice movement has also helped by reintroducing home care for dying persons to many communities. Even so, many children are still insulated from death and often are discouraged from attending funerals. It is not unusual to find adults in their forties who have never attended a funeral [16]. The diminished awareness of mortality that begins in childhood, then, is often carried on into adulthood.

THE DEVELOPMENT OF CHILDREN'S
LITERATURE

Prior to the development of a literature intended specifically for children in the middle of the seventeenth century, there were two characteristic ways in which children were considered. The first was a holdover from the age of the Greeks and Romans, in which children were perceived as miniature adults. Another manner of perceiving children, as something infra-human, was distinguished by Michel de Montaigne, the French humanist and essayist of the sixteenth century. It is difficult, however, from a modern perspective, to be sympathetic to Montaigne's assertion that children possessed "neither mental activities nor recognizable body shape" [17, p. 229].

Authors writing children's literature in the eighteenth century were primarily interested in educating children and assisting them to become socially acceptable human beings. Beyond providing just a certain amount of book learning, they also sought to teach the correct ways to behave. For this reason, all the tales of Perrault had an emphatic moral at their end. They were cautionary tales of what could happen to a child if he or she didn't act in a proper fashion. Some of Perrault's titles were: La Belle au Bois Dormant (Sleeping Beauty) [18], Le Petit Chaperon Rouge (Little Red Riding Hood) [19], and Les Fées (Toads and Diamonds) [20]. As pointed out by Maria Tartar in *Off With Their Heads!*:

> From its inception, children's literature had in it an unusually cruel and coercive streak—one which produced books that relied on brutal intimidation to frighten children into complying with parental demands. This intimidation manifested itself in two very different forms, but both made examples of children. First, there were countless cautionary tales that managed to kill off their protagonists or make their lives perpetually miserable for acts of disobedience. Then there were stories about exemplary behavior which, nonetheless, had a strange way of also ending at the deathbeds of their protagonists [21, p. 9].

In 1658, John Amos Comenius's *Orbis Sensualium Pictus* (A World of Things Obvious to the Senses Drawn in Pictures), a Latin school book, was published. This teaching device was the first picture book for children [22, p. 16], and it was also the first to respond to the recognition that children needed their own literature because they were not scaled-down adults. It was still almost a century, however, before children's literature began to come into its own. In 1744, John Newberry wrote *A Little Pretty Pocket Book* for children [23]. This book is credited as signifying the "real" start of children's literature in England.

FAIRY TALES

Fairy tales provide an excellent example of the fashion in which themes that came to be considered distressing to children have been moderated over time, and insulation of children from an awareness of mortality can be traced through the progression of different versions of typical stories. A generalization can be made about fairy tales as they came to be thought of specifically as children's stories: the sexual content was diminished, and the amount of violence tended to be increased. This process can be seen in successive editions of the Brothers Grimm's Fairy Tales. To understand this evolution, it is necessary to have a picture of the environment in which it took place. According to the perception of children's needs current at the time that the Brothers Grimm were writing, children did not need to be protected from portrayals of violence.

William Jordan in *Divorce Among the Gulls* provides a dramatic context for the state of life that was not untypical for children in London a mere one hundred years after the time that a children's literature came into being:

> I doubt that any of us can comprehend how brutal the fight for survival has been throughout evolution. We ignore our prehistoric, evolutionary legacy, a world in which most children died in infancy or childhood, where teeth rotted out by the age of twenty, where gangrene took the lives of the injured, where thirty-five was foul old age. Even as recently as 1750 in London, the toll of disease staggers the mind: Of 2,239 children born that year, only 168 were still alive five years later [24].

From its inception, literature for children has been motivated by a belief that children needed written material not so much for entertainment but to prepare them for life. The majority of books published and intended for children up through the 1800s can be compared to James Janeway's *A Token for Children: Being an Account of the Conversion, Holy and Exemplary Lives, and Joyful Deaths of Several Young Children* (1671-72) [25]. The London Bills of Mortality for the period shortly following the publication of Janeway's book show that the mortality rate of children age five and under was running as high as 66 percent [21, pp. 14-15]. Writers of this era commonly concurred with Janeway's position that they held a sacred duty to salvage the souls of those who were "not too little to go to Hell." The exemplary stories in *A Token for Children* were also designed to provide comfort to children faced with the tragedy of a sibling's death or confronted with their own mortality when visited by some dread disease [21, p. 87].

The violence and death in stories written for children takes on a different light when put in the context of such high rates of mortality. The practice of abandoning unwanted children either at the Foundlings' Hospital or on church steps was increasing in the seventeen hundreds. It was not just the poor but all classes who contributed to the ranks of abandoned children. The foundling institution was established to make it possible to dispose of infants without leaving any record. Buffon noted in 1772 that about one-third of all children born in Paris that year were abandoned. Jean-Jacques Rousseau (1712-1778) claimed to have turned his five children over to the state, leaving them at the Foundlings' Hospital at birth [26, pp. 590-591].

A high mortality rate for children was reflected in children's literature. As Freud noted in *The Interpretation of Dreams*, half the human race failed to survive the childhood years [27]. The characteristically romanticized depiction of an afterlife that was superior to the life of this world was seen as a way to help children cope with the brutal facts of the life they had no choice but to lead. In the seventeenth and eighteenth centuries, children were routinely required—not just encouraged—to attend public executions so that they could see the price of criminal behavior. This says much about the methods of child rearing believed appropriate in this era [21, p. 46].

The Brothers Grimm's story "Aschenputtel," or "Cinderella," shows an emphasis on punishment that was lacking in the earliest oral versions, and that increased in intensity in subsequent editions. In the early version, taken by Perrault from the oral tradition, Cinderella forgave her stepsisters for mistreating her and introduced them at court. Grimm's first version has Cinderella's sisters turning pale and being horrified when Cinderella becomes a princess, but in the second edition the sisters are punished by being blinded by pigeons that peck out their eyes [21, p. 7].

In the Brothers Grimm's "Hansel and Grethel" there is a description of how horribly the witch howled when Grethel pushed her into her own oven and how " . . . Grethel ran away, and therefore she was left to burn, just as she had left many poor children to burn" [28, p. 57]. The use of violence as punishment for bad behavior is typical in fairy stories. And violent occurrences were frequently shown to be the result of even minor misdeeds. This tendency is evident in the collection of stories found in *Struwwelpeter*. In these short tales Little Pauline plays with matches and goes up in flames, and Conrad the Thumbsucker gets his thumbs sliced off. As Tartar points out the interesting point here is that " . . . the weight is given to the punishment (often fully half the text is devoted to its description) and the disproportionate relationship between the childish offense and the penalty for it make the episode disturbing" [21, p. 34].

The removal of sexuality from books intended for children was a development that paralleled the evolution of housing in Europe. In the Middle Ages houses were rarely more elaborate than was necessary. Few homes had more than one room. The poor had hovels which were little more than a shelter for sleeping. Family life tended to be compromised. Because there was no room for children, only for infants, the older children were commonly sent away to work as apprentices or servants.

The living quarters of the bourgeois would typically be above a store or artisans shop. It generally consisted of a single large room in which the household cooked, ate, transacted business, entertained and slept. Households of up to twenty-five people were not uncommon. Privacy was unknown [29, p. 28], and children were not sent to bed in their own rooms so that racy stories could be told to adults only. Beds were generally large because they were intended to hold more than one or two people. Children lived and worked alongside adults and listened to the same stories. Since children were in the company of adults who were not their parents, but were employers or other servants, there was not the same concern about what children were exposed to that parents of today have.

By the seventeenth century, this living arrangement had evolved into one in which there tended to be a greater segregation between the quarters allocating to working, food preparation, and sleeping. There still tended to be a main room used for dining, entertaining, and receiving visitors, but servants and children began to be separated into smaller rooms adjacent to the central, common areas [29, p. 38]. It was at this time that fairy stories began to be transformed into works intended more strictly for children. This transformation of living spaces coincides with other changes that had great impact on children, including attitudes about how children should be taught about proper behavior and about death and dying.

By looking at the changes in one fairy tale, Little Red Riding Hood, we can observe the changes in attitudes toward death, children, and their education. The earliest known oral version of the tale of Little Red Riding Hood, for example, would not generally be considered suitable entertainment for children today. In the version of the story traditionally told in Brittany, Little Red is unwittingly led by the wolf to eat her grandmother's flesh and drink her blood, and she performs a provocative striptease for the disguised wolf before climbing into bed with him. Little Red later escapes from the wolf when she goes outside to relieve herself. As this tale was originally told, its primary purpose was to entertain adults, so it was not as heavily encumbered with the admonitions and advice that later came to distinguish versions of this tale intended for children.

The earliest written version of Little Red Riding Hood was recorded in French by Charles Perrault in 1696-97. The title of the story in French was 'Le Petit Chaperon Rouge'. The "chaperon" was a hat worn in the Middle Ages, which suggests an even earlier oral tradition [30, p. 22]. One of the fullest texts faithful to the traditional, oral versions of "Little Red Riding Hood" was also recorded in France at the end of the nineteenth century [21, p. 37].

Perrault's first version of the tale was published in *Histoires au Contes du Temps Passé* (Stories [Tales] of Times Passed), subtitled *Contes de Ma Mère L'Oye* (Tales of My Mother Goose). Perrault included seven other tales along with the tales of Little Red Riding Hood. Each of these tales had a moral in verse at the end. In this version of Little Red's tale, the grandmother and Little Red are both eaten by the wolf, and both perish. Although Perrault did not have Little Red's mother giving her any initial warnings before she departed for her grandmother's house, he did conclude the story with a moral suitable for the intended audience of children: Do not speak to strangers or you, too, may provide a wolf with his dinner. The violence of this story is later moderated in the Brothers Grimm retelling by the introduction of an additional character, a hunter or woodcutter, who is able to rescue Little Red and her grandmother by slicing open the wolf and letting them out.

The version of Little Red's tale as told by the Brothers Grimm also gives an expanded role to Little Red's mother, who gives Little Red many warnings and much advice before sending her off through the forest to Grandmother's house. Little Red is admonished to "make haste . . . go straight . . . behave prettily and modestly . . . do not run . . . and do not forget to curtsy and say "good morning" to everyone who knows you" [28, p. 109]. These initial admonitions served to educate the young audience of the story in the manners that were expected of them, and they provided a framework in which the resulting action of the story would be played out. The Brothers Grimm vividly portrayed the consequences of not heeding Mother's advice. Interestingly, in this version, the hunter refers to the wolf as "old sinner" [28, p. 112], perhaps as an oblique reference to risqué incidents excised from the children's version but remembered from the oral tradition.

In a popular nineteenth-century retelling of Little Red's tale found in *Old Favorite Fairy Tales*, Grandmother still gets eaten by the wolf, but Little Red survives and learns to play closer attention to her mother's words: "For she saw the dreadful end to which/A disobedient act may lead" [28, p. 112]. This version of the tale has an interesting emphasis on avoiding any unnecessary suffering of the characters. Here is the depiction of the wolf putting an end to Grandmother:

> He jumped up on the bed, and ate her all up. But he did not hurt her so much as you would think, and as she was a very good old woman it was better for her to die than to live in pain; but still it was very dreadful of the wolf to eat her [30, p. 20].

The editor of *Old Favorite Fairy Tales* was apparently undecided about whether Grandmother's fate was good or bad. When the woodcutter arrives on the scene to rescue Little Red, he advises her that one shouldn't "tell one's affairs to strangers, for many a wolf looks like an honest dog,"—an interesting way of warning a young girl that looks can be deceiving!

In later versions the hunter arrives in time to shoot the wolf before he eats either Little Red or her grandmother, and in still other versions, even the wolf is spared to escape through an open window, or to become Little Red's pet. The moral or message of the story also evolves with the transformation of the events depicted in the story. In the traditional, oral version of Little Red Riding Hood, Little Red was not forewarned by her mother about the dangers of talking to strangers, therefore Little Red cannot be seen as naughty or disobedient. In Perrault's original written version the mother does not give Little Red any cautions, either, while in later versions the mother often gives many instructions and admonitions to her daughter. Upon rescuing Little Red from the dire misfortune she brings upon herself, the hunter/woodcutter inevitably gives her a lecture on obedience and points out to her that she now knows what can happen if she disobeys her mother's warnings. The role that mortality plays in the changing tale of Little Red Riding Hood is seen to diminish as the tale evolves; rather than being the graphic and unmourned event as Perrault depicted it, it becomes unrealistically softened in the later versions, eventually being banished to the periphery of the young audiences' attention.

WHAT IS A FAIRY TALE?

To better understand the significance of the place that fairy tales and other tales told to children have in determining the formation of attitudes relating to death and dying, it is helpful to become familiar with some of the different definitions that these tales have been given. Fairy tales have been defined in various ways by different people. Rollo May considered fairy tales to be " . . . our myths before we become conscious of ourselves" [31, p. 196]. Bruno Bettelheim wrote:

> The figures and events of fairy tales . . . personify and illustrate inner con-
> flicts, but they suggest ever so subtly how these conflicts may be solved, and
> what the next steps in the development toward a higher humanity might be . . .
> presented in a simple homely way . . . Far from making demands, the fairy
> tale reassures, gives hope for the future, and holds out the promise of a happy
> ending [32, p. 26].

Madonna Kolbenschlag writes:

> Fairy tales are the bedtime stories of the collective consciousness. They
> persist in cultural memory because they interpret crises of the human condi-
> tion that are common to all of us. They are shared wish fulfillments, abstract
> dreams that resolve conflicts and give meaning to experience [33, p. 2].

Edwin Krupp makes a distinction between fairy tales and the rest of children's literature,

> The term 'fairy tale' is sometimes used for all children's stories, but the fairy
> tale really has its own special character. It involves or takes place in another
> realm or world, not in the one in which we usually reside. Fairy tales are really
> stories of the supernatural. Other laws prevail in them, and the creatures that
> inhabit them do not belong to ordinary reality [34, p. 11].

All of these definitions are good and even have merit in their own context, yet they are unsatisfying in their failure to consider the origin of these tales in adult entertainment and the purposeful manner in which they were converted into tales intended for children.

There is an easily confusing overlap between fairy tales, folk tales, and myths. Myths are the most easily distinguishable, as they are mainly stories intended to provide explanations for the occurrence of natural phenomena, generally by personifying a natural effect as an animistic or anthropomorphic deity. The depiction of the sun in its course as Apollo driving his fiery chariot, and winter being caused by Demeter mourning for the six months of Persephone's captivity in Hades, are typical of mythological stories. Even though in their later elaborations myths might come to deal with models of behavior and other topics commonly found in fairy tales, their origins can be found in the earliest explanations of natural phenomena. Broad definitions like Rollo May's seem to apply more clearly to myths than to fairy tales.

Folk tales and fairy tales are not as easily distinguished, as indicated by the fact that published collections of folk tales and fairy tales may very well contain some of the same stories.

A characteristic of fairy tales is the flexible way that they have been perceived by authors. Authors in different times and places have recognized that fairy tales are capable of carrying a message that can be tailored to fit their particular needs. Existing as they do in the common domain, fairy tales and their characters provide an easily accessible medium for both writers and their audience. The task of the audience is eased by the familiarity of the characters and situations with which they are presented, and the writer's burden is lightened as he brings stories from an earlier time into conformity with the standards he is trying to represent. The subtle or obvious manner in which a fairy tale departs from its audience expectations while still fulfilling their desires is a measure of its successful telling. A current example of this phenomenon is the bestseller *Women Who Run With the Wolves* [35], in which many fairy tales are retold with emphasis on their pertinence to the modern female experience.

Fairy tales are also significant in the wide range of characters and situations that may be found in them. Children are presented with characters that they can identify with in fairy tales, commonly in the guise of a child not so unlike herself or himself who is faced with an adverse situation in which he or she is called upon to make new judgments and exhibit mature behaviors. Children can be exposed to a range of novel situations through the fairy tale and exposed to models for their own behavior to fit a variety of their needs. The most popular fairy tales, especially, have always been adapted as adult perceptions of children's needs have changed and adult needs to communicate various lessons to children have changed [36, p. 80].

In distinction to fairy tales, folk tales often concern the actions of pseudo-historical or typical personages who are engaged in activities that represent cultural standards that children are expected to aspire to. The unerring accuracy of William Tell is related in a folk tale, as is George Washington's chopping down of the cherry tree and his precocious, unwavering honesty. The adventures of Paul Bunyan and his gigantic blue ox, Babe, are folk tales that recast popular stories from the era of the westward expansion of the United States as "tall tales" with a common main character.

It cannot be maintained, as Bettelheim's definition suggests, that a fairy tale invariably holds the promise of a happy ending. The Little Mermaid, which is a definite fairy tale, has been subjected to a great deal of distortion, or "artistic license," to produce a happy ending. At the conclusion of the tale as Hans Christian Anderson originally wrote it, the Little Mermaid choose death for herself rather than murder the Prince, which would have enabled her to regain her form as a mermaid. The only consolation for the Little Mermaid, who had already sacrificed her home, family, and voice to pursue her love for the mortal, human Prince, is that after performing deeds of kindness for three hundred years as a "daughter of the air," she might gain a human soul and join the Prince in heaven. The very morning that the Little Mermaid sacrifices herself and spares the Prince, he marries a princess from another land whom he mistakenly believes had rescued him from drowning, when actually the Little Mermaid had saved him. Only in Disney's version does the Little Mermaid manage to displace the "other woman" and marry the Prince. Disney justifies this alteration by casting an evil sea-witch in disguise as the other princess.

The classic fairy tale "Blubeard" also presents a problematic ending. In this fairy tale, one of three sisters marries a wealthy but mysterious man, distinguished primarily by a beard of blue color. After the wedding, the wife is given access to all Bluebeard's possessions, but she is forbidden to use one small golden key. When she inevitably opens the door the key closes, she discovers the bloody bodies of Bluebeard's previous wives. When Bluebeard discovers his wife's transgressions, he prepares to add her to his collection. At the last moment, the wife is saved by the sudden appearance of her brothers, who hack her husband into pieces before her eyes. The happiness of the ending of this tale must be considered more one of degree; although the latest wife did not meet the fate of her predecessors, is it really a happy ending to have your brothers murder your husband? This tale also leaves unresolved the dilemma of the wife's part in the action. Her disobedience is a necessary part of the story, yet there is no clear resolution to this issue. The fast and easy way to conclude a fairy tale is to recite "and they lived happily every after," yet when one takes a close look at fairy tales there are many which do not have a "perfect" ending.

THE FUTURE OF FAIRY TALES

When folk and fairy tales existed solely in an oral medium, every story teller was able to tell a version of a story that was personalized by the demands of his or her time, place and audience. When stories came to exist more exclusively in printed form, they began to reflect more enduringly the nature of the time and place in which they were recorded. For this reason, it is especially odd that we continue to read to our children—often without the slightest degree of critical reflection—unrevised versions of stories that are imbued with the values of a different time and place. L. Frank Baum, the originator of the tales of the land of Oz (1900), recognized this predicament, and recommended that it was time for a new set of 'wonder tales', and that previous fairy tales should be classed as 'historical' [21, p. 19].

There is a growing perception that children are capable of having an understanding of dying and death as natural processes, and that the lifelong relationship a person has to dying and death is based in no small measure on the experiences of childhood. In the last twenty years, there has been a revolution in the practices and perceptions surrounding dying and death, yet little has been effectively done to transmit these changes to children. Adults are beginning to recognize the difficulties they have experienced as a result of being sheltered from an awareness of mortality and the need is felt for a way to transmit a realistic awareness of mortality to children.

Denoting traditional fairy tales as "historical" would help distinguish the changes in values and behaviors that have occurred in the many years since they were recorded, and would encourage parents and teachers to more critically examine just what they are presenting to children. Modern editions of fairy tales have enormous appeal, demonstrated by the lavishly illustrated editions that have been offered recently by some of the large publishing houses. It is interesting to note that reviews of these books have concentrated on the beauty of the illustrations, the size of the book, the quality of the paper . . . in other words on everything but the content. The assumption seems to be that the buying public already knows what the content is and that no explanation is necessary.

But it is important to consider the implications of fairy tales in our modern world. Perhaps it is time to begin transforming them to reflect the tremendous changes that have occurred in a world increasingly forced to accept the limits of medical technology, where death is being acknowledged again as a necessary and inevitable counterpart to life.

Reading with a child is a wonderful activity; introducing someone to the world of books is to offer them the promise of a greater and better world. Fairy tales can be an important part of this process, because their "real" existence is in the imagination of a child, and through the action of a fairy tale a child can learn that he or she can confront circumstances that are new or frightening and be able to do the right thing. It is important that the tales we tell to our children reflect what we ourselves believe. Rather than continuing to insulate children from the realities of death and dying, especially by providing the unsuitable types of messages that Saturday morning T.V. provides, fairy tales can provide a medium for children to be introduced to the types of situations that they will encounter all their lives.

One of the few activities that hasn't changed since the eras of our parents and grandparents is tucking a child into bed with a story, even down to the story we might choose to read. There is a comfort in this nostalgia, and a sense of continuity in this activity that can make all involved believe in the truth of the final " . . . and they lived happily every after." A cartoon in a recent edition of the *New Yorker* magazine illustrated this, while also showing the capacity fairy tales have to portray facets of the world that are not necessarily easy to explain. The cartoon showed a mother reading a bedtime story to her daughter with the caption "She married and then divorced, and then she married and divorced, and then she married and lived happily ever after."

Although this cartoon was certainly intended to be ironic, it still points out the purpose of providing moral instruction that fairy tales can fulfill. With the expanding use of hospice programs, and the corresponding increase in opportunities for children to be exposed to meaningful death experiences, and with the increase of the awareness of the lethalness of AIDS, it is important that even the tales told to children come to reflect current perceptions of dying and death.

BOOKS ABOUT DEATH FOR CHILDREN
AND YOUNG ADULTS

The following list of books is a sample of general books (fiction and non-fiction) about death available for children.

Non-Fiction

Bernstein, J. and Gullo, S. J., *When People Die*, Dutton, New York, 1977.

Le Shan, E. J., *Learning to Say Good-by: When a Parent Dies*, Macmillan, New York, 1976.

Richter, E., *Losing Someone You Love. When a Brother or Sister Dies*, Putnam's, New York, 1986.

Rofes, E. and The Unit At Fayerweather Street School, *The Kids' Book About Death and Dying*, Little, Brown & Co., Boston, 1985.

Segerberg, O., Jr., *Living with Death*, Dutton, New York, 1976.

Stein, S. B., *About Dying*, Walker, New York, 1974.

Zim, H. and Bleeker, S., *Life and Death*, Morrow, New York, 1970.

Fiction

Alcott, L. M., *Little Women*, Grosset & Dunlop, New York, 1947. (originally pub. 1869) (sister—illness)

Alexander, S., *Nadia the Willful*, Pantheon, New York, 1983. (brother—accidental—bereavement)

Aliki, *Two of Them*, Greenwillow, New York, 1979. (grandfather—old age)

Bartoli, J., *Nonna*, Harvey House, 1975. (grandmother—natural death)

Blume, J., *Tiger Eyes*, Bradbury, Scarsdale, New York, 1981. (father—murdered in robbery)

Brown, M. W., *The Dead Bird*, Addison-Wesley, Reading, Massachusetts, 1965. (wild bird—natural death)

Bunting, E., *The Empty Window*, Frederick Warne, New York, 1980. (friend—illness)

Coerr, E., *Sadako and the Thousand Paper Cranes*, Putnam, New York, 1977. (Hiroshima—leukemia caused by radiation)

Craven, M., *I Heard the Owl Call My Name*, Doubleday, New York, 1973. (young priest—illness)

de Paola, T., *Nana Upstairs and Nana Downstairs*, Putnam, New York, 1973. (great-grandmother and grandmother—natural death)

Douglas, E., *Rachel and the Upside Down Heart*, Price, Stern, Sloan, Los Angeles, 1990. (father—heart attack)

Gerstein, M., *The Mountains of Tibet*, Harper & Row, New York, 1987. (reincarnation)

Hermes, P., *You Shouldn't Have to Say Good-bye*, Harcourt, New York, 1982. (mother—illness)

Hickman, M. W., *Last Week My Brother Anthony Died*, Abingdon, Nashville, Tennessee, 1984. (infant brother—congenital heart condition)

Kantrowitz, M., *When Violet Died*, Parent's Magazine Press, New York, 1973. (pet bird—natural death)

Mann, P., *There Are Two Kinds of Terrible*, Doubleday, New York, 1977. (mother—illness)

Miles, M., *Annie and the Old One*, Little, Brown, Boston, 1971. (Navajo Indians—grandmother—natural death)

Paterson, K., *Bridge to Terabithia*, Crowell, New York, 1977. (friend—accidental death)

Saint Exupery, A. de., *The Little Prince*, Harcourt, New York, 1943. (death—general)

Smith, D. B., *A Taste of Blackberries*, Crowell, New York, 1973. (friend—bee sting allergy)

Talbert, M., *Dead Birds Singing*, Little, Brown, Boston, 1985. (mother, sister—car accident)

Tobias, T., *Petey*, Putnam, New York, 1978. (gerbil—illness)

Varley, S., *Badger's Parting Gifts*, Lothrop, Lee & Shepard, New York, 1984. (personified animals—remembering someone after death)

Viorst, J., *The Tenth Good Thing About Barney*, Atheneum, New York, 1971. (pet cat—natural death)

Warburg, S. S., *Growing Time*, Houghton Mifflin, Boston, 1969. (pet dog—natural death)

White, E. B., *Charlotte's Web*, Harper & Row, New York, 1952. (death as a natural consequence of life)

Wilhelm, H., *I'll Always Love You*, Crown, New York, 1985. (pet dog—natural death)

Williams, M., *The Velveteen Rabbit*, Holt, Rinehart & Winston, New York, 1983 edition. (life and death—general)

Zolotow, C., *My Grandson Lew*, Harper & Row, New York, 1974. (grandfather—remembering him)

REFERENCES

1. L. A. De Spelder and A. L. Strickland, *The Last Dance*, Mayfield Publishing, Palo Alto, California, 1992.

2. E. P. Lamers, The Dying Child in the Classroom, in *Children and Death*, King's College, London, pp. 175-186, 1986.
3. *McGuffey's Eclectic Readers*, Vols. 2-6, Van Nostrand & Reinhold, New York, 1920.
4. W. Wordsworth, We Are Seven, in *McGuffey's Eclectic Readers*, (Third Reader), Van Nostrand Reinhold, New York, p. 163, 1920.
5. E. Waller, Old Age and Death, in *McGuffey's Eclectic Readers*, (Sixth Reader), Van Nostrand Reinhold, New York, p. 95, 1920.
6. C. Dickens, The Death of Little Nell, in *McGuffey's Eclectic Readers*, (Sixth Reader), Van Nostrand Reinhold, New York, p. 96, 1920.
7. T. Gray, Elegy in a Country Churchyard, in *McGuffey's Eclectic Readers*, (Sixth Reader), Van Nostrand Reinhold, New York, p. 108, 1920.
8. E. Barrett Browning, He Giveth His Beloved Sleep, in *McGuffey's Eclectic Readers*, (Sixth Reader), Van Nostrand Reinhold, New York, p. 195, 1920.
9. Anonymous, My Mother's Grave, in *McGuffey's Eclectic Readers*, (Fourth Reader), Van Nostrand Reinhold, New York, p. 253, 1920.
10. E. B. White, *Charlotte's Web*, Harper & Row, New York, 1952.
11. L. M. Alcott, *Little Women*, Grosset & Dunlop, New York, (originally pub. 1869), 1947.
12. A. Douglas, *The Feminization of American Culture*, Anchor Press, New York, "The Domestication of Death," pp. 200-226, 1988.
13. M. W. Brown, *The Dead Bird*, Addison-Wesley, Reading, Massachusetts, 1965.
14. D. L. Guth, *Letters of E. B. White*, Harper & Row, New York, 1976.
15. E. Kubler-Ross, *On Death and Dying*, Macmillan, New York, 1969.
16. F. I. Newton, *Children and the Funeral Ritual: Factors that Affect Their Attendance and Participation*, Master's Thesis, California State University, Chico, 1990.
17. Encyclopaedia Britannica, Children's Literature, Macropaedia, Vol. 4, p. 229, 1976.
18. C. Perrault, La Belle au Bois Dormant (Sleeping Beauty), in *Favorite Fairy Tales*, J. Mulherin (ed.), Granada Publishing, London, p. 12, 1982.
19. C. Perrault, La Petit Chaperon Rouge (Little Red Riding Hood), in *Favorite Fairy Tales*, J. Mulherin (ed.), Granada Publishing, London, p. 22, 1982.
20. C. Perrault, Les Fées (Toads and Diamonds), in *Favorite Fairy Tales*, J. Mulherin (ed.), Granada Publishing, London, p. 52, 1982.
21. M. Tatar, *Off With Their Heads! Fairytales and the Culture of Childhood*, Princeton University Press, Princeton, New Jersey, 1992.
22. C. Johnson, *Old-Time Schools and School Books*, Dover, New York, (reprint of the Macmillan 1904 edition), 1963.
23. J. Newberry, A Little, Pretty Pocket Book, 1744, in *Children's Literature*, Macropaedia, Vol. 4, Encyclopaedia Brittannica, p. 231, 1976.
24. W. Jordan, *Divorce Among the Gulls*, Harper Collins, New York, 1991.
25. J. Janeway, A Token for Children: Being an Account of the Conversion, Holy and Exemplary Lives, and Joyful Deaths of Several Young Children (1671-72), in *Off With Their Heads! Fairytales and the Culture of Childhood*, M. Tatar (ed.), Princeton University Press, Princeton, New Jersey, p. 14, 1992.
26. D. J. Boorstin, *The Creators*, Random House, New York, 1992.

27. S. Freud, The Interpretation of Dreams, Vol. 4 of the Standard Edition, James Strachery (trans.), (London: Hogarth, 1953) p. 254, in *Off With Their Heads! Fairytales and the Culture of Childhood*, M. Tatar, (ed.), Princeton University Press, Princeton, New Jersey, p. 46, 1992.
28. L. Owens, *The Complete Brothers Grimm Fairy Tales*, Avenel, New York, 1981.
29. W. Rybcznski, *Home: A Short History of an Idea*, Penguin, New York, 1987.
30. J. Mulherin, *Favorite Fairy Tales*, Granada Publishing, London, 1982.
31. R. May, *The Cry for Myth*, Delta, New York, 1992.
32. B. Bettelheim, *The Uses of Enchantment*, Vintage Books, New York, 1977.
33. M. Kolbenschlag, *Kiss Sleeping Beauty Good-Bye*, Bantam, New York, 1981.
34. E. C. Krupp, *Beyond the Blue Horizon: Myths and Legends of the Sun, Moon, Stars, and Planets*, Harper Collins, New York, 1991.
35. C. P. Estés, *Women Who Run With the Wolves*, Ballantine Books, New York, 1992.
36. N. Tucker, *The Child and the Book*, Cambridge, New York, 1982.

CHAPTER 12

Saying Good-Bye to Tomorrow

Inge B. Corless

Saying good-bye to tomorrow connotes the lack of continuity of the present social reality for an individual or group. Although it could be perceived as living in the present, saying goodbye to tomorrow implies loss and, in particular, death. In this chapter, I will examine a more recent addition to the lexicon of death and dying terminology, namely multiple loss. This term, used to describe the experience of loss for members of the Gay community, will be analyzed along with such other terms as multiple losses, chronic sorrow, depression, pathological grief, bereavement overload, burnout, and post-traumatic stress disorder. To illuminate its idiocratic aspects, multiple loss will be contrasted with such phenomena as disease due to cultural contact, random violence, the Holocaust (with which it is often compared), natural disaster, and other epidemics. This background will be used to bring into relief the AIDS- related bereavement experience of Gay men.

Multiple loss has come to be accepted as a descriptor for the experience of loss in the Gay community [1-3]. Multiple loss while applying to the death of individuals has meaning in terms of the group. It denotes prematurity of occurrence and implies threat to the capacity for coping. Multiple deaths or "people losses" also occur in the experience of the elderly [4]. To the extent that any death is "too soon," there may be the feeling of prematurity, but for the elderly death occurs in an overall context of the expectation of loss. Sadly, it is an age-appropriate phenomenon.

Multiple deaths also occur in combat both of soldiers and civilians. Prematurity of death is expected for soldiers and is honored as making a sacrifice for one's country or cause. Thus death while premature is given meaning; a vital consideration to the maintenance of social control and the continuance of risk-taking. Multiple deaths take place and are tallied in body counts. Overemphasized in terms of the enemy and minimized with regard to one's own combatants, deaths in combat are viewed in the aggregate and are rarely considered from the perspective of the individual [5, 6].

Expectation of death as appropriate is specified in health care institutions as applicable to those which occur due to the overwhelming insult to the physiological integrity of the individual or the gaps in current scientific knowledge or technology to address these challenges. Prematurity is not at issue when malfeasance is not an issue, at least, from a systems perspective.

From the perspective of a health care provider the young person dying from cardiac malfunction creates greater distress than the death of an older person. Here prematurity is very much to the point. And while there may be similarity in age to the soldier dying in combat, there is not the readily available access to meaning— at least in the secular world.

The dilemma for post-modern man (and woman) is the segregation of religion to the periphery of contemporary life and the lack of satisfactory explanations for the Job-like traumas which transpire. As with Frankl, there is the search for meaning [7]. This question of meaning will be revisited later in this chapter.

To this point several characteristics of multiple loss have been identified; prematurity, that is early death, for which there is no readily available ascription of meaning, and deaths which occur in numbers to members of one's social network. These are not deaths in the abstract but deaths which have personal significance.

Multiple losses, by way of contrast, encompass changes in physiological function, behavior, social and financial status, housing, and significant relationships [8]. The latter losses, namely those of significant relationships, result not only from death, but from the loss of individuals who cannot handle the illness of a friend or family member, or who are homophobic, or from the alienation of family for whom the acknowledgement of the sexual preference of their offspring is unacceptable. For these individuals human immunodeficiency virus (HIV) disease is tantamount to public dishonor and the perceived dishonor is of greater moment than the dying of their family member.

The elderly also experience multiple losses but are not explicitly stigmatized. Implicitly, in a fitness worshipping, youth enshrining society, blemishes in figure and function are noted with a subtle, devaluing of the individual. Values such as honoring one's elders are more likely to reside in traditional societies than in modern ones. The accumulation of wealth, however, is valued in most societies and, in a perverse way, is the great equalizer. All sorts of otherwise stigmatized conditions are less impairing in the presence of wealth. That is not to say that loss is not experienced. It is to say that prosperity provides economic resilience, an external buffering system. Such buffering is also provided by social support about which more will be said.

Multiple losses are also experienced in chronic sorrow [9]. However, these losses are of a continuing nature and relate to a single source such as a handicapped child, multiple sclerosis in a young adult, or dementia in an elderly person

[9]. Chronic sorrow may be conceptualized as having multiple points of sadness [10]. It is described as being progressive, periodic, pervasive and permanent [9, p. 31]. Related to chronic illness, chronic sorrow is considered a normal response.

By way of contrast depression, often described as anger turned inwards, is of concern to clinicians. Schneider notes that depression is "characterized by negativism, helplessness, lowered mood, and reduced self-esteem" [11, p. 161]. Further, and significant in delineating the similarities and differences with multiple loss, and for Schneider, with grief, "There may not be a recognizable loss by the depressed, or the loss is seen as punishment" [11, p. 163]. Whereas grief is other directed, depression is "me" focused.

Pathological grief is grief prolonged, grief unending, and grief all-consuming. It may also be death denied. In this sense it differs from multiple loss wherein the death is acknowledged cognitively and the difficulty lies in emotional integration.

How then is multiple loss, multiple losses, chronic sorrow, depression, and pathological grief to be distinguished from yet another concept, bereavement overload? In describing bereavement overload Kastenbaum mentions multiple losses or as he phrases it "Sorrow upon Sorrow, Loss upon Loss" [12, p. 153; 13]. Bereavement overload is having too much grief to bear, usually in too short a period of time. And while Kastenbaum initially makes reference to the elderly, the concept has been extended by Lehman and Russell to the Gay community [1]. "A similar phenomenon is seen with AIDS: young adults are experiencing the loss of many friends within a few months or years. This is particularly devastating and frightening within the homosexual community" [1, p. 180].

The issue is one of multiple sources of loss and not the multiple levels of loss associated typically with the loss of a spouse wherein the death may entail physical, psychological, and social sequelae. Both multiple loss and multiple losses may result in bereavement overload in which the capacity to cope is challenged by the size of the bereavement burden (see Figure 1).

Chronic sorrow, the result of continuing losses associated with a long-term impairment, is also related to bereavement overload as is evidenced by these caregivers of elderly dementia patients. "Several caregivers said they took life one day at a time. It was too painful to perceive at one time all the sorrows they had or to contemplate all the sorrows of the future" [9, p. 78]. These caregivers illustrate a mode of coping with chronic sorrow and preventing bereavement overload.

Bereavement overload exhausts the carrying capacity for loss leading, in the case of professionals, to burnout. A term used to describe health care worker response to work-related stress, burnout typically is applied to caregivers in situations involving serial deaths such as in hospice care or work with individuals with HIV disease. Burnout describes the response of the individuals to perceived stresses [14].

A loss of spirit, burnout directs our attention not just to the magnitude of the loss, whether individual or multiple, but also to the individual and his or her capacity to experience loss. This capacity is modulated not only by personality

Phenomenon (A)	Trajectory of Loss (B)	Preparation	Size of Bereavement Burden (A + B)	Individual Coping Capacity	Social Support	Responses	Outcome
Individual	Discrete	Expected	Manageable	Intact	Adequate	Grief	Resolution
						Depression	
Multiple Loss	Continuing	Unexpected	Bereavement Overload	Impaired	Inadequate	Pathological Grief	Impairment
Intimates							
Friends						Chronic Sorrow	
Acquaintances						Post Traumatic Stress Syndrome	

Figure 1. Factors Influencing Responses to Death

174

characteristics but by personal interests, professional and social support. In hospice care, the carrying capacity for loss is evaluated prior to employment. Persons newly bereaved are usually advised to wait with employment in a hospice environment for at least a year or until after they've had adequate time to resolve their grief. And while employers have a responsibility to structure support for their health care provider employees, the individual also has a responsibility. Burnout occurs when the individual no longer has the resiliency to cope with the various employment-related stresses including death.

Burnout, grief, depression, pathological grief, and chronic sorrow are all responses to loss. A response with similarities to burnout, post-traumatic stress disorder (PTSD) received renewed attention when the needs of Viet Nam veterans began to be recognized. More recent investigations by researchers in Israel describe a soldier suffering from PTSD under the heading of normal grief [5]. While one might question whether this is usual or normal grief, under the circumstances described, that of a young soldier whose tank crew was ambushed resulting in the death of the crew and subsequently his best friend, perhaps any other response would have been unusual. Initially found wandering in the desert, he was "apathetic-looking, disoriented and confused." "After 2 days . . . He remained sensitive to noise, sleepless and had bouts of restlessness and hand-wringing alternating with bouts of passive immobility and apparent apathy" [5, p. 427]. After treatment, "The picture evolved into one of extreme anger, social withdrawal, sadness, and nightmares together with occasional involuntary invasive visual pseudo-hallucinations of his friend dying" [5, p. 427].

PTSD as a grief response has as its source traumatic death occurring over a discrete period and in the illustration above the usual sense of social order was disrupted by the surprise of the ambush and the death of the commander. It may also be a delayed response as was observed in some veterans of the Viet Nam conflict. These elements of multiple deaths, the disruption of the social order and the potential for a delayed response are also found in multiple loss.

In the next section of this chapter the focus will shift from concepts describing death and responses to loss such as PTSD to the phenomena which result in multiple deaths. The last section of this chapter will utilize this analysis to highlight the bereavement experiences of Gay men suffering from multiple loss.

Phenomena which result in multiple deaths may be classified as either man (sic)-made or natural disasters. Man-made disasters range from the unintended, such as that caused by cultural contact with individuals from previously unknown social groups naive to the others' microorganisms, to the intentional transmission of disease; from random violence, such as that which happens in so-called modern society, to concerted, planned violence as happens in war, or in the Holocaust. Natural disasters include those which result from typhoons, earthquakes, tornadoes, hurricanes, floods as well as those epidemics/ pandemics which arise from new pathogens. Clearly HIV disease has elements of both a natural disaster and one promulgated, both intentionally and unintentionally, by man.

The multiple loss experienced by the American Indian due to disease after contact with whites has been commented on by Tafoya [15]. " 'Because American Indians had no immunity to European diseases, 92 percent of them died within two generations of their initial contact with whites', said Dr. Tafoya, an Indian himself. 'So there is tremendous parallel in the Native American experience and what the gay community is going through in the 90's' " [15].

There are also differences. Contagiousness varies with the route of transmission. Direct sexual transmission is easier to limit than is spread by respiratory droplets. When mosquitoes or rodents bearing fleas are the vectors of transmission, understanding of this intermediary role is required if effective intervention is to be undertaken. Another distinction is whether part or all of the community are affected and if only part, which part—the reputable or disreputable, the honored or the disposable. The latter distinctions do not apply to the Native Americans who died from disease as a result of cultural contact with whites. The tribe was affected by unintentional disease transmission. Other Native Americans perished intentionally, as a result of contact with outsiders, in battle and other hostilities and as a concomitant of forced marches for purposes of relocation on reservations.

While not the result of a forced march, members of minority groups live together in another version of reservations called the inner city. In these ghettoes individuals experience the random violence associated with firearms, gangs, and drugs. There are multiple losses and deaths particularly among young African-American males. The experience of multiple losses bears similarity to the experience of the elderly. As in multiple loss, the relative youth of the affected indicates that this is an age inappropriate phenomenon for persons in a country of the North. In countries of the South, formerly termed developing countries, multiple losses are part of the lives of most citizens.

Random violence in the inner city is to be distinguished from the loss encountered in war, during the Holocaust and as a result of nuclear attack. A major question is whether the enemy can be identified. Does one know "us" from "them"? The participation of Viet Cong women in native attire in the violence against South Vietnamese forces and their supporters in the Viet Nam conflict, increased the difficulty of knowing us from them and thus increased the terror and the violence. So-called "friendly fire" directed at young officers also clouded the boundaries between ally and foe.

These boundaries were disrupted during the Holocaust in Germany wherein neighbor and friend could easily become foe. For German Jews, the country to which their allegiance was sworn betrayed the trust of its citizens by identifying religious group membership as an inherent threat to the state. In countries which Germany invaded, the threat was from without and differentially applied. Here, too, neighbor might betray neighbor and national leaders collaborated with the invader. However, the national response could also be one of common identity with the threatened citizen as in Denmark where all wore a Star of David. In so doing the Danes demonstrated their integrity and affirmed their common identity with the oppressed.

For Jews in Europe, the Holocaust was clearly a time of unimaginable loss. Lifton addresses the totality of that destruction when he states that "holocaust means a total disaster; the physical, social and spiritual obliteration of a human community" [16, p. 113]. Horrific destruction of massive proportions also occurred with the bombing of Nagasaki and Hiroshima. Here the enemy was external and the subsequent misery was shared by all citizens in the bombed cities. With the Nazi holocaust, the enemy was perceived to be within, although considered "other," as is evidenced by Himmler's remarks to his Gruppenführer. "We had the moral right vis-a-vis 'our' people to annihilate [umzubringen] 'this' people which wanted to annihilate us" [17, p. 17]. Indeed "this" people was no longer a part of "us."

The use of force and the power of the state are questions that continue to challenge American society as we strive to uphold the inalienable rights to life, liberty and the pursuit of happiness. Clearly, the power of the state continues to support these rights, albeit with deviations. Thus to contrast the multiple loss experienced by the Gay community and others with the Holocaust is to overstate the case. Nonetheless, the Gay experience of multiple loss in a societal environment perceived at the very best to be uncaring resonates with the Holocaust experience of Jews dying, beseeching aid from other countries and having others turn their backs to the impending tragedy.

One might query the appropriateness of examining HIV disease under the category of natural disasters when what some say is the duplicity and ineptness of various interest groups, has accelerated spread of the disease, or at the very least, has not impeded it [18, 19]. Apart from cultural contact with previously unencountered sources of transmission which for the purpose of this analysis is considered a man-made disaster, albeit unintentional, other experiences such as the hantavirus outbreak which occurred principally among the Navaho in 1993 is considered an example of a natural disaster [20].

Natural disasters caused by various atmospheric and geological phenomena are usually time-delimited in their immediate impact but have numerous secondary consequences. This series of continuing losses is similar to that encountered in the depiction of chronic sorrow. Tyhurst in his description of individual behavior in community disasters describes "three overlapping phases—a period of impact, a period of recall, and a post traumatic period" [21, p. 769].

The Buffalo Creek flood which occurred in Appalachia destroyed homes forcing people into refugee camps. Although still residing in the same community, individuals were no longer with neighbors and the integrity of the social fabric was rent. The "democratization, disorientation and loss of connection" experienced by survivors of the Buffalo Creek disaster address some of the implications for the social network created by a natural disaster [22].

A similar situation would be the destruction of the Castro district in San Francisco. Although many Gays live elsewhere both in and outside San Francisco, the Castro district has served as a locus for Gay-related establishments and housing. Its' visceral familiarity facilitates the sense of community which binds residents of this area; a community all the more significant given the severance, or frequently the attenuation, of ties to other locales and other social networks. Thus natural disasters for communities such as Buffalo Creek or the Castro District, destroy the physical structure and have consequences for the social fabric which supports the individual [22]. Some might argue that HIV disease has been akin to such a disaster.

The Buffalo Creek disaster also involved individuals with a paucity of personal resources. One suspects that more affluent and mobile individuals and those less tied to the land might have responded differently; that individuals with greater resources would have no longer been dazed after a year, as the Buffalo Creek survivors clearly were. The reliance on a physically proximate support network effective in other circumstances and destroyed by the flood, limited the available social support. Physical dispersion resulted in social displacement.

Another type of natural disaster, epidemics, do not typically result in permanent physical displacement. The multiple loss resulting from such epidemics has an impact on the social network. It differs from a geological natural disaster in the accretion of additional deaths over time and may not necessarily involve physical displacement in the way geological disaster does.

Attention will now be turned to the question of whether the multiple loss experienced by the Gay community is the same or different from the loss experienced in other epidemics? The question here is not one of the size of the epidemic nor its length timewise. Clearly in prior epidemics the wealthy fled from the places of plague, retreating to what they perceived to be places of relative safety—often in "the country." This was the case in the various epidemics which affected Boston in the seventeenth century, Philadelphia in the eighteenth century and Chadwick's England of the nineteenth century. As is evident, as a society we've never all been in this together. Exposure to harm is usually buffered by social and economic resources. The wealthy have always used their resources to protect themselves leaving the less affluent to fend for themselves—often in the city.

What is different from the epidemics of previous centuries is our expectation of the role of government in such circumstances. The expectation is that government will use the people's resources to inhibit disease transmission and care for those affected. What makes the multiple loss experienced in the Gay community all the more poignant is the sense that government has abandoned the afflicted, contributing thereby to the magnitude of loss. Government has, as it were, fled to the country leaving the afflicted to their own devices. Or so it is perceived. And in the city (and countryside) people are dying.

Multiple losses acquires literally new shadings of meaning when this concept is applied to the "dying family." The dying family is composed of HIV infected mother, frequently husband or partner, and child or children. There may or may not be uninfected siblings of the child. Grandmothers often care for their ill children and grandchildren. What does the death of succeeding generations mean to these individuals? The literature discusses the death of a child and not the deaths of children and grandchildren other than as isolated events of violence or ill-fortune.

Multiple loss takes on a very special meaning for HIV disease infected and affected families whose HIV disease-related grief frequently occurs in the inner city's context of multiple losses. And while not strictly applicable to the dying family's bereaved, in that the numbers of deaths may not approach those experienced in the Gay community, the magnitude of the loss suggests that the dying family be included in the discussions of multiple loss.

In this regard, the orphans of dying families require special attention. Sustaining multiple loss and multiple losses, these youngsters likely have profound needs. How does a child cope with such devastation? Clearly children have experienced the deaths of their parents through other mechanisms. Further attention needs to be paid to the similarities and differences in the bereavement experiences of dying families.

Frameworks for intervention need to be explored with the bereaved of dying families—the adults and the children. Pheifer and Houseman discuss such a framework for adults, based on the work of Worden [23, 24]. Issues of cultural sensitivity, elder and child bereavement need to be reconsidered in the context of HIV disease.

The literature on multiple loss addresses the bereavement experience of members of the Gay community. Biller and Rice using Rando's formulation of avoidance, confrontation and reestablishment as responses in normal grief, found in their study of five gay males and two lesbian females that the boundaries of these phases were "fragile" [2, 25]. They make the important observation that "Interestingly, after each new loss, survivors seemed to further grieve the loss they had identified as most significant" [2, p. 288]. This observation of the lack of closure is explicated by the respondent to a study of multiple loss who said, " 'This is cumulative. You can never finish with one before another happens. You can never fully process a loss; it's a dangerous thing, two or three more happen and I haven't even finished with the others, and they are friends' " [26, p. 12]. The psychosocial process used to cope with multiple loss and to maintain involvement with both individuals and the community is depicted as one of a balance between functional/dysfunctional engagement and detachment [26, p. 11].

Approaches to coping with multiple losses are to be distinguished from grieving for the loss of an individual in the context of multiple loss and losses although they are related. McGaffic and Longman study the latter and find two major psychosocial processes, connecting and disconnecting [27]. Processes involved in connecting included "sharing the death, caring for the person with AIDS, legitimizing the relationship, memorializing, and AIDS-related work." Disconnecting was characterized by "performing death related tasks, letting go of the relationship, and passage" or the establishment of new relationships.

The social processes studied by McGaffic and Longman which implicitly suggest a trajectory should be distinguished from the psychological consequences of multiple loss [28, 29]. Connecting and disconnecting are processes associated with grief and mourning. McKusick, citing Worden and Rando, describes "grief as the acute stage of mourning. Grief is the process of experiencing the loss; mourning refers to the processes that promote undoing the bonds, adapting to the loss, and learning how to live in a healthy manner in the new world" [3, p. 3]; the disconnecting described by McGaffie and Longman. McKusick states "In the communities devastated by HIV, we are in a constant state of mourning, even though we are not necessarily in a state of acute grief" [3, p. 3].

Mourning speaks to the adjustment necessary to accommodate to the loss of a significant individual in one's emotional network. It is more than simply the cognitive acknowledgement of the death of an acquaintance as a disruption to one's social world. McKusick seems to be suggesting that in multiple loss there is chronic mourning. He also has stated that multiple loss syndrome is comprised of three processes—grief, a post-traumatic stress-like syndrome and burnout [30].

This seeming incongruency can be resolved if multiple loss is conceptualized as encompassing the loss of intimates, friends and acquaintances. Whereas the loss of intimates and some friends results in both grief and mourning, the loss of other friends and acquaintances may not result in a profound grief response but will still constitute a loss in the larger network of friends and acquaintances, a loss of potential social support. McKusick has added here the notion both of delayed response and the satiation of carrying capacity and thus inability to process further loss characterized by burnout.

Several authors comment that multiple loss includes other losses and most particularly the loss of a pre-AIDS lifestyle [26, 31]. "Gay men today grieve not only for their dead and dying friends but also for a way of life that is gone and may never come again" [31, p. 24]. From a public health perspective resumption of an aspect of that lifestyle namely anonymous, unprotected sex is clearly a risk factor for acquiring HIV disease. Unfortunately some Gay men have relapsed in their practice of safer sex and other, younger men have not adopted such practices. In this respect they do not differ from their heterosexually oriented counterparts, that is, many young people, and adolescents in particular, have failed to adopt consistent safer sex practices.

The title of this chapter "Saying Good-Bye to Tomorrow" challenges the assumption that a social world as it is known currently can be expected to continue into the future. Indeed the multiple losses sustained by the social network suggests a more profound grief related to the continuity of the assumptive world. Leon McKusick, in a session at the Eighth International AIDS Meeting in Amsterdam, spoke of his fondest wish to grow old with his partner [30]. His recognition that this was not likely to occur, though unspoken, was readily apparent.

The loss of the future, a future together with others significant in one's life is one of the losses accompanying multiple loss. Another is the loss of individuals who constitute a support network. Thus the very individuals who would provide the support necessary to buffer a death may themselves be ill, or dying or dead. Inadequacy of social support has been related to more intense grief [32]. The parallel to the experience of the elderly is striking.

Another feature observed in the bereaved is guilt. Demi and Miles state that "Guilt feelings may be expressed as Role Guilt, Grief Guilt, Moral Guilt or Survival Guilt" [33, p. 176]. It seems likely that the grief of multiple loss is increased by survival guilt particularly where the "survivor" engaged in similarly risky behaviors and is HIV negative. "I've had unsafe sex, . . . Why was I spared while my friends and lovers test positive?" [34, p. A13]. The other types of guilt identified by Demi and Miles are likely to compound these feelings.

For those who are HIV negative there is the concern about growing old alone. " 'Am I going to be the only one left?' " [34, p. A13]. And like those who are HIV positive and whose lovers and friends are dying, there is the concern about who will be here for me when I'm ill, when I'm dying.

Dying alone is not a comforting thought and is literally in apposition to the picture of the "happy ending" surrounded by loved ones. That traditional picture has been disrupted by the advent of high "tech" medicine and the mobility and distant residences of many family members and friends. The peripheral position of religion for many individuals has contributed further to the sense of loss of tradition. Thus each death is a death in isolation devoid of meaning and not one which is inexorably tied to the tradition of predecessors. Without a religious or cultural tradition, the individual dying of cancer or any other disease dies the death of an individual if not an isolate and is grieved for as an individual.

The AIDS Quilt has stitched together all of the individuals dying of HIV disease into a larger whole. Thus the person dying of HIV disease dies connected to the whole—all of those with this disease—and is grieved for both individually and as part of a larger community of loss. And while individual meaning may still elude these deaths, the isolation has been overcome. In death the person dying of HIV disease and his or her bereaved who have contributed a panel to the Quilt, are no longer alone. And meaning is ultimately achieved through the continuing involvements of the bereaved in HIV disease-related activities.

The Viet Nam Memorial, that black wall inscribed with the names of all who died in the Viet Nam conflict has transformed individual grief into collective grief and mourning. The Memorial provides a permanent gathering place for mourners and others to acknowledge the ultimate sacrifice made by these soldiers. The Quilt is displayed at various gatherings, growing organically as deaths from the epidemic increase, its ultimate resting place unspecified. The Quilt and the Memorial are not merely symbolic. Each has contributed to a sense of belonging, providing some meaning, particularly in the case of the Quilt, where formerly there was none.

In the broader definition of multiple loss suggested in the latter part of this chapter, multiple loss encompasses multiple losses. And as the title of this chapter indicates multiple loss entails saying good-bye to the tomorrow of one's assumptive world. The AIDS Quilt (and the Viet Nam Memorial) preserve the memories of our yesterdays and todays for future generations. Let those who survive speak out so that further deaths are curtailed and so that as a society we do not forget. Failing that, the lessons painfully learned will be for nought and thus without meaning. And we will have said good-bye to yesterday as well as to tomorrow.

REFERENCES

1. V. Lehman and N. Russell, Psychological and Social Issues of AIDS and Strategies for Survival, in *Understanding AIDS*, V. Gong (ed.), Rutgers University Press, New Brunswick, New Jersey, pp. 175-189, 1985.
2. R. Biller and S. Rice, Experiencing Multiple Loss of Persons with AIDS: Grief and Bereavement Issues, *Health and Social Work, 15*:4, pp. 283-290, 1990.
3. L. McKusick, Meeting the Challenges of Grief and Multiple Loss, *HIV Frontline*, #6, Center for AIDS Prevention Studies (CAPS) at the University of California, San Francisco, February 1992.
4. J. E. Garret, Multiple Losses in Older Adults, *Journal of Gerontological Nursing, 13*:8, pp. 8-12, 1987.
5. R. Garb, A. Bleich, and B. Lerer, Bereavement in Combat, *Psychiatric Clinics of North America, 10*:3, pp. 421-436, September 1987.
6. P. Z. Fischer, Letting To—Mourning a Fallen Soldier, in *Dying, Death and Bereavement: Theoretical Perspectives and Other Ways of Knowing*, I. B. Corless, B. Germino, and M. Pittman (eds.), Jones and Bartlett, Publishers, Inc., Boston, Massachusetts, 1993.
7. V. Frankl, *Man's Search for Meaning*, Washington Square Press, New York, 1963.
8. L. A. Govoni, Psychosocial Issues of AIDS in the Nursing Care of Homosexual Men and Their Significant Others, *Nursing Clinics of North America, 23*:4, pp. 749-765, December 1988.
9. C. L. Lindgren, M. L. Burke, and G. G. Eakes, Chronic Sorrow: A Lifespan Concept, *Scholarly Inquiry for Nursing Practice: An International Journal, 6*:1, pp. 27-40, 1992.
10. I. M. Martinson, Response to "Chronic Sorrow: A Lifespan Concept," *Scholarly Inquiry for Nursing Practice: An Interdisciplinary Journal, 6*:1, pp. 41-42, 1992.
11. J. M. Schneider, Clinically Significant Differences Between Grief, Pathological Grief and Depression, *Patient Counselling and Health Education*, (Fourth Quarter), pp. 161-169, 1980.
12. R. J. Kastenbaum, *Death, Society and Human Experience* (3rd Edition), Charles E. Merrill Publishing Company, Columbus, Ohio, 1986.
13. R. J. Kastenbaum, AIDS, Society and Human Experience, in *Death, Society and Human Experience* (4th Edition), R. J. Kastenbaum (ed.), MacMillan, New York, pp. 127-145, 1991.

14. I. B. Corless, Spirituality for Whom, in *In Quest of the Spiritual Component of Care for the Terminally Ill*, F. Wald (ed.), Yale University School of Nursing, New Haven, pp. 86-96, 1986.

15. E. Rosenthal, Struggling to Handle Bereavement as AIDS Rips Relationships Apart, *New York Times National*, p. 1, December 6, 1992.

16. R. J. Lifton, The Concept of the Survivor, in *Survivors, Victims and Perpetrators—Essays on the Nazi Holocaust*, J. E. Dimsdale (ed.), Hemisphere Publishing Company, Washington, pp. 113-126, 1980.

17. Speech by Himmler at Gruppenfuhrer meeting at Poznan, October 4, 1943, PS-1919, quoted by R. Hilberg, The Nature of the Process, in *Survivors, Victims and Perpetrators—Essays on the Nazi Holocaust*, J. E. Dimsdale (ed.), Hemisphere Publishing Company, Washington, pp. 5-54, 1980.

18. R. Shilts, *And the Band Played On*, Viking Penguin Inc., New York, 1987.

19. P. S. Arno and K. L. Feiden, *Against the Odds*, Harper Collins Publishers, Inc., New York, 1992.

20. CDC. Update: Outbreak of Hantavirus Infection—Southwestern United States, *Morbidity and Mortality Weekly Report, 42*:23, pp. 441-443, 1993.

21. J. S. Tyhurst, Individual Reactions to Community Disaster—The Natural History of Psychiatric Phenomena, *American Journal of Psychiatry, 107*, pp. 764-769, January-June 1951.

22. K. T. Erikson, Disaster at Buffalo Creek. Loss of Communality at Buffalo Creek, *American Journal of Psychiatry, 133*:3, pp. 302-305, 1976.

23. W. G. Pheifer and C. Houseman, Bereavement and AIDS—A Framework for Intervention, *Journal of Psychosocial Nursing, 26*:10, pp. 21-26, 1988.

24. J. W. Worden, *Grief Counseling and Grief Therapy*, Springer, New York, 1982.

25. T. Rando, *Grief, Dying and Death*, Research Press, Champaign, Illinois, 1984.

26. B. Carmack, Balancing Engagement/Detachment in AIDS-Related Multiple Losses, *Image: Journal of Nursing Scholarship, 24*:1, pp. 9-14, 1992.

27. C. M. McGaffic and A. J. Longman, Connecting and Disconnecting: Bereavement Experiences of Six Gay Men, *JANAC, 4*:1, pp. 49-57, 1993.

28. J. L. Martin, Psychological Consequences of AIDS-Related Bereavement among Gay Men, *Journal of Consulting and Clinical Psychology, 56*:6, pp. 856-862, 1988.

29. L. L. Viney, R. M. Henry, B. A. Walker, and L. Crooks, The Psychosocial Impact of Multiple Deaths from AIDS, *Omega, 24*:2, pp. 151-163, 1991-92.

30. L. McKusick, Multiple Loss, Eighth International AIDS Meeting, Amsterdam, The Netherlands, July 21, 1992.

31. S. J. Klein and W. Fletcher III, Gay Grief: An Examination of Its Uniqueness Brought to Light by the AIDS Crisis, *Journal of Psychosocial Oncology, 4*:3, pp. 15-25, 1986.

32. M. C. Lennon, J. L. Martin, and L. Dean, The Influence of Social Support on AIDS-Related Grief Reaction among Gay Men, *Social Science and Medicine, 31*:4, pp. 477-484, 1990.

33. A. S. Demi and M. S. Miles, Bereavement Guilt—A Conceptual Model with Applications, in *Dying Death and Bereavement: Theoretical Perspectives and Other Ways of Knowing*, I. B. Corless, B. Germino, and M. Pittman (eds.), Jones and Bartlett Publishers, Boston, pp. 171-188, 1993.

34. M. Navarro, Healthy, Gay, Guilt Stricken: AIDS' Toll on the Virus Free, *The New York Times*, New York, p. 1, B6, January 11, 1993.

CHAPTER 13

Horrendous Death:
Linking Thanatology and Public Health

Daniel Leviton

The Horrendous Death concept is a link between Thanatology and global public health. The ultimate outcome of the model is to eliminate Horrendous Death. The vitality of the concept in providing a purpose in life for the author—a health educator, husband and parent is described.

LaRouchefocauld was wrong. It *is* possible to stare into the threat of personal death just as it is the sun. There are problems, yet one has a choice. Stare into the sun for a time and the price will likely be loss of vision. On the other hand, at a given moment one may turn one's head to avoid the sun's intensity. There is a time to avoid harm—it has survival value. So it is with the steady contemplation of personal death: The outcome can be despair, psychological growth and insight, or both. Epictetus, a "late" stoic, was right: For every evil there is a good and for every good there is an evil [1].

There are lessons to be learned from staring at the glare of personal death. Death takes many forms and shapes. My particular interest is *Horrendous Death* (HD) [2, 3]. Its ubiquitous, murderous nature has and does destroy world populations. Ironically, HD, its threat and actuality, has the power to improve the quality of health and well-being to a level higher than has been known in the twentieth century—a century referred to by Barbara Tuchman as the age of violence [cited in 3, p. 15]. HD is the link between thanatology, and public health and public health policy. *Its elimination is one of the most pressing public health problem of our time.*

PURPOSE OF THE CHAPTER

The purpose of this chapter is to explain the HD concept, and its relationship to individual and global health and well-being. HD provides a conceptual framework and motivation for my work as a health educator, citizen, and parent. It provides a philosophy that links past, present and future, and may contribute to one's purpose in life. It has to mine, and that, too may be a story worthy telling.

I have always been inclined toward *action*. Faustian-like study for the sole purpose of acquiring knowledge is dull. It is in the application of knowledge and insight into practice that is exciting. I like to design and develop projects that improve health and well-being. When things go right I feel like Faust, who exulting in his new found vigor and youth, exclaimed, *restless doing is the only way for man* [4, p. 62]. It is the awareness of death that offers an opportunity (again citing *Faust*) to *sate our ardent passion* [4, p. 62]. My passion (ardent to one degree or another) is to act to reduce the actuality and threat of HD, and thus contribute to improving the quality of individual and global health. Another is to follow my daughter's career in writing and my son's in baseball. The two are linked. More of this later.

The quest is often Don Quixotian. It is a roller-coaster ride. On the one hand, it is depressing that politicians, and leaders of other domains of power (media, business, medicine, religion, science, education, the community, and the military) fail to address the public health problem of eliminating HD. In my own field, *Health Education*, progress has not been earth shaking. I have never been successful influencing my peers or my professional organizations. Don't misunderstand. There have been many in my field and in other endeavors who have been supportive, but my closest allies have been my family, the senior staff, board of advisors, and members of the Adult Health & Development Program at the University of Maryland at College Park (ADHP/UMCP), the leadership of the Association for Death Education & Counseling, and many other individuals.

On the other hand, the HD project is a no-lose situation. If something of significance is accomplished we are all better off for the effort. If nothing is accomplished, then like Don Quixote I'll meet my end with the satisfaction of knowing that the effort was worthwhile, at least, in my own mind.

WHAT IS HORRENDOUS DEATH?

HD, Type I is characterized by being:

1. man-made (the sexist terminology is intentional)
2. motivated by the desire to kill, maim, injure, torture, or otherwise destroy another
3. torturous in quality
4. premature
5. deadly to large numbers of people.

Examples are thermonuclear and conventional war, assassination, terrorism, homicide, death resulting, indirectly or directly, from racism and ethnic hatred, man-made starvation and the like. HD, Type I is the focus of this chapter.

In another type of HD (HD, Type II), the motivation to kill another is lacking. Examples are death because of motor vehicle, environmental, and other accidents, and drug and tobacco abuse. For convenience I shall use, *HD*, to refer to HD, Type I.

Since HD is caused by people it could be eliminated if we would put our will to the task. The penultimate question is how to get people and institutions to act in their best health interests by eliminating HD. As a health educator-thanatologist, I know that *having suffered* the HD or threat of HD to loved ones is often a stimulus to action. What about the *general, impersonal threat* of HD? Paradoxically the threat, by itself, is not enough for most people. Even though the headlines and television scream highly of the toll of HD few act as a result. Typical headlines are:

- Teen-ager's Slaying Stuns Peaceful Gaithersburg—Hye Ja Yi (age 18) had been sexually assaulted and then stomped to death, Montgomery County police said—*Washington Post*, April 30, 1985.
- Decapitated Body of Boy Found—*Washington Post*, January 13, 1986.
- Loaded Gun Taken From Fifth Grader's Desk—*Washington Post*, February 4, 1986.
- Nearly 220 teen-agers and children have been shot or stabbed in Washington during the first eight months of the year (1988), an average of about one young victim a day—*Washington Post*, October 12, 1988.
- Gunplay Blights Childhood in D.C. Hundreds become victims in epidemic of shootings—*Washington Post*, September 14,1992.
- Dozens of U.S. Items Used in Iraq Arms—*Washington Post*, July 22, 1992.
- Selling {arms and munitions} to Scoundrels: Why We Won't Stop—*Washington Post*, November 15, 1992.
- 30 Million Hungry in U.S., Report Says—*Washington Post*, September 7, 1992.
- Childhood Poverty Rate Rose During Prosperous '80—*Washington Post*, July 8, 14, 1992.
- U.S. Tolerated Iraqi Fronts, Gonzales Says: The U.S. government knew an Iraqi network of front companies was buying equipment for weapons of mass destruction before the Persian Gulf War but "decided to tolerate his activity"—*Washington Post*, August 11, 1992, p. A4.

We read this and shudder—but only momentarily—as the mind shifts its focus to other matters. But what if *one's child, grandchild, beloved other, or oneself* are substituted for the victims in the headlines?

What is the effect? This sort of contemplation of futurity, with its threats to *everyone's* health, *everyone's* life and limb, and *everyone's* future should be maddening. Ernest Becker elaborated on Pascal's observation:

> Men are so necessarily mad that not to be mad would amount to another form of madness. . . . If we had to offer the briefest explanation of all the evil that men have wrecked upon themselves and upon their world since the beginning of time right up until tomorrow . . . I would be simply in the toll that his pretense of sanity takes, as he tries to deny his true condition [5, p. 29].

That condition is one where we know we and our loved ones are mortal and vulnerable to HD while at the same time we think we are invulnerable.

THE HEALTH (MORTALITY) COST OF HD

There is little mention of HD in the international and national health establishment's official publications and statistics. The only HD-related data included in the *World Health Statistics Manual* are motor vehicle traffic accidents, and suicide and self-inflicted injury [6].

In the United States, deaths resulting from *accidents and adverse effects, suicide, and homicide and legal intervention* are the only forms of HD listed in the government's public health literature [7].

Estimates of mortality due to three causes of HD, Type I (genocide, homicide, and war) affirm the deadly cost of HD, that is, the number of preventable deaths. However, the true mortality picture is obscured because the disease, physical and mental illness, and suffering associated with HD are not included.

Genocide

Rummel, in his painstaking investigation of genocide, estimates that since 1900, over 120,000,000 people have been murdered by their governments (from the review of *Democide: Nazi Genocide and Mass Murder*, in the *Internet on the Holocaust and Genocide*, 1991, Issue No. 34) [8-10].

Homicide

Among the industrialized countries the United States leads, by far, the world in homicide rates [11]. The United States is also higher in childhood mortality due to homicide than eight other developed countries (Federal Republic of Germany, France, The Netherlands, England and Wales, Sweden, Canada, Japan, and Australia). Homicide is the third leading cause of death for elementary and middle school children [12]. In the United States in 1991, 26,513 people were killed due to homicide and legal intervention. They are the leading cause of death for the African American population for those aged 15-24 [7].

War

William Eckhardt, Research Director of the Lentz Peace Research Laboratory, calculated the war and war-related deaths (including *interventions* and *invasions*) by region and country, from 1500-1990 [13]. Absolute numbers of civilian and military deaths were reported. The total number of deaths for civilians was 75,649,000, and for the military was 63,709,000 for a total of 141,901,000 men, women, and children killed in war.

QUALITY OF GLOBAL HEALTH

With an understanding of the concept of HD, Quality of Global Health (QGH) is defined as $QGF = LF_{max}/HD_{min \ or \ elim}$ where HD is minimized or eliminated and Lifegenic Factors (LF) are maximized. *Lifegenic factors* increase the probability of living long and well. Examples are:

1. Meaningful education
2. Meaningful employment
3. Meaningful love and friendship relationships
4. Financial security
5. Quality health care
6. Opportunity for self-actualization
7. Opportunity for enjoyable leisure, recreation and play
8. Purpose and meaning in life
9. Opportunity to achieve spirituality needs
10. Opportunity to maximize health
11. Opportunity for artistic and creative expression

Thus, a high value would show a high QGH Index.

A goal for a highly civilized global society is the elimination of HD and maximum LF.

HOW DID THE HD→GLOBAL HEALTH AND
WELL-BEING CONCEPT DEVELOP

The linkage between health and Thanatology led to HD→Global Health and Well-Being concept. Thanatology is the systematic study of death-related phenomena. It first gained respectability as an academic discipline and science in 1959 with the publication of Herman Feifel's, *The Meaning of Death* [14]. As Freud saw repressed sexuality as a powerful factor explaining human behavior, so Feifel saw death. Feifel felt that the meanings given death influenced our fear of old age, for old age and decrepitude were stark reminders of death and decay. Fear of death, too, might well be a powerful factor contributing to our denial of reality.

He wrote, "Our socially repressive outlook encourages neurotic anxieties about death" [14, p. 11]. On the other hand he knew that

> ... if we accept death as a necessity. ... This might possibly mute some of the violence of our times, for energies now bound up in continuing attempts to shelve and repress the concept of death would be available to us for the more constructive aspects of living, perhaps even fortifying man's gift for creative splendor against his genius for destruction (my emphasis) [14, p. 12].

As a professional health educator I was struck by Feifel's message. My variation of Feifel's insight was that the meaning given death very much affected personal and social health-related behavior. My guess was that if people *fantasized* or otherwise faced the *reality* of themselves or *loved ones* murdered, greater priority might be given to preventing homicide, one type of HD.

I observed that those people most active in reducing HD were those who suffered the HD of someone close to them. An example: At a conference at King's College in London, Ontario, I asked the president of the organization, *Parents of Murdered Children*, whether, in her wildest imagination, she would have predicted the murder of her child. Her response was "Never!" After her child was murdered, she started the organization. Prevention of murder had become salient for her. A similar scenario prompted the development of *Mothers Against Drunk Driving* (MADD). Do our children have to be murdered or killed by drunk drivers before we act to prevent their premature, unnecessary death? Is this the only way we can be motivated to act? Experience is the toughest teacher. There must be less costly ways for people to learn. That is the behavioral health question of our time: *How can we increase the probability that people act in their best health and well-being interest?* Specifically, *How can we get people to act to eliminate forms of HD?*

The elimination of HD is an appropriate challenge for my profession, health education. It has yet to be met. If there is an example of institutional denial it is within the health education professional associations. Health education is not alone. HD, as a public health issue, is essentially avoided by organized medicine (with the exception of *Physicians for Social Responsibility, International Psychoanalysts Against Nuclear War*, and others of that type), education (with the exception of *Educators for Social Responsibility* and like-minded groups), the corporate sector, and other institutions. On the other hand, the Association for Death Education and Counseling provided a platform for discussing HD in the late 1970s.

Governments, like people, tend to deny the fact that HD is inimical to health and well-being. *Health United States 1986 and Prevention Profile* and other publications of the U.S. Public Health Service and National Center for Health Statistics say little of the health and well-being costs of HD. Some mention is made of violent behaviors such as homicide and legal intervention, suicide, accidents, and child and spouse abuse [11, 15]. Whether this is unintentional or intentional is unknown but the result is the same.

it is only when one reads such mind-boggling, but objective gems as *The State of the World Atlas* [16], an annual publication, *World Military and Social Expenditures* [17], and *State of the World* [18] that the enormous economic and health costs of HD for present and future generations are realized.

THE SENSE OF BETRAYAL

There was another reason for becoming involved. I felt betrayed by institutions and individuals responsible for the general well-being and happiness of the population. Regardless of the institution, its ultimate goal is to improve the quality of global health and well-being for its constituency. This concept was central to the sanguine philosophy of Francis Hutcheson written during the pre-revolutionary war period. His *Essay on the Nature and Conduct of the Passions and Affections* articulated a philosophy that was the opposite of the Hobbesian view that people were selfish and aggressive [19, p. 26]. Hutcheson felt that *kind and generous affections were potent sources of human bonding and the good society* [19, p. 27]. Jefferson, influenced by Hutcheson, intentionally included *happiness* rather than *property* in the trinity of *pursuit of life, liberty, and happiness* in the Declaration of Independence [19, p. 42]. In a similar vein the Preamble to the Constitution provides for the common defense and *promoting the general welfare*. Both *happiness and general welfare* are operationally similar to our definition of *quality of global health and well-being*, that is, the absence of HD and maximum of lifegenic factors. This country has invested billions in arms and precious little in promoting the general welfare.

Let me make the transition to the community where I live. I grew up in Washington, D.C. No one can say to me, without me laughing in his face, that I have things better now than when I was growing up around Edgewood Playground and McKinley High School in Northeast Washington during the post World War II era. My kids and your kids unlikely will never enjoy the pleasure of similar neighborhoods that were relatively free of violence, environmental pollution, and other forms of HD.

Washington wasn't Nirvana. There were injustices and need for social reform. Still, hostility was settled on the athletic field, with the mouth, or in a short-lived fist fight. Endemic homicide? Referring to women as bitches? Child, woman, and elder abuser? Animal torture and brutality? Talking back to a teacher or police officer? No way. Their occurrence was an aberration, and the perpetrators were viewed as strange and abnormal.

Something happened over those fifty years. The public received a royal screwing from those in positions of influence and power. Not just from those in politics but industry, education, religion, medicine, the military, the media, and other domains of influence and power. The rich are richer (as likely from cheating and price gouging), and the middle class and poor are poorer. Oceans, lakes, rivers and bays are polluted, and the air stinks.

I look at this, cynically smile, and say to myself, "You've been had!" However, as a father I don't smile. I am furious! Why? Because the prospects for my kids and yours are dismal. I know that my kids can be murdered any time, any day.

I worry that my kids might be called upon to fight a war over oil or other aspects of *realpolitik.* Children report the same cynicism of government. In a *Washington Post* story (*Children seen losing trust in government,* Sept. 14, 1992), it was reported that less than half of the more than 300,000 children in grades two through six who were surveyed, said they believed their government can be trusted to do what's right.

Ross Perot tapped this anger and fear with the slogan, *It's the economy, stupid!* But it is more than economics. It is anger and fear over *diminishing prospects for the future,* and increased probability of HD.

My credo? My kids will never go to war unless the children and grandchildren of the power brokers, and/or those who profit from war, lead the way by ex-ample—that is, in the frontlines of the infantry. And if they are stupid enough to play Abraham ready to sacrifice their Isaac, count me out. I won't play that deadly and stupid game.

My work was cut out for me.

HUSBAND-AND FATHERHOOD

Responsibility for others such as mate and children changes one's views of death. It makes the threat of death more fearsome. It is not personal death but death of the beloved that takes priority. As a bachelor, I could tease death with adventures and escapades. As a parent and husband, premature death, especially HD, must be avoided at all costs. HD has no redeeming virtue. That it occurs is a testament to our stupidity, tendency to conform, and denial of death.

Aware that my wife and children could die, at any time, HD serves as a stimulus to action. In don't think most people react this way simply because, for them, it is next to impossible to think of their loved one's dying a HD. Yet the denial could be removed enabling us to imagine our most beloved others dying a HD, we might be moved to action. Imagine your most beloved person or pet brutally murdered— the throat slashed, and stomach ripped open by knife. Evisceration. Does the imagery have an effect? If you and I would periodically and systematically imagine our children starving would it prompt us to do what we could to make sure that all children were nourished well? I think it increases the odds. Why?

Because the meaning given life and death, and health and well-being would become more *personally* salient. *Hunger* and *homicide*, as examples, would lose much of their abstract quality. The ultimate goal, again, is to increase the probability that the individual *acts*.

The HD concept focuses on whoever the target person loves the most. It may be oneself or the *most beloved other*. In my case, it is my children. I suspect that I can face my own dying and death—but the HD of my kids? That has the potential of arousing one to action. But the denial that one's own child can die is powerful. Is a key to action, then, the removal of the denial of the HD threat? I think it is part of the answer.

HD → FEAR OF DEATH → REMOVAL OF DENIAL → ANTICIPATORY GRIEVING → ACTION → HEALTH AND WELL-BEING OUTCOME LINKAGE

The perception of the quality, circumstances, and type of death are related to the *level* of denial (or awareness). For example, when my parents were alive, I *feared* their death in old age because of cancer, heart disease, or other chronic diseases associated with old age, that is, the category of deaths that I labeled *Other*. That fear was related to a certain *level* of psychological *denial*. I knew they could die at any moment due to a host of causes but, I denied it (that middle knowledge of which Weisman wrote) [20]. The prevention of my parents' inevitable death was important to me, and we did what we could to *prevent* the inevitable: Countless visits to physicians, tests, medications and the like. *I took some action to prevent their deaths*.

Now take the threat of death of my children. How? Say, in excruciating pain by means of *burning to death* (napalm), *bayonet, nuclear blast* (not an immediate death in the nanosecond of the nuclear flash but prolonged suffering), *torture, lynching, rape-murder*, or *evisceration*. The fear of these sorts of HD happening to our children and grandchildren is the highest. Consequently, the accompanying denial is highest, and the probability of action to prevent such a death is very low. A curvilinear relationship is hypothesized: *The more horrible the type or style of dying and death is perceived, the greater the fear; the greater the fear, the greater the denial; and, the greater the denial, the less chance of action to eliminate the very causes of such torturous deaths. On the other hand, low fear of HD is also associated with low probability of action.*

DENIAL OF HD

Again, the removal of the *denial* of HD is crucial to eliciting systematic action to reduce the probability of HD. As Freud and others have suggested denial is a universal adaptation to the threat of personal death [21-23]. World War I disillusioned Freud. He was horrified by the eradication of the rules of civilized moral and social conduct, and the brutality with which men could inflict death and suffering upon people whether soldiers or civilians [24]. How could people be so barbaric? His answer was psychological denial of personal death. "Our own death is indeed imaginable," he wrote. " . . . at bottom no one believes in his own death, or to put the same thing in another way, in the unconscious every one of us is convinced of his own mortality" [25, p. 15].

Ernest Becker agreed when he wrote that "This narcissism is what keeps men marching into point-blank fire in wars: at heart one doesn't feel he will die, he only feels sorry for the man next to him" [5, p. 2].

Yet, Lifton is correct when he observes,

> And our resistance to that knowledge, our denial of death, is indeed formidable. . . . But the denial can never be total; we are never fully ignorant of the fact that we die. Rather we go about life with a kind of 'middle knowledge' of death, a partial awareness of it side by side with expressions and actions that belie that awareness [21, p. 17].

Removal of denial of HD is central to motivating people to act to eliminate that form of preventable death.

ANOTHER WAY OF REMOVING DENIAL: HORRENDOUS DEATH IMAGERY— THE HOLOCAUST

It was mentioned that an efficient way to remove the denial of HD is to have intimate experience with HD. It is a tough way to learn. Is it possible to learn vicariously through education with a subsequent gain in insight and wisdom? Can education prompt action to eliminate HD? The answer is unknown but we make our effort.

Since 1965 I have been teaching Death Education at the University of Maryland. Each semester the issue of HD is covered usually using the Holocaust, homicide, or a ongoing war, or act of genocide as an example. When I focus on the Holocaust, I am amazed how few students are aware that it even happened, and its profound implications for the potential for evil in people. The exceptions are most Jewish students and others who lost loved ones in the Holocaust. Students have come up to me after class with tears in their eyes asking what could be done to prevent such carnage from happening again. One young lady, herself a Christian, could not believe that Christians participated in the genocide and that others like the United States and the Catholic Church stood by making little effort to stop the killing until late in the war. She, too, wanted to know what to do. It was important to point out to her that many Christians and countries such as Holland, went to great lengths, often jeopardizing themselves, to save the victims of Naziism. In keeping with self-efficacy theory it was almost important to recommend a task for her. She ultimately joined *Amnesty International.*

Lest we forget such a hideous event, I show the film, *Genocide,*[1], or a similar film,[2] to serve as a stark reminder of HD. The film severs several purposes, that is, to:

- Recognize that genocidal acts occur as a function of state policy, and that no nation, institution, or individual is immune from committing genocidal acts [26-29]
- Allow discussion, even venting of anger against responsible forces and leaders for allowing such horrors to occur. It is a time when students will talk of the deaths of their grandparents and other relatives
- Motivate students toward action to reduce the probability of genocide.

The bitter lesson of history is that we *do* forget—and *avoid.* Yet there are those who never forget, and who learn from history and experience. Organizations and their publications such as *The Institute of the Holocaust and Genocide*, and the *Institute for the Study of Genocide* are invaluable for their research efforts to understand genocide, and alert us to potential trouble spots throughout the world.[3]

Another lesson concerns the complexity and power of *the herd effect, or conformity.* All levels of German citizenry participated in the conduct of the Holocaust: Physicians, Ph.D.s, lawyers, and (the greatest irony for me), health educators. Robert Lifton wrote of the psychological processes (such as psychic numbing, psychic splitting, conformity, and rationalization) enabling the pillars of German society—physicians—to participate in the torture and execution of over six million people. Affectionate fathers and husbands, and accomplished in their professional field—on one hand, and on the other—mass killers [26, 30]. It can happen here. Even now we are numb to the homicides and poverty in our cities, the genocide in Bosnia, Rwanda, and Somalia, and fail to act toward their elimination.

---

[1] For information write to the Simon Weisenthal Center, 9760 West Pico Blvd., Los Angeles, CA 99035, or telephone (213) 553-9036. Also see Grobman, A. & Landes, D. 1983. *Critical issues of the holocaust: A companion to the film Genocide. Los Angeles: Simon Weisenthal Center.*

[2] Recently, I have shown a videotape, *Special Report: After the War with Bill Moyers.* Order from Public Affairs Television, 356 West 58th St., New York, NY 10019. It is a masterful documentation of the after effects of the war against Iraq especially the harm done civilian populations. This was, ostensibly, the war of *smart bombs* which *always* targeted or hit military targets exclusively. We know that sometimes civilians were targeted or decimated as the SCUDS went off course.

[3] Write to: The Institute on the Holocaust and Genocide, P.O.B. 10311, 91102 Jerusalem, Israel. Its publication is *Internet*, and the basic subscription is $25.00; and The Institute for the Study of Genocide, CUNY, 899 Tenth Avenue, Room 623, New York, NY 10019. It publication is the *ISG Newsletter*, and its membership fee is $25.00.

GRIEVING THE FUTURE,
PREMATURE HORRENDOUS
DEATH OF ONE'S OWN CHILD

Once denial of HD of the child is removed, and the imagery of the torturous but preventable death confronted, *anticipatory grieving* is thought to occur. By going through the process of anticipatory grieving the probability of health protective *action* increases.

Dennis Klass' *Parental Grief: Solace and Resolution* explains the process of grieving for one's dead child [31]. The death of one's child is one of life's most profound stressors, and a health risk increasing the probability of premature death and morbidity [32, p. 283].

The death of a child is a psychological indictment concerning parental competence. "The child is a part of the parent's self," writes Klass [31, p. 12]. This identification is part of the parent-child bond. When the child dies it is often likened to an amputation. Not only has a part of the self been killed but the psychological and physical pain is excruciating. The death of a child destroys plans and expectations for the future. In a real sense the future dies with the child.

The HD of a child is different from, say, death by means of childhood cancer. Besides identification with the dead child, that is, incorporating the dead child as part of the parent's ego, the patient internalizes the dead child's pain and suffering. The parent of a killed child cries out for vengeance and retribution and rest does not come easily until it is achieved [31]. For our purposes, the difference between anticipatory grieving of the fantasized and actual HD of one's child lies in the modification and channeling of vengeance. If the child is literally killed, the odds are good that vengeance would be directed toward the killer or a killer-substitute (e.g., country, political leader, flag, etc.). It is possible that the need for retribution might be channeled toward constructive outcomes, but most of us have yet to achieve control over such primal drives.

On the other hand *anticipatory, fantasized grieving* over the death of the beloved child *in the future* elicits screams, fear, and trembling of what might be. Themes of hatred and vengeance toward the fantasized killer individual, group or state are subordinate to the need to *prevent* such a death and to subsequently survive and survive well. Thus, in the conceptual framework presented here, the probability of personal *action to eliminate HD* is thought to increase if the individual experiences the anticipatory grieving resulting from the imagery of the dead child killed by forms of HD. Obviously, arousal toward action is increased (at least in me) if the real life situation (war, racial and ethnic antagonism, poverty, homicide, etc.) reinforces the imagery. If you live in my county, country, or globe, HD is real. HD, then, is a link between individual and global health, and Thanatology. HD gives new meaning to *health* for it makes us consider *time*, and *perception*.

DEFINITIONS OF HEALTH

The World Health Organization's definition of health reads, "Health is a state of complete physical, mental, and social well-being and not merely the absence of disease and infirmity" [33, p. 4].

A modification is suggested with special reference to the meaning given *time*. Think of your limited mortality. Think of the world as you will leave it to your children and grandchildren. How is your view of the future affected (with special reference to what Lifton calls themes of continuity, connection, and futurity) [21]? Think of your history (past time)? What legacy were you left by your parents, grandparents, and others? What legacy do you wish to leave? That meaning can affect health-related behavior. It should serve to motivate to action.

My modified definition is: *Health is the process toward*, and *perception* of acceptable physical, mental, and social well-being and not merely the absence of disease and infirmity here and now, and *as expected in the future* (emphasis is mine). The person filled with "fear and trembling" and dread over what tomorrow might bring is not healthy according to our definition. Suicide is an example.

SUICIDE

Many public health professionals see suicide as an indicator of the health of the social group or community similar to unemployment, homicide, infant survival rates and the like. Generally, perceiving the future with a chronic sense of hopelessness and lack of meaning is an indicator of suicide. Hopelessness is present and future-oriented. One sees no way out of the box here and now, and in the future. Is it any wonder that many individuals confined to Nazi concentration camps committed suicide [34]?[4] Coupled with the anguish and grief over the miserable death of loved ones was their own perceived loss of control and sense of hopelessness as they contemplated their present and foreseeable future. Toward the end of this chapter I discuss the need for individuals and groups to have (or expect) *prospects for the future*. If one has something to live for one lives.

SYMBOLIC IMMORTALITY AND HEALTH

Robert Lifton thoughtfully comments about the linkage between death and life, that is, continuity. He feels that the link is "symbolic immortality," that is, how we perceive ourselves symbolically living on after death. According to Lifton we

---

[4] It is just as interesting to ask why so many concentration camp sufferers did *not* suicide? Reasons given include the strong social support and sense of sharing within the camps, the desire for vengeance upon the Nazis, the prohibition against suicide while emphasizing life in Judaism, the desire and hope for reunion with loved ones at some point in the future, and that a direct cause for the misery could be identified [34, 35].

hope to live on through several modes: *Biology* (our children); *creativity* (our work . . . Beethoven lives!); *theology* (themes of resurrection, rebirth and the like); *nature* (the mountains, trees and rivers live on as my spirit lives on); and *experiential transcendence* (" . . . a psychic state so intense and all-encompassing that time and death disappear") [21, pp. 3-35]. Lifton writes,

> A *sense* of immortality, then is by no means mere denial of death, though denial and numbing are rarely present. Rather it is a corollary of the knowledge of death itself, and reflects a compelling and universal inner quest for continuous symbolic relationship to what has gone before and what will continue after our finite individual lives. *That quest is central to the human project, to man as cultural animal and to his creation of culture and history. The struggle toward, or experience of, a sense of immortality is in itself neither compensatory nor 'irrational'*, but an appropriate symbolization of our biological and historical connectedness [21, p. 17].

Personal sense of *health* in the present and the future, too, is central to our existence. Nearly every survey inquiring about life satisfaction, life's priorities, or factors contributing to happiness, finds "health" among the highest values and priorities of people. That sense of health pertains not only to oneself but to loved ones as well. How can I feel healthy if my loved ones are sick or dying, or *threatened* with sickness or death? Perhaps at a different level of awareness, health may be affected when *others within the global community are threatened with sickness and death.* If for no other reason than to maintain personal health and well-being we must insure the health and well-being of our neighbor.

Our perception of threats to our sense of futurity is increasing. That is, threats to our need for connection, symbolic immortality, our hopes and plans, and expectations of health and well-being for ourselves and children are increasing geometrically.

RESPONSIBILITY

> Louis Ludborg, the former chairman of the board of the Bank of America, who has said that, in the final reckoning, the quality of life in its total meaning is the only justification for any corporate activity. But Ludborg was never able to turn the Bank of America around in its own decision-making so that it would include the environment in its calculations and deliberations.
>
> —The Case for an Environmental Ethic in
> *The Center Magazine*, March 1980

The ultimate goal of all institutions is the improvement of the quality of civilized life, that is, global health and well-being. Because of the multidimensional quality of "health and well-being," attaining, maintaining, and improving it becomes more than a medical, and individual endeavor or responsibility. Political institutions, the corporate sector, religion; education, science and medicine, the media, and, the military—all of us have the responsibility to improve health and the perception of health of individual and society both here and now and in the future. Health, quality of civilized life, and "general welfare" have in common the goal of increasing the probability that people live long and well.

MY TERROR, MY FUN

Terror is the realization that my family can die a HD at any moment. Terror is the knowledge that I will be unable to prevent it. Children and adults are intentionally and unintentionally murdered everyday. Caught in a crossfire between hoodlums, or in warfare they die. A person machine guns and kills a crowd of children in a fast food restaurant whom he has never seen or met before. *What if my family and I were dying due to man-made starvation in Somalia, or in the United States, the land of milk and honey? I am terrified because I lack control of the situation.*

Good coping skills, ability to function well, and mental health are related to our sense of control. We like to think that we are "John Wayne." That is, able to accomplish any task, overcome obstacles, and move mountains with perseverance and "true grit." We can invent the computer, throw a baseball 100 miles an hour, and whip the Iraqis on the battlefield in days with *destructotech*. Yet we can't conquer death. John Wayne couldn't. He couldn't beat Cancer. John Wayne was never supposed to die. He symbolized the common hero myth linking immortality and performing good deeds.

Joe Louis was a bonafide hero who symbolically beat death. When Louis knocked out Max Schmeling in their second fight, Louis symbolically defeated Death, specifically HD. He defeated the entire Nazi movement: The Brown Shirts, Black Shirts, Storm Troopers, the Gestapo, Hitler, Goering, Goebbles, Hess—all of them. If *he* could beat the invincible, scowling Schmeling, there was hope for us. He gave us confidence, and hope for the future by reducing our terror—our fear of HD. He was every person's idol. A hero when he was alive or dead. He is immortal.

Some years after Mr. Louis retired, I met him. At that time, the heavyweight champion, Mohammed Ali was preparing to fight at the Capitol Center in Landover, Maryland. It so happened that a public health conference was in session in the hotel where Ali, Louis, and others were staying. When I entered the foyer of the hotel I saw Mr. Louis in the crowd talking with a group. For awhile I enjoyed watching and listening to the colorful fight crowd when I noticed that he was free. I introduced myself and said, "You know, when I was a kid, I thought the Nazis would conquer all, and ultimately torture, and mutilate all of us. You were a hero to this Jewish kid." He smiled, and allowed how he appreciated my comment. Then he paused, looked me up and down, and quietly asked, "Am I that much older than you?"

Today's leaders, by their actions, have done little to assuage the terror of the possibility of HD. Undoubtedly, there has been progress between the former Soviet Union and the United States to reduce the nuclear stockpile such as the START I and II agreements. But by and large the threat of HD remains, and possibly increases in certain areas.

U.S. presidents are assumed to be noble and virtuous. Show me one, in recent times, who hasn't lied, or sold arms and weapons to our enemies, and I'll buy you a beer. In many cases they are the colleagues of death as they start their wars within and between nations in the name of *realpolitik*. They have their hand on triggers of all types and have pulled or come close to pulling those triggers. President Kennedy and the Cuban missile crisis, and presidents Johnson and Kennedy and Viet-Nam come to mind. How close we came to annihilation.

We wish politicians and leaders in other domains to be heroic and models and models for us and our children. Former vice-president Agnew? Former presidents Nixon, Reagan, and Bush? Mike Miliken? There is no Mother Theresa, Ghandi, or Martin Luther King in that group. Influential CEOs, presidents, and others need to know what I know. They nor their children and grandchildren can escape HD. They need to join with us in eliminating HD, and improving the quality of global health.

The FUN part is working to eliminate HD. The first lesson learned is that we act in ways best suited to our personality, situation, and training. Years ago I talked with a friend, and octogenarian activist, Carlos Van Lear. Carlos was a Dartmouth graduate, witty as well as an accomplished banjo player. He has gone to jail several times for acts of civil disobedience protesting civil rights inequities, the nuclear weapons buildup, the Viet-nam war, and degradation of the environmental. I commented once that I was envious of him for he had "put his action where his mouth was." He laughed. After a moment he asked how many students and others I taught each semester. I estimated that around 800 people enrolled in my Death Education, and Adult Health & Development Program each year. He asked if I discussed the topic of HD, and the need to act? I replied, "Every semester, one way or another." "Well," he said, "you influence more people to do the right thing in one semester than I have in a lifetime." His point was that we each do *our own thing in our own way*. No matter how kind Carlos' words were, he and other activists *do* have more courage than I. Still we need to act in our own way.

Projects naturally developed from the HD concept. One is the Adult Health & Development Program and the National Network for Intergenerational Health, and the other has to do with efforts to convene a Manhattan type project to eliminate HD. The former is an actuality, while the latter is only beginning.

THE ADULT HEALTH & DEVELOPMENT PROGRAM
(AHDP) AND NATIONAL NETWORK FOR
INTERGENERATIONAL HEALTH (NNIH)

The AHDP is an intergenerational health promotion and rehabilitation program where older institutionalized and non-institutionalized adults (called *members*) are paired on a one-to-one basis with a trained *student-staffer* to improve health, well-being, physical fitness, and health knowledge [36-41]. The proliferation of AHDPs to colleges and universities throughout the United States and elsewhere is the NNIH. The NNIH consists of AHDP's located at Aurora University, Northern Virginia Community College, Nicholls State University, Bloomsburg State College, Gallaudet University, and Israel. Universities soon to open their Programs include University of Delaware, University of Miami at Oxford, Utica College, Western Colorado University, Clark-Atlanta University, Banneker High School, Paine University, and Florida A & M University.

How does the AHDP/NNIH contribute to reducing HD? One goal is to reduce ethnic, racial, age, and other stereotypes and labels which contribute to hostility and aggression between and among individuals and groups. How? By *integration of diverse groups*. The AHDP's members vary in terms of ethnicity and race, socio-economic background, health, age, experiences, etc. Staffers also vary in their age, ethnicity and race, academic major, and experiences. It has been said that the AHDP represents a miniature United Nations in the make up of its members and staffers. Integration of diverse groups is intentional, and a requirement for acceptance into the NNIH. Also, the nature of play, fun, physical activity, and health education are non-threatening and serve as a means to bond the staffer and member regardless of social class, racial or ethnic differences.

Of course, my personal satisfaction is immense. The pleasure is in seeing the older adult member improve in health, well-being, physical activity status, and simply having fun with their staffers. The staffers—with special reference to the senior staffers—they are something else. Over the years, I watched them become confident, develop into leaders, and grow. I have seen them operate under stress. Their word is their bond. Is it any wonder that the only students for whom I write recommendations are staffers?

HD AS A STIMULUS TO
IMPROVE THE QUALITY OF GLOBAL HEALTH:
THE MANHATTAN PROJECT MODEL

Another endeavor which naturally developed from the HD concept was a variation of the Manhattan Project. If you recall, the Manhattan Project was the major effort during World War II, to develop the first atomic bomb, and thus speed the end of the war. Marshalled together in common purpose were the best brainpower and equipment. Money was no object. The focus upon accomplishing the task was tunnel vision *par excellence.*

Why not emulate the Manhattan Project to address the complex problem of eliminating HD? I had been writing and talking about this and other approaches for years. It was time for action. The idea was to start small. Was it possible to convene a group of "gatekeepers" who were influential and in their sphere of influence to discuss the idea? Frankly, the answer is not yet in.

VIEWING THE WORLD FROM THE GLOBAL HEALTH PERSPECTIVE

In order to elicit change in the direction of global health the population needs to be informed. But knowledge is not enough to prevent HD. A sense of responsibility and a global health ethic must be developed resulting in action. How? Through informal (by way of parenting, religious education, by emphasizing sportsmanship in athletics, etc.) and formal health education. What is needed is a substantial segment of the population that is health educated, persevering, and action-oriented to work toward becoming *influential.* Influence toward the end of achieving global health and well-being.[5] It is illusory to believe that the HD $\rightarrow$ Global Health & Well-being concept will be universally supported. Unfortunately, too many of the world's population are preoccupied with attaining basic needs even though they are as susceptible to HD as anyone else. Others will be resistant for one reason or another, or simply will not care.

Leaders and the electorate, in order to live both long and well, will be well served by adapting a universal value system and way of looking at the world. Some of those values are discussed below.

VALUING THE INDIVIDUAL AND HIS/HER CULTURE

Individuals from different nation-states, and the nations-states themselves need to be seen as fellow inhabitants of our planet and given the respect which we would give our family, friends, and neighbors. The stereotype, perhaps even, the word, *enemy,* is best forgotten unless it refers to HD, the enemy common to us all.

Some forms of HD (preventable by definition) increase in probability because of negative perceptions about people. Homicide, racism, political torture, and wars are examples. In the United States there is a widening division between white and African-American communities. On black-oriented radio and television I hear of fears of a formal plan of genocide conjured up by the white establishment similar to that practiced by Nazi Germany upon Jews and other non-Aryans during

---

[5] The domains of global power are politics-government, labor, corporations-business, religion, education, science and medicine, the media, the military, and the community.

World War II. It is a fear based upon the more valid perception that blacks are expendable victims—as soldiers in war, victims of homicide, victims of poverty, and victims of drugs.

The fact that this *perception* of planned systematic genocide exists in the African-American community should be of concern to everyone. Why? Two reactions to any *threat* are variations of *flight or fight*. Fight? One can expect increased race-related homicides even race war in the future. Variations of flight are just as defeating. An individual or group can lose hope. An entire race can become a permanent demoralized underclass at best, or clinically depressed, and/or suicidal at worst. In either case, the rich potential of the ethnic or racial minority individual and culture to contribute to the health and well-being of the global community is lost. Thus, a view of the world is necessary which values the potential and worth of each human being, and his or her culture.

That which encourages the elimination of stereotypes and labels is to be encouraged. Intermarriage is one means. It is difficult to feel hostility toward someone of another race or ethnic background when your own children are a member of that group. Alexander the Great was wise when he encouraged his soldiers to marry the women of the enemy, learn their language and live among them.

Unless children and youths are valued, learn to respect and like themselves and others, the alternate is self- and other-hatred. Children shoot one another for staring. Their behavior is similar to that of children raised in war torn environments who become numbed to death. They get a "kick" out of killing. They have no conscience, no remorse, and no humanity. Parents and governments in countries such as Iran, Iraq, Viet-Nam, and Cambodia have allowed their children to be used as killers. Deadly and dead children are now a social problem of increasing magnitude in the United States and other western countries as well. The threat of class war looms larger each year. Imagine a nine-year-old murdering your nine-year-old. Impossible you say? Read the papers.

PARENTAL, SOCIAL, AND INSTITUTIONAL SUPPORT OF THE DEVELOPING CHILD TO INSTILL A POSITIVE SELF-CONCEPT

The birthright to a "decent minimal share of world resources by virtue of being born" is not enough. Concerned with the increasing scarcity of natural resources and their effect on survival, *Richard Barnet's first principle for evolving a survival strategy is that "every person born has political and economic rights and has a vested right to a decent minimal share of world resources by virtue of having been born. The explicit purpose of a global resource system is to serve the world population,* and that must mean everybody on earth" [42, p. 310].

That birthright must include love and social support. If we wish people to be loving and peaceful human beings, to respect and value animal and human life, and the ecosystem they must have self-esteem while eliciting the respect and friendship of others. The key to this is in the love, education, support, and nurturing of the developing child provided by the 1) intact family, 2) community, 3) educational system, and 4) social institutions such as government, business, labor, religion, law, and the media.

For example if the data clearly indicate that a child's development and well-being is related to the presence of a loving parent-child relationship it follows that such behaviors should be reinforced by every means possible. A means to that end would be compulsory, formal, health education courses concerned with the art and science of parenting. Think of it. Any damn fool can hold two of the most profound occupations in the world without benefit of education or training: Parenthood and politics!

Barnet puts it another way. His second principle for evolving a survival strategy is the protection of communities. He writes, "A rational planning system should start with the goal of community health—physical, economic, and spiritual" [42, p. 311].

The minimum wage, and income tax system need to be adjusted allowing parents to rear their children with a minimum of economic stress. Certainly, the opportunity for upward mobility must be provided if we are to improve the health and well-being of people. Why are such recommendations made? To insure social stability, and individual and social health and well-being. It is worth the price.

THE VALUES OF GLOBAL HEALTH
AND FUTURITY

The elimination of HD, while enhancing lifegenic factors, for the benefit of present and future generations should be the top priority of all nation-states. Where does one place his or her priorities when it comes to life? Is it the acquisition of material goods? Education? Travel? Children? One has to be alive in order to enjoy such pleasures. There also needs to be a future for us as well as our children. We need to value the quality of life in the future, and leave a legacy of a healthy planet. A planet without HD.

Specifically, what forms of HD would you eliminate first? Is the elimination or reduction of nuclear and conventional weapons number one? Or is it the elimination of the close relatives of war, such as homicide, genocide and holocaust, or terrorism? Is it the elimination of poverty and undernutrition? Racism? Threats to the environments? Do we need to place priorities? My view is that the elimination of HD *as a class* is the priority. This view of the world considers present and future generations.

Writing in, *Peace Review*,[6] Renner cites Wendell Barry:

[6] For information write to *Peace Review Publications Inc.*, 2439 Birch St., Suite 8, Palo Alto, CA 94306.

To what point . . . do we defend from foreign enemies a country that we are destroying ourselves? In spite of all our propagandists can do, the foreign threat inevitably seems diminished when our air is unsafe to breathe, when our drinking water is unsafe to drink, when our rivers carry tonnages of topsoil that make light of the freight they carry in boats, when our forests are dying from air pollution and acid rain, and when we ourselves are sick from poisons in the air. Who are the enemies of the country? [43, p. 22].

ESCHEWING GREED, AND VALUING ALTRUISM, TRUST AND OTHER VIRTUES

Viktor Frankl is the existential philosopher, who found meaning to life while a prisoner of the Nazis in their hellish Nazi concentration camps. On the value of altruism he wrote, "Only in the service of a cause higher than ourselves, and only through the love of a person other than ourselves do we become really human, and do we actualize our real selves" [44, p. 7].

The opposite of altruism is described by Hobart Rowan of the *Washington Post*. He found it ironic that the Bush administration opposed a $4.55 minimum wage while Mike Miliken, a Drexel Burnham junk bond salesman earned $550 million dollars in 1987. A CEO of Ralston Purina received $1 million in salary in 1988 and $12 million in stock-options profits [45]. How much money does a person need to live an enjoyable life? I argue that there is survival value in sharing the wealth, and in narrowing the gap between haves and have nots. Would you steal to feed your starving child while abundant food was available to those who could afford it, and conspicuous consumption and greed were seen as virtuous and desirable? I would.

In order to eliminate HD trust between people, their leaders and institutions must again become part of the social contract. I mentioned earlier that the American public casts a suspicious eye upon its leaders. Members of so called "noble" professions fare little better than politician in the public's view. Some scientists under pressure to show statistically significant results, in order to obtain grants, and/or attain or maintain status, falsify data. According to one survey of 211 medical doctors, 33 percent "would mislead survivors if hey knew their treatment error had contributed to the patient's death" [46]. As a member of the faculty at a large eastern university for well over twenty years I've learned that all academics, especially administrators, cannot be trusted.

When James E. Hansen, director of the Goddard Institute of Space Studies, starkly warned of the immediacy of the greenhouse effect and its ultimately deadly effects on the biosphere his comments were altered, without his permission, by the White House [47]. Why was a scientist prevented from expressing his professional opinion concerning global health and well-being?

The United States is not alone. *Izvestia*, a Soviet newspaper, accused a government ministry of trying to cover up accidents at nuclear plants. Apparently, increasing "nuclearphobia" in the Soviet Union following Chernobyl provoked the cover up [46].

Plaintively, the columnist, Haynes Johnson, asked the Bush administration to provide presidential leadership. He wrote,

> Wisdom and honesty: the very qualities of Americans have yearned for in their presidents since the first George so long ago—and the same ones Bush will most need in the White House to lead America in the 1990s [48, p. A1].

Shortly after the Johnson article appeared, the Speaker of the U.S. House of Representatives, and the Japanese Prime Minister were cashiered out of office for malfeasance.

There is a price to be made when we lose faith in our leaders. Whether in athletics, government, education or entertainment, people need altruistic models to emulate. That which reinforces altruism in the family, the schools, and the community should be encouraged.

VALUING LEADERSHIP BY EXAMPLE
AND REWARD

It is a view of the world which realizes that the super military and economic powers: China, France, Germany, Great Britain, France, Japan, the former Soviet Union, and the United States can best provide leadership in improving the quality of global health by good example and positive reinforcement rather than rhetoric and force. Does the United States wish Iraq to halt planned or actual production of chemical and biological weapons? Then the United States cannot continue production of binary and other exotic chemical weapons. How can we expect north Korea, Pakistan or Brazil to refrain from producing nuclear weapons if we continue increasing our overkill capacity? If we wish nation-states and their citizens to trust and value representative democracy then we cannot endorse and support brutal dictators like former "President" Marcos of the Philippines or the former Shah of Iran simply because they wave the flag of anti-communism.

The impoverished hearken to that political-economic system that provides health and well-being (e.g., food, employment, shelter, education, and health services) rather than rhetoric.

VALUING THE ECOSYSTEM

It is a view of the world which understands the interdependence of the constituent parts of the ecosystem upon one another. Increasingly, nation-states are dependent upon one another economically and in trade. All one has to do is observe the United States' dependency upon foreign oil and capital, or the former

USSR's need to trade for wheat. Barnet writes that since the Earth's natural resources are limited we need to realize:

> In just 300 years a high clunk of the geological capital of the ages was consumed as if it were an ever growing annuity guaranteed until the end of time. . . . The fundamental philosophical choice—can human beings dominate nature or are they limited by nature—now divides both capitalism and socialism. It may well be the issue on which a true "convergence" of the market economies and the centrally planned economies takes place [42, p. 301].

From the perspective of global health and well-being maintaining the ecosystem take priority over extraordinary unnecessary consumption, and luxurious living. Would you rather retain the ozone layer or have hair sprayers pressured by chlorofluorocarbons which destroy the atmosphere? Desire nuclear power? What will you do with its waste products?

VALUING ANIMAL AND HUMAN LIFE

Preserving the life of one's tribe is a universal value of all cultures except under certain conditions, e.g., warfare, self-defense, etc. The proscription, thou shall not kill, must be extended beyond kinfolk and tribal members to all human beings. We need to return to valuing human life.

Two world wars, and the Nazi Holocaust imprinted mass murder upon the public's consciousness. While generally accepted by civilized people as an abomination still the collective conscious of the Allied nations (United States, Great Britain, France, China, and the Soviet Union) during the early part of World War II was numbed by the high numbers of murders and the efficiency of the gas chambers and lethal injections. If the German citizenry denied such mass death even as box cars of prisoners rumbled past their towns and the odor of burning flesh permeated the air so did religious institutions and governments within and outside of Germany.

An ethical and psychological schism exists between the accepted social contract (thou shall not kill) and the reality of HD. The result of this conflict between our "good" and "dark" sides is individual and group anxiety. How did this come to be? Barnet makes an interesting and, to my way of thinking, valid observation. He writes,

> The three traditional impulses for protecting human life have been deadened by progress. One is religious. The obligation to respect the individual is derived from a duty to a supreme being or supernatural source. There is a transcendent value to each soul. . . . The religious commandments in the Old and New Testaments that worshipping God requires ministering to the poor and the helpless have lost much of their force [42, p. 304].

One does not have to be religious in a formal sense to appreciate and see the necessity of the values derived from religion for getting on well with global neighbors. The two icons of the Christian-Judaic religions, "Love thy neighbor," and "Do unto others as you would have them do unto you" serve well as a basis for civil behavior among people. Why not add, "Serve well those who will inherit the earth."

A second "impulse for valuing life is a sense of community . . . the traditional obligations to family and village" where each individual has a duty to protect the other members of the community [42, p. 304].

We need to develop a sense of community, a sense of the commons in which the protection of children from HD is a community responsibility. The studies of children who grow up in a violent environment indicate that they become numbed to the value of life because their life is meaningless. Thus, any plan to eliminate HD and enhance global health and well-being should develop a strong sense of values and community—emphasizing the healthy nurturing of children.

A community is not inherently warlike. Johan Galtung, a pioneer in the relatively new field of peace research,[7] feels that peace and war are not part of human nature but influenced greatly by *culture* and *learning* [49]. Certain religious cultures such as Buddhism and Hinduism are very peace and love oriented while others, such as Christianity and Islam, are known to be friendly to the sword depending upon the circumstances. In terms of *structure*, nomadic social structures such as the Eskimo, compared to sedentary groups, tend to be peaceful. To paraphrase Dr. Galtung, we need more Buddhist Eskimos if we wish peace. On the other hand we can emphasize and teach the religious values of ahisma, shalom, brotherhood, peace, and love in our social structures (family, schools, community, government, business, military, etc.) regardless of our personal, formal religion.

Anything that denigrates life, and which numbs us to suffering does not contribute to our scheme of global health and well-being. A mark of highly civilized society is the care and nurturing provided the dependent: Children, the aged, the impoverished, and animal life. A word about the latter. The legitimation and institutionalization of hunting and fishing contribute to a devaluing of life. It is easy to become hardened to the suffering and death of the hunted deer, the baited bear, the "fighting dog." Animals should never be considered "pets"—a more civilized term and way of thinking would be "companion animal."

As a former athletic coach and participant I have always felt that hunting and fishing were never "sport." The term implies equal opportunity for each participant to "win" the contest. When was the last time a doe killed a hunter, or a

---

[7] The peace research movement started in the late 1950s as a result of the devastation and horrendous deaths caused by World War II. One of the first organized efforts was the Norwegian International Peace Research Institute in 1959.

trout, a fisherperson? You might say that hunting animals is one thing, but humans would never condone or participate in the brutal killing of fellow human beings except soldiers killing soldiers in times of war, or in self-defense. The Nazi Holocaust, and the other state sponsored programs of genocide under Stalin, Pol Pot, Idi Amin, our own disgraceful behavior in My Lai, and the carnage in Bosnia ended the myth that civilized people are beyond inflicting mass death upon their fellows. It is easy to abandon the veneer of civil and civilized behavior. We need to modify culture and, provide structures which value life, not death. Education is an efficient way.

THE INTEGRATION OF HEALTH EDUCATION AND DEATH EDUCATION

I suggest an integration of classical, health, and death education to produce a leadership based upon virtue in the Aristotelian sense of the word, that is, courage, integrity, a sense of altruism and mission to serve future generations. Children and adults need to study and emulate those who have acted to improve the lot of humankind even at risk to their own personal reputation and safety. Socrates, Einstein, Ghandi, Jesus, Martin Luther King, Ralph Nader, Paul Robeson, and Rachel Carson are examples.

Classical education refers to the *Great Books*[8] and as defined by Robert Maynard Hutchins and Mortimer Adler, and other classical literature, drama, and visual arts. The value of the classics is its emphasis on wisdom more so than merely the acquisition of facts. Values which underscore the responsibility we have to one another to improve health and well being.

Classical literature is the bedrock of democratic institutions. It includes the study of civics, geography, history, human relations, philosophy, the role of institutions, ethics and morality, virtue, and the universal problems of life. To that I would add the study of cultures, as means to understanding the great and rich diversity of people the world over. It is also a valuable means to reducing ethnocentrism. That which promotes affection and understanding between cultures and people are to be encouraged. Thus education should encourage student exchanges, overseas study programs, and programs such as the Peace Corps and ACTION.

If the classics utilize the wisdom of the past to resolving the problems of today, health and death education are concerned about the problems relating to living long and well today and tomorrow. The classics, and health and death education have the potential to help improve the quality of global health and well-being.

What should be the subject matter of health education?[9] If *health* and *well-being* are the Yin, Thanatology is the Yang. Each is a side of the same coin. Health

---

[8] A legitimate criticism of the *Great Books* is the need to include works of people of color and women who also meet the established criteria for inclusion.

education should enhance the value of life and living by describing the fragility and interdependence of all life. I would include the causes, and *emotional, economic, physical and social effects* of HD [17, 43, 50-56]. I would educate students enabling them to become agents of change to act in their best interests.

Today, formal school health education is primarily concerned with prevention of disease such as AIDS, coronary heart disease, diabetes, kidney diseases, and others by modification of health behaviors such as exercise, diet, smoking, and stress. I think health education should be concerned with more than disease prevention.

BASEBALL, A CIGAR, AND OTHER JOYS OF LIFE

Knowing that I can die at any moment helps establish priorities. Nothing takes priority over attending my son's baseball games. Obligations such as departmental meetings (ugh!) are avoided whenever possible.

If I were younger I would rhapsodize over the joy of playing sport. At age sixty-three, going to my son's games in the company of wife, daughter, often the family dog, and friends while puffing on a Partagas No. 1 cigar is heaven. Baseball symbolizes joy and life. It is also death in life. A mediocre performance, or a loss that should have been a win are, for the moment, equivalents of death. I can put up with this. When dead there are no ball games to enjoy or suffer through.

Baseball, at the competitive level played by my son, has a pristine even existential quality. No one cares about socioeconomic status. Yet there are universal absolutes. For example, some years ago, when I was an active player, a team mate told my manager that I was pursuing a Ph.D. He economically summarized his values when he replied, "As long as Dan or anyone else on this team can hit the ball, throw the ball, and catch the ball, he'll play." He continued, "When he can't, he'll sit—Ph.D. or not." I didn't fault him then nor now.

My daughter was an English major who recently graduated from the University of Maryland (1994), and is employed in her field. Eventually she will return for graduate studies enabling her to be more critical of my writing. She, too, is quite competent. It is also fun and pleasurable sharing her work and her life.

Both children are *prospects*. Matt was drafted by the Baltimore Orioles in June 1994 but will attend the University of South Carolina on an athletic scholarship instead. He is a left-handed pitcher, eighteen years of age, 6'4", and 190 pounds. He is fast having been clocked at 87 miles per hour on the *fast gun* (as the baseball is released from his hand). Leslie is neither 6'4" nor 190 pounds but she, too, is a prospect in her field. We look forward to her career.

---

[9] Content has been more fully discussed in my two edited volumes [2, 39].

This is intoxicating stuff for me. The *present*, here and now, is fine. Oh, the world is not perfect. I would much prefer being at another university, earning an appropriate wage, and having a supportive chairperson. But the academic stresses and strains of my department are certainly manageable.

Yet, the present and future, the hopes and fantasies can be wiped out by fate—an accident, an injury to Matt's arm—or HD happening to either child. That is the intolerable threat. Thus, HD is my motivator without peer. The idea of HD both sweetens and nullifies life.

Thanatology, too, magnifies that which is joyful in life and living. I need to say a word about friends and projects in general. In the early 1970s a small group of us formed and developed the *Association for Death Education & Counseling* (ADEC). Over the years it has blossomed into the highly respected professional-educational-scientific organization. My friendship with the leadership, and members has been fun and enjoyable—they are the salt of the earth. Their yearly conference is filled with new information and insights.

I feel the same way about the senior staff and members of the AHDP. Some of us have worked together for over twelve years. Thus, awareness of mortality has influenced my professional life. It has influenced past accomplishments and future directions. On the one hand, it has helped me endure a mediocre work situation (hey, I could be dead). On the other hand, it has reinforced the pleasures of family, friends, baseball, dog an 175 pound English Mastiff, and a Partagas No. 1 cigar. Awareness of mortality has its rewards.

REFERENCES

1. J. Choron, *Death and Western Thought*, Collier Books, New York, 1963.
2. D. Leviton, *Horrendous Death and Health: Toward Action*, Hemisphere Publishing Corporation, New York, 1991.
3. D. Leviton, *Horrendous Death, Health, and Well-being*, Hemisphere Publishing Corporation, New York, 1991.
4. J. W. v. Goethe, *Faust: Part One & Part Two*, The Bobbs-Merrill Company, Inc., New York, 1965.
5. E. Becker, *The Denial of Death*, Free Press, New York, 1973.
6. World Health Organization, *1992 World Health Statistics Annual*, World Health Organization, New York, 1993.
7. National Center for Health Statistics, *Advance Report of Final Mortality Statistics, 1991*, Public Health Service, Hyattsville, Maryland, 1993.
8. R. J. Rummel, *Lethal Politics: Soviet Genocide and Mass Murder Since 1917*, Transaction Publishers, New Brunswick, 1990.
9. R. J. Rummel, *China's Bloody Century: Genocide and Mass Murder Since 1900*, Transaction Publishers, New Brunswick, 1991.
10. R. J. Rummel, *Democide: Nazi Genocide and Mass Murder*, Transaction Publishers, New Brunswick, 1991.

11. A. Reiss J., Jr., and J. A. Roth, *Understanding and Preventing Violence*, National Academy Press, Washington, D.C., 1993.
12. B. Vobejda, Children's Defense Fund Cites Gun Violence, in *The Washington Post*, Washington, D.C., p. A3, 1994.
13. R. Sivard, *World Military and Social Expenditures, 1991*, World Priorities, Box 25140, Washington, D.C., 20007, Washington, D.C., 1991.
14. H. Feifel, *The Meaning of Death*, McGraw-Hill Book Company, Inc., New York, 1959.
15. National Center for Health Statistics, Health United States, 1986, U.S. Department of Health & Human Services, Washington, D.C., 1986.
16. M. Kidron and R. Segal, *The State of the World Atlas*, Simon & Schuster, New York, 1981.
17. R. Sivard, *World Military and Social Expenditures, 1987-88*, World Priorities, Box 25140, Washington, D.C. 20007, Washington, D.C., 1987.
18. L. R. Brown, A. T. Durning, C. Flavin, H. F. French, J. L. Jacobson, N. Lenssen, M. D. Lowe, S. L. Postel, M. Renner, J. Ryan, L. Starke, and J. Young, *State of the World: 1991*, W. W. Norton & Company, New York, 1991.
19. J. M. Burns, *A People's Charter*, Vintage Books, New York, 1991.
20. A. D. Weisman, *The Realization of Death: A Guide of the Psychological Autopsy*, Jason Aronson, New York, 1974.
21. R. J. Lifton, *The Broken Connection*, Simon & Schuster, New York, 1979.
22. W. W. Meissner, Impending Nuclear Disaster: Psychoanalytic Perspectives, in *Psychoanalysis and Nuclear Threat*, H. B. Levine, D. Jacobs, and L. J. Rubin (eds.), The Analytic Press, Hillsdale, New Jersey, pp. 89-110, 1988.
23. H. Segal, Silence is the Real Crime, in *Psychoanalysis and the Nuclear Threat*, H. Levine, D. Jacobs, and L. Rubin, et al. (eds.), The Analytic Press, Hillsdale, New Jersey, pp. 35-58, 1988.
24. S. Freud, Thoughts for the Times on War and Death, in *Civilisation, War and Death: Sigmund Freud* J. Rickman (ed.), Hogarth Press, pp. 125, 1968.
25. J. Rickman, *Civilisation, War and Death: Sigmund Freud*, Hogarth Press, London, 1968.
26. R. J. Lifton, *The Nazi Doctors: Medical Killing and the Psychology of Genocide*, Basic Books, New York, 1986.
27. I. W. Charny and D. Fromer, The Readiness of Health Profession Students to Comply with a Hypothetical Program of Forced Migration of a Minority Population, *American Journal of Orthopsychiatry, 60*, pp. 486-495, 1990.
28. E. Markusen and J. B. Harris, The Role of Education in Preventing Nuclear War, *Harvard Educational Review, 54*, pp. 282-303, 1984.
29. M. Rosenbloom, The Holocaust Survivor in Late Life, *Journal of Gerontological Social Work, 8*, pp. 181-191, 1985.
30. R. J. Lifton and E. Markusen, *The Genocidal Mentality: Nazi Holocaust Social Work, 8*, pp. 181-191, 1985.
31. D. Klass, *Parental Grief: Solace and Resolution*, Springer Publishing Company, New York, 1988.
32. M. Osterweis, F. Solomon, and M. Green, *Bereavement: Reactions, Consequences, and Care*, National Academy Press, Washington, D.C., 1984.

33. P. Steinfels, Introduction, *Journal of the Hastings Center, 1*, pp. 3-6, 1973.
34. Z. Ryn, Suicides in the Nazi Concentration Camps, *Suicide and Life Threatening Behavior, 16*, pp. 419-433, 1986.
35. R. G. Roden, Sexuality and the Holocaust Survivor, *Israel Journal of Psychiatry and Related Sciences, 22*, pp. 211-220, 1985.
36. D. Leviton and L. Santa Maria, The Adults Health & Development Program: Descriptive and Evaluative Data, *The Gerontologist, 19*, pp. 534-543, 1979.
37. D. Leviton, Intergenerational Health Education: The Adults Health and Development Programme, *Hygie, 8*, pp. 26-29, 1989.
38. D. Leviton, Horrendous Death as a Stimulus to Intergenerational Health Protective Action and Global Well Being, in *Proceedings of the 32nd ICHPER Anniversary World Congress*, S. Haberlein and H. Cordts (eds.), Frostburg State University, Frostburg, Maryland, pp. 15-21, 1990.
39. D. Leviton, Toward Rapid and Significant Action, in *Horrendous Death and Health: Toward Action*, D. Leviton (ed.), Hemisphere Publishing Corporation, New York, pp. 261-283, 1991.
40. D. Leviton, The Adult Health and Development Program: More Than Just Fitness, in *Physical Activity, Aging and Sports: Volume II: Practice, Program and Policy*, S. Harris, R. Harris, and W. S. Harris (eds.), Center for the Study of Aging, Albany, pp. 232-250, 1992.
41. D. Leviton, D. Redman, N. Cordova, and S. Hin, The Adult Health & Development Program: Retaining Minority Students and Motivation High School Students to Attend the University, *Retention 2000*, unpublished paper, University of Maryland, College Park, 1993.
42. R. J. Barnet, *The Lean Years: Politics in an Age of Scarcity*, Touchstone Books, New York, 1980.
43. M. G. Renner, Who are the Enemies?, *Peace Review, 1*, pp. 22-26, 1989.
44. V. E. Frankl, Viktor Frankl on Aging, Meaning, and Death, in *The Aging Connection*, p. 7, 1989.
45. H. Rowan, Minimum Wages, Maximum Greed, in *The Washington Post*, Washington, D.C., p. A23, 1989.
46. J. Van, Most Doctors Willing to Lie, Study Suggests, in *The Washington Post*, Washington, D.C., p. A7, 1989.
47. C. Peterson, Experts, OMB Spar on Global Warning, in *The Washington Post*, Washington, D.C., p. A1, 1989.
48. H. Johnson, in *The Washington Post*, Washington, D.C., p. A1, 1989.
49. J. Galtung, *There Are Alternatives: Four Roads to Peace and Security*, Dufours Editions, Chester Springs, 1984.
50. W. Bank, *World Development Report*, Oxford University Press, New York, 1988.
51. J. Brenner, *Mental Illness and the Economy*, Harvard University Press, Boston, 1974.
52. L. Duke, Race: Gray Areas of Health Data, in *The Washington Post*, Washington, D.C., p. A-19, 1992.
53. V. R. Fuchs and D. M. Reklis, America's Children: Economic Perspectives and Policy Options, *Science, 255*, pp. 41-45, 1992.

54. C. Gorlick, Unemployment and Poverty: Correlates of Morbidity/mortality, in *Horren-dous Death, Health, and Well-being*, D. Leviton (ed.), Hemisphere Publishing Corporation, Washington, D.C., pp. 191-204, 1991.
55. M. G. Renner, National Security: The Economic and Environmental Dimensions, in *Worldwatch Institute*, 1989.
56. B. J. Tidwell, *The State of Black America 1992*, National Urban League, New York, 1992.

CHAPTER 14

Death and Beyond:
A Hindu's Perspective

Aruna Mathur

Day to day experiences and observations of the living world are filled with "starts" and "ends," births and deaths. Rarely do we observe complete recycling. As a member of the egocentric human race, observation of death/end scares us and heightens our awareness of mortality. This awareness acquires enormous proportion because we have attachments, we enjoy the world we live in and work hard for our comforts. No wonder that our awareness of mortality frightens us all. Our capacity to deal with the mortality issue depends greatly on the beliefs we harbor. Many of these beliefs have philosophical and religious roots. Rightly so, because the physical and biological sciences point only to a final end.

Let me share with you my own experience and beliefs.

An automobile accident on Highway 401 took away the life of a friend and his sixteen-year-old daughter. The aftermath of this event triggered an unending quest in me to reconcile and understand better "death and beyond." Suddenly all readings of philosophical and religious works seemed to be put to critical re-examination over and over again in my thoughts until acceptable answers could emerge to numerous but related questions regarding mortality. Knowing that we are mortals and that death is inevitable for all living species in the world, why is it not often expected and accepted? What is death? Who dies? Who survives? If there is survival after death, should death be mourned or rejoiced? Why do people do what they do for the dead?

Thinking about death also raises the question of pain for the dying a well as for those bereaved. Pain for the dying person is not only because of the physical suffering, in fact, the greater pain is inflicted due to separation from dear ones and regrets for not completing important tasks. Given that death is inevitable, could a better understanding of death and beyond lessen, if not take away, the pain of the inevitable mortality?

Fear of dying or losing a dear one has always been and, more than likely, will always be there. In fact if paying a price could avert it, virtually every living person may be a potential buyer. This reminds me of a Buddhist parable which is summarized below.

A lady, fear stricken by the thought of some day death of her beloved son, approached the enlightened Gautama Buddha and asked him if he could make her beloved son immortal. Gautama Buddha immediately recognized that the love and attachment of the woman for her son has masked the ultimate reality of death from her. Therefore, he chose to indirectly enlighten the woman and suggested that if she could fetch some mustard for him from a family which had never experienced death, he would make her son immortal. The woman searched far and wide, found people willing to give her any amount of mustard but, as one would expect, she did not find any family which had escaped death. The ultimate reality was thus revealed.

There is no question or uncertainty that every person who is born will, sooner or later, die. Nobody has lived forever; nobody will live forever. When we talk about death, the inevitable end, we mean ceased functions of the physical body organs, such as stoppage of brain functions or heart beat or the like. It is pointless for the purpose of this discussion to argue that not all bodily functions stop simultaneously and therefore, the instant of clinical death is ill defined. What is certain is that after death one's body is of no further value to the dead person, even if the body parts of the deceased are transplanted in another person and continue to function.

The mention of one's body raises a philosophical enquiry: who is the possessor of the body? The body and all its parts seem to belong to someone else. Who? Who is the real "I" when I assert that it is my body. We know that everybody ages, falls into disrepair, and eventually ceases to function. Does it mean that "I" or the possessor of the body dies with the body?

For ages Hindus have made a clear distinction between the physical body and the subtle body and have introduced the concept of soul [1]. The belief is that just as in this consumer world "a person casts off worn out garments and puts on new, likewise an embodied soul casts off a worn out body and takes on a new." Thus spoke Lord Krishna in Bhagavad Gita (Chapter 2) to reveal the ultimate reality to Arjuna. Recognition of soul as the very essence of life and its nondestructability dates back to Vedas [2] (about 1500 B.C.) and Upanishads [3] composed in 800 to 700 B.C.

In Katha Upanishad [4], these thoughts appear in an ancient story in which a teenager, Nachiketa, asks Lord Yama, the lord of death: "When a man dies, this doubt arises: some say 'he is' and some say 'he is not,' please teach me the truth."

Lord Yama acknowledges that even the gods had this doubt in times of old; for mysterious is the law of life and death and goes on to say:

The all knowing Self was never born,
Nor will it die. Beyond cause and effect,
This self is eternal and immutable.
When the body dies, the self does not die.
If the slayer believes that he can slay
Or the slain believes that he can be slain
Neither knows the truth, the eternal self.
Slays not, nor is ever slain [5, p. 223].

The challenge to understand death is, therefore, age old. In this scientific age, where if an idea is to be accepted it must be proven, unfortunately we have not yet been able to resolve the issue of who dies? Who survives? The fact is that those who are dead cannot tell us about their experiences and those who claim to have a better understanding are actually inexperienced. There is, however, some indirect acceptance of the soul or spirit or consciousness which transcends the body. The ceasing of the heartbeat was the age old acceptance of the moment of death. But modern skills of the resuscitation of cardiac arrest patients, even subsequent to permanently and irreversibly ceased brain functions can, perhaps, be equated to the departure of the spirit or soul from the body [6].

"Hindu philosophy equates death with life. The two are regarded as different modes of the same consciousness that pervades the continuum of space-time. When located in temporal space-time, this consciousness manifests as life; while pervading infinite space-time, it appears as death" [7]. Death is taken as a preparation for fulfilling the higher goal, for fuller life. In a long journey of life, death is only a stop and then the journey continues.

Hindus believe life to be an endless process and death or rather physical death is just a moment in that process. The word "life" is not restricted in its meaning to the span of time between birth and death of a person. "Life is a process, there is no process without change, no change without becoming and no becoming without the intervening moments of discarding dispensable elements of the life process. Death is one such moment" [8, p. 9]. In the life process when the elements of the physical body disintegrate, that moment is called death, but life goes on. It is not an annihilation of existence or a total destruction, it is simply a change into another kind of existence in a non-physical state which is normally not perceived by our senses. Therefore a statement like "this person is dead" simply means that this physical body is no longer usable for life, but not that it is the end of the life.

The word "life" which is a translation of a sanskrit term "Prana" is used with two meanings. Commonly used it means the existence of the individual between birth and death on earth. It also means, the cosmic energy or the connecting thread of multiplicity. When life as connecting thread (Sutratman) leaves the body, the body disintegrates into separate elements that compose it and dies [9].

This cosmic energy or connecting thread is part of the divine which never dies. It continues existing endlessly.

Hindus believe that an individual is a combination of material body which is mortal and soul, which is immortal. The first is physical. It is composed of five elements: water, earth, fire, air, and ether. The other is spiritual, divine in nature and completely different from the physical body [10]. The essential nature of a person is this changeless spiritual entity known as soul which exists in the form of pure consciousness, the divine spark, the connecting thread of life. The physical body serves as an instrument only and works because of the presence of the soul within. When this soul leaves the body, the person is declared dead, or lifeless. But the soul is reborn in a new body with fresh opportunities, this is called "transmigration of soul." Thus physical death is not the end, it is the beginning of a new life.

Acceptance of immortality of consciousness, therefore, lessens the pain of death. The event of death, generally regarded to be the end, could be seen to be the beginning of a new life. As for the body, it disintegrates into various elements. These very elements reconstitute to give birth to a new body. This would be acceptable if examined in scientific terms because we are told that nothing is ever totally destroyed—it merely transforms.

Close linkage of birth and death is deeply rooted in Hindu mythology [11]. Lord Brahma is identified to be the creator of the universe. Having created the universe, he did not want it to grow uncontrolled. Therefore, the creator himself also created "Mrityu" or death to hold the balance. It is very attractive to consider the cycle of birth-life-death-birth in infinite space-time continuum and accept birth and death as mere events in an unending process. Once the terminal concept of death, as it is generally perceived, is discarded, a comforting understanding develops which makes it easier to accept death as an event. Since this understanding relieves fear and lessens emotional pain a good case can be made to place faith in it even if it were to be only to lessen the pain of anticipating death. Hindus firmly believe in "soul" which is "pure consciousness." It is considered to be divine and the connecting thread of life. In fact there are a number of other religions and schools of philosophy in the East and West which also believe in the existence of soul. However, what is unique in Hinduism is the belief of transmigration of soul upon death from one body to another body. Transmigration being governed by one's deeds performed in one's life span in this world. This is known as the law of Karma. The Karmas (deeds) not only determine the quality of one's future life, they also determine the continuity of life cycle. One's thoughts, words and deeds have an ethical consequence in fixing one's lot in future existence. It is believed that there is nothing uncertain or accidental in this world. If a person performs honorable deeds and lives a good life, one will be born in a higher state of life. Transmigration seems to work automatically as cause and effect without any divine intervention and yet it is a divine expression.

Shvetashvatara Upanishad [6, 16] declares: "He is the maker of all . . . the cause of transmigration and of liberation of continuance and of bondage."

Transmigration affirms not only survival of death but life before birth—pre-existence. If more than one life on earth is admitted, there appears to be no limit to births and deaths. The law of Karma should logically admit no deliverance from the consequences of action until a full penalty has been exacted. Even for the noblest, according to mythology, it may take many births before deliverance. For example in Buddhist scriptures (Jatakas) 550 lives of Buddha are recorded before he attained full enlightenment and nirvana.

The Bhagavad Gita personifies the transcendental vision in Lord Krishna in whom all beings are seen to return. The purpose of transmigration is thus interpreted to be an opportunity for betterment, continual upgrading until nirvana or moksha or merger of the soul or pure consciousness takes place with the supreme divine.

Death, when accepted to be the imminent beginning of the next life, a stage in an evolving process of continuous improvement, for continuous refinement, a stage closer to the ultimate merger in the supreme divine, has the promise to be anticipated with expectations. The resulting comfort may even outweigh the remorse of separation from dear ones or physical possessions. There could even be satisfaction and contentment in having completed the much-needed good Karmas in one's life as death approaches. As well, there may be the longing for a better life in the next birth. And finally, there may be a belief that after death one has to live one life less in the total lives required prior to nirvana. These thoughts may provide comfort which may, at times, more than compensate, for the dying, the pain of separation from the dear ones as well as leaving behind one's life time accumulation of worldly possessions. These thoughts may be comforting not only for the dying but, as well, for those attending a dying person. In fact, even in the totally unexpected accidental death of a relative or a friend, the pain may be reduced, if one reconciled that the departed had completed all required deeds in this life and has proceeded to the next life.

The biggest challenge arises in reconciling the presence of divine (soul or atman or pure consciousness) in a person, transmigration of soul, consequence of karmas of this life in the next life, eventual merger of soul in the supreme divine, when one asks—why does it all happen?, and, for what purpose? If the supreme divine exists why does he put all beings through this cycle?

Hindu Scriptures anticipate such questions and explain the entire creation, its sustenance and some day end for a new beginning, to be the 'Maya' or the divine play [12]. It requires a leap of faith to accept it because it is a given and not really a reasoned explanation. Such beliefs in divine play exist in most religions whether it is to explain one life or in multiplicity of life cycles implied in the concept of transmigration of soul. Let there be light or let there be life are attributed to divine play.

In a dynamic world, birth and death, beginning and end are characteristic cyclic events. These must coexist and do coexist even within the observable world. Let alone the absence of one or the other, even a slight imbalance can create decaying or explosive situations.

Hindu mythology has many situations where men through good deeds had acquired supernatural powers including control on death [13]. Corrupted by the seeming assurance of immortality these good men turned supermen (Ravana, Bali, Kansa, Hiranakashyapa) stopped distinguishing between good and evil and indeed created anarchy. Because every being born must die, in these extraordinary situations, the God himself had to reincarnate as a human being and through special provisions which invalidated protection of these supermen from death, put them to death. The incarnate God himself (Narasimha, Rama, Krishna) ended his human life by death.

Whether one believes in mythological stories or not, the ultimate truth is—death is a must for every being.

Through belief in transmigration, reincarnation, Hindus have trivialized death. One would question—are Hindus totally above attachment to life, attachment to people, attachment to things? No, not quite so. There may be only a difference in degree but for most Hindus the attachment is there. Hindus are therefore also grief stricken when confounded with death. The fear of one's death is always there and so also is the pain of death of dear ones. I too was grieved and disturbed for a considerable period of time at the accidental death of our friend. I am still trying to reconcile. The question therefore is—How and in what way does the belief in Hindu philosophy practically help?

It helps in several ways. It forces one to accept death as inevitable. It helps in reducing undue attachment with the human body. Partially, it takes away the fear of death. It changes the perception of death from darkness, falling into a bottomless void to a journey towards light in anticipation of a better life. It motivates people to perform good deeds for improving their next life as well as it softens the misery of misfortunes by regarding these to be the consequences of one's misdeeds (Karmas) in the previous life which cannot be undone.

Hindus divide a (100 year) lifespan into four spans (ashramas) each of twenty-five years duration [14]. The first is dedicated to acquiring knowledge, the second for marriage and raising family, the third for retirement and the fourth for renunciation. The last two stages prepare one to depart from this world content and with ease. This division into ashramas is based on the concept that each life is a pilgrimage and there is a duty to be performed in each of the four ashramas. Satisfactory discharge of duties in each span leads to content and to gradual detachment. For the dying the prospects of improving one's next life by ending this life immersed in good thoughts and remembering God brings peace rather then horror of death. It is for this reason that friends and relatives of a dying person chant and sing prayers as death approaches. For example, on January 30, 1948, the world watched and listened to Mahatma Gandhi recite "Hey Rama, hey Rama, hey Rama" (Oh God, Oh God, Oh God) prior to succumbing after being shot.

As death approaches, it signals the end of one phase, in preparation to take a new body and new attachments. Farewell is offered by all near and dear ones to a dying person, consequently crowding around the person is usual as the person nears death. A family member, friend or priest reads from scriptures, particularly from Bhagwad Gita, those parts which emphasize the immortality of soul, reminding the dying person as well as friends and relatives of the ultimate nature of life so that giving up the body and attachments become less painful for the dying. It has another purpose. As Hindus believe that the final thoughts of a dying person influence their life in the next birth, these thoughts are directed towards God by scripture recitations. Other important traditions include—offering sacred water from Ganges and placing the body from bed to ground. Both initiate psychological acceptance of the last moment of this phase of life.

Hindus observe death rites into two groups. One of those, which is performed immediately after the physical death and the others must be performed periodically for a longer period of time.

The first group of rites relate to the disposal of the dead. Started in Vedic times approximately 1500 B.C. [15], they are still in practice with very few variations in different parts of India. In India, the dead body is cremated as early as possible to prevent decay. Cremation is an act of disposing a corpse by fire. Before taking the body to a cremation ground, it is washed and anointed with water and aromatic substances, then dressed in new garments, usually white for a man and red for a woman (e.g., red wedding sari if married). The body may be decorated with jewelry and flowers according to one's status when alive. This all is done in the house by family members. A priest is usually invited to perform the last rite (samskara) in the form of a worship, chanting vedic mantras. The body is placed on a stretcher and carried on the shoulders of immediate relatives, such as, son, husband, grandson, accompanied in a large procession of relatives and friends and taken to the cremation ground. With a special flame, the eldest son lights the funeral pyre and the body is cremated. Thereafter all present at the cremation purify themselves by taking a bath either right on the cremation ground or at home before entering the house. One of the requirements of a good cremation ground is that water should be available there or near by. Usually, that day no food is cooked in the house. It is provided by relatives or neighbors.

On the third day (in most cases) following cremation, left-over charred bones and ashes are collected to be scattered in the holy river Ganges at Hardwar. Hindus believe that this washes away all evil and even the last trace of the body is purified by the holy water of Ganges.

What has been said so far was the traditional way of disposing of the dead body which is still the practice in most parts of India. However, in some big cities, electric crematoriums have replaced wood pyres. Exceptions to cremation are young children under three or so, still born and ascetics who are known to be already dead to the world. Burial is a standard practice for children and babies.

Mourning is performed by family members of the departed person for usually twelve days. This can vary according to family traditions. In this period devotional songs are sung, scriptures, particularly Bhagwad Gita [16], are recited to lighten the grief by repeated reminder of the immortality of soul. Generally family members cry aloud when friends, neighbors or relatives visit to express condolences. Visiting the family of the deceased is an important practice as it reinforces the support of relatives and friends for the family. Crying aloud perhaps provides a good psychotherapy.

The other kind of rites which are performed periodically are to show reverence and remembrance to the departed soul. This begins right from the moment a death occurs in the family and continue for a long period of time. On the eleventh day following death, a homage ceremony is performed known as "Sraddha." A number of gifts like food, clothes, perfume, umbrella, bed, cow, etc. are given as alms to a priest in the name of the departed, to show respect. Similar Sraddha although on a smaller scale is performed every month, preferably on the new moon day with the final one in the end of one year. Thereafter Sraddha is performed every year, for at least three generations on both paternal and maternal sides.

At Sraddha, mantras are chanted which mean: "May the entire universe comprising all worlds, the Gods, Risis, Munis (saints and seers) and humans—as also forefathers including those on the mother's side (mother's mother and others) be happy. Those that are friends, related and those not related (in the present life) as also those who were related in other lives—let all of those now desirous of this water offering be happy eternally. May all those belonging to innumerable past generations, who once dwelt in the seven continents, be happy in their three worlds (heaven, sky and earth) with this water offered by me" [17].

From a religious point of view the responsibility of death is charged to lord Yama. Death is personified as a woman beautiful but wearing dark clothes to signify mystery (Mrityu). Upon death one is said to encounter weightlessness as the burden of the worn out body is left behind and one travels towards bright light. Death is expected but not feared.

As life is regarded to be a beautiful experience, death is regarded but only a stop prior to the fresh start of a new beautiful experience. Mortality may therefore not be feared.

Perhaps we can all lessen the pain and fear of death only if we think about it often and plan for this major journey into the next life even if half as much as we do for small travels within this life.

The inevitable will catch up with us one day. We are all mortals. Let us not fear death rather accept it gracefully.

REFERENCES

1. Upanishads; (Chandogya Up. V1, 8-9, Katha Up. 1, 34, Brahadaranyaka Up. IV, 4, 3), Bhagwad Gita Ch. 2, also Vedanta Sutra Ch. 1 and 2.

2. Rig Veda; X, 16, 3.
3. Chandogya Upanishad; VIII, 3-12.
4. Katha Upanishad; I, 1-20.
5. E. Easwaran, *Dialogue with Death: A Journey into Consciousness*, Nilgiri, California, 1992.
6. *Diagnosis of Death*, memorandum, Conference of British Royal Medical College (1979), cited in "*Hindu Concept of Life and Death*" Shyam Ghosh, p. 22, 1989.
7. S. Ghosh, *Hindu Concept of Life and Death*, Munshiram Manoharlal, New Delhi, p. 1, 1989.
8. F. H. Holck (ed.), *Death and Eastern Thought*, Abingdon, New York (Raju, P.T.), p. 9, 1974.
9. ibid, p. 14.
10. F. H. Holck, (ed.), *Death and Eastern Thought*, Abingdon, New York, Radhakrishnan, S., Death: *Awakening into a New Life*, p. 188, 1974.
11. Mahabharata, Drona Parvan,50-52.
12. Rig Veda (VI, 4, 18; X, 54, 2). Prashna Upanishad (1, 16), Svetasvatara Upanishad (IV, 10), Bhagwad Gita (IV, 5-7, XVIII, 61) Brahma Sutra (II, 1, 4; 11, 3, 30).
13. Mahabharata, Ramayana (Bal Kanda and Uttar Kanda), Vishnu Puran.
14. Manusmriti (9), Rig Veda (7, 66, 16).
15. These rites found in Rig Veda hymns and later in the Brahmanas and Aranyakas, then developed in prescribed form in Grhya Srauta and Asvalayana Sutra.
16. Bhagwad Gita chapters 2 and 18.
17. S. Ghosh, *Hindu Concept of Life and Death*, Munshiram Manoharlal, New Delhi, p. 151.

Contributors

INGE BAER CORLESS, a graduate of the Bellevue School of Nursing in New York City, attended Hunter College and graduated from Boston University with a bachelor's degree in nursing, the University of Rhode Island with a master's degree in sociology, and from Brown University with a PhD in sociology. As a Robert Wood Johnson Clinical Scholar, Dr. Corless did postdoctoral study at the University of California-San Francisco. She has held academic positions at Russell Sage College, the University of Michigan, the University of North Carolina-Chapel Hill, as well as her current position at the MGH Institute of Health Professions at the Massachusetts General Hospital. Dr. Corless served as program director of St. Peter's Hospice in Albany, New York and as a short term consultant for WHO at the Western Pacific Regional office. A Fellow of the American Academy of Nursing, Dr. Corless has written on hospice and HIV disease and is co-editor with Mary Pittman-Lindeman of *AIDS: Principles, Practices and Politics*, and with Mary Pittman-Lindeman and Barbara Germino of *Dying, Death and Bereavement: Theoretical Perspectives and Other Ways of Knowing. A Challenge for Living: Dying, Death and Bereavement*, co-edited with Mary Pittman and Barbara Germino, 1994.

KENNETH J. DOKA, Ph.D. is professor of Gerontology at The College of New Rochelle. He has authored over 40 articles and three books: *Disenfranchised Grief, Death and Spirituality; Living with Life-Threatening Illness* and *Death and Spirituality*. He is past president of the Association for Death Education and Counseling, and the associate editor of OMEGA, Journal of Death and Dying.

ROBERT KASTENBAUM is a professor of communication at Arizona State University. A graduate scholarship in philosophy at University of Southern California somehow led to a Ph.D. in psychology (1959), and then to the emerging fields of gerontology and thanatology. He is the author of *The Psychology of Death* (revised edition, 1992), *Death, Society, & Human Experience* (4th edition, 1991), forthcoming, *Defining Acts: Aging as Drama* (a set of plays dealing with themes of aging and/or death) and *Dorian Graying*. He also serves as editor of *Omega, Journal of Death and Dying*, and *International Journal of Aging and*

Human Development, as well as *The Encyclopedia of Death* (with Beatrice Kastenbaum, 1989), *The Encyclopedia of Adult Development* (in press), and advisory editor to the first "all-death" issue of *The Monist*, a journal of general philosophy.

JEFFREY KAUFFMAN is a psychotherapist specializing in loss and mourning. He lives and practices near Philadelphia, Pennsylvania. He is a training and clinical consultant for loss and mourning to many groups, including nursing homes, schools, mental health agencies, developmental disability agencies, hospices, diverse social service agencies, MAAD, Families of Murder Victims, and others. He is the author of numerous articles on loss and mourning.

KJELL KALLENBERG, B.A., Ph.D. is the author of numerous books and articles about a variety of spiritual and ethical issues, including psychological and social care following major accidents and disasters, abortion, bereavement, and suffering. Following parish work, he became Chaplain of the General Hospital in Örebro, Sweden, in 1977, and still holds that post; he is also a member of the Örebro County Council Group for Ethics in Medicine, and advisor in medical ethics to the Church of Sweden's Board of Bishops. From 1980 to 1985 he was a member of the Board for the Postgraduate Education of Hospital Chaplains, and from 1982 to 1984 served as Chairman of the Board of the National Association of Hospital Chaplains. He lectures widely and has a particular interest in ethical leadership and management in commercial and industrial life.

ELIZABETH LAMERS holds a BS cum laude from the State University of New York at New Paltz and an MA in education (reading) from Sonoma (Cal.) State University. She is credentialled as both a classroom teacher and a reading specialist. She has worked with terminally ill and bereaved children for the last ten years. She has conducted workshops and lectured extensively on the dying child and return to the classroom, children and grief, children's literature and death. She is a member of Kappa Delta Pi (Honorary Education Society), the International Reading Association, the International Work Group on Dying, Death and Bereavement, the Los Angeles County Bar Association Bioethics Committee, The Education and Prevention Task Force for the AIDS Regional Board for the County of Los Angeles, and chairs the AIDS Task Force for the American Red Cross, Santa Monica Chapter. She has written many book chapters and journal articles.

DANIEL LEVITON, Ph.D. is a professor of health education, and director of the Adult Health & Development Program (AHDP) at the University of Maryland, College Park, Maryland. He was one of the founders, and first president of the *Association for Death Education & Counseling*, founded and directs an intergenerational health promotion and rehabilitation program (the AHDP), has supervised its spread to 12 universities in the United States and Israel, and serves on the editorial board of *Omega*. Much of his spare time is spent coaching his son as they seek the Holy Grail of baseball pitching—excellent mechanics and a 90 mph fastball. Both goals are within reach and, hopefully, shall be attained before Dr. Leviton's death.

DR. ARUNA MATHUR, born and educated in Jodhpur, India, accompanied her husband to Leeds, Great Britain where she completed the remaining part of her Ph.D. Dissertation, Comparative Philosophy of East and West: Samkara and Spinoza. She immigrated to Winnipeg, Canada in 1969. While raising her family she taught part-time at the Universities of Manitoba and Winnipeg. Since 1987 she has lived in London, Ontario and has taught at the University of Western Ontario and Huron College. Currently an Assistant Professor at Huron College, she teaches courses on Living Religions of the World, Oriental Philosophy and Understanding India in a new program on Modern Eastern Civilizations. She has a deep interest in mysticism and philosophy of religions.

JOHN D. MORGAN is Professor of Philosophy and Director of the Centre for Education about Death and Bereavement at King's College of the University of Western Ontario, London, Canada. Dr. Morgan has been teaching courses about death and bereavement since 1968 and has coordinated the King's College International Conferences on Death and Bereavement since 1982. Dr. Morgan is editor of *Thanatology: A Liberal Arts Approach; Suicide: Helping those at Risk; Death Education in Canada; The Dying and the Bereaved Teenager* and *Young People and Death.* Dr. Morgan is the Consulting Editor for the Death, Value and Meaning Series published through Baywood Publishing Company. Dr. Morgan's research interests focus on issues of cultural attitudes related to death and bereavement.

GALEN PLETCHER studied philosophy at Kalamazoo College (B.A.) and the University of Michigan (M.A., Ph.D.). He has taught since 1970 at Southern Illinois University at Edwardsville, where he is currently Associate Provost and Associate Professor of Philosophical Studies. His teaching and research interests are philosophy of religion, ethics, and twentieth century analytic philosophy. His current research work centers on the problem of meaning in life.

DAVID J. ROY is the founder and director of the Center for Bioethics, Clinical Research Institute of Montreal. He is research professor in the Department of Medicine at the Université de Montréal and has coordinated and taught courses in Medical Ethics and Jurisprudence in the Medical Schools of McGill University in Montreal and the Université Laval in Quebec City. Dr. Roy holds degrees in mathematics, philosophy and theology. He earned his Ph.D. from the Westfälische Wilhelms Universität, Münster, West Germany, in 1972. Dr. Roy serves as consultant to doctors, health care professionals and government on ethical problems in medicine and clinical research, and devotes most of his time to research on ethical issues in clinical medicine and biomedical science. Dr. Roy is also Editor-in-Chief of *The Journal of Palliative Care.*

VICTOR L. SCHERMER, M.A., C.A.C. is a clinical psychologist in private practice and clinic settings in Philadelphia, Pennsylvania. He is Executive Director of The Study Group for Contemporary Psychoanalytic Process, faculty member of the Institute for Psychoanalytic Psychotherapies, and on the Board of Directors of The Institute for Spirituality and Psychological Healing. Mr. Schermer is coauthor of *Object Relations, the Self, and the Group* and coeditor of

Ring of Fire, about primitive affects and object relations in group psychotherapy. He has had a long-standing interest in psychoanalytic theory. His special interest in the problems of mortality, grief and loss, came about as a result of his work with addictions and, more recently, with clients suffering from AIDS.

ADRIAN TOMER teaches in the Department of Psychology at Shippensburg University in Pennsylvania. He has done consulting work on the applications of Structural Equation Models and has written on many subjects including gerontology and death anxiety.

DR. BILL WARREN is an Associate Professor in the University of Newcastle, Australia, where he teaches philosophy. He is the author of *Death Education and Research: Critical Perspectives*, and numerous other articles in the field of death and dying, as well as a wide range of papers in philosophy and psychology. In addition to his academic appointment he is a Clinical Psychologist in Private Practice and holds an Honorary position at the Royal Newcastle Hospital.

Index